Elizabethan Revenge Tragedy

1587-1642

ELIZABETHAN REVENGE TRAGEDY

1587-1642

BY

Fredson Bowers

PRINCETON

Princeton University Press

Copyright, 1940
Princeton University Press

ISBN 0-691-01259-8

First PRINCETON PAPERBACK Edition, 1966
Second Printing, 1969
Third Printing, 1971

Printed in the United States
of America

TO

GEORGE LYMAN KITTREDGE

PREFACE

IN this book I have endeavored to give a broad view of the background, the origin, and the chronological development of the Tragedy of Revenge, by tracing the dramatic currents and the literary and ethical influences which affected dramatists working in the type between the years 1587 and 1642. Since the only possible value of this work lies in its attempt to isolate and then to study a single type of drama, I have considered the individual plays not as many-sided works of dramatic art but instead only as representatives of the larger pattern of revenge tragedy. Thus I have usually ignored aspects of plays which were unrelated to my subject and have emphasized the general influences of the period rather than the personal influence of one dramatist on another. The importance of aligning the revenge tragedies with Elizabethan ethical thought and practice, combined with the paramount necessity of sketching the modifications in type of these tragedies throughout the whole period, has made it impossible for me always to treat an individual play with the fullness it deserves.

Shakespeare's *Hamlet* furnishes the most conspicuous example. Within the space that could have been allotted to *Hamlet* there was nothing new of any real importance that I could have added to the published investigations, particularly to those of Professor A. H. Thorndike. To try to give *Hamlet* the treatment it deserved, and adequately to trace its influence on later revenge tragedies, would have thrown completely out of balance the scale and proportions of my more general survey. The whole was more important for my purpose than any one of its parts, even when that part was Shakespeare; hence I have written more about the *Ur-Hamlet* than Shakespeare's *Hamlet*.

The dating of the plays follows that of Sir Edmund Chambers in *The Elizabethan Stage,* supplemented by Felix Schelling's list in *Elizabethan Drama* and Alfred Harbage's in *Cavalier Drama,* except where recent researches have altered their findings. A formal bibliography has been omitted in favor of full footnotes on the first references to quoted books. In sixteenth, seventeenth, and eighteenth century books the place is London unless otherwise indicated, and the date is that of the first edition unless preceded by the abbreviation "ed." which indicates a later edition used for reference because it alone was available. A single quotation from an Elizabethan book or manuscript is sometimes employed to buttress some specific point about the dramatic ethics of a play. I should perhaps mention that I have in no instance based my point solely on this one quotation, but have instead chosen it from a number as the most appropriate to my purpose. Usually similar quotations will have been found in the preliminary background chapters, and the quotation is to be considered as an illustration rather than a proof.

There remains the pleasant duty of acknowledging the help of many friends. To Professor George Lyman Kittredge I am most indebted for the searching criticism and the numerous suggestions which he lavished on the earliest version of this work. Professor R. Gale Noyes of Brown gave me valuable references, as did Professor Theodore Newton of McGill, Professor Arthur Sprague of Bryn Mawr, and Dr. William Ringler of Princeton. Mrs. Sutphen Bowers typed several early drafts. The manuscript of this book has been read and criticized in various stages by Professor Hyder Rollins of Harvard, Professors Hoyt Hudson and Thomas Parrott of Princeton, Professors Armistead Gordon and Archibald Hill of the University of Virginia, and Mrs. Jeremiah Finch. For permission to use their collections I am indebted to the librarians of the Harvard College Library, the British Museum, the Bodleian Library, the Cambridge University Library, and to the Master of Emmanuel College, Cambridge. Harvard University generously awarded me a grant for study in England.

F.B.

The University of Virginia
January 20, 1940.

POSTSCRIPT

This paperback edition is of a book originally published in 1940, condensing a diffuse Harvard dissertation of 1934. Yet however much one may wish to treat one's early ventures in publication as by-blows, I cannot disown this, for graduate students still seem to find it of use and its publication in two previous editions has effectively inhibited the production of other surveys on the same subject. There may, thus, be some reason to continue to keep it in print, as its original publishers have charitably proposed.

Since its composition dates back at the latest to 1938, footnote references to pertinent scholarship conclude even earlier. Small alterations in the present text have been made on pages 85, 86, 98, 204, and 219. Otherwise, the book must stand as it was first printed, substantive revision being impracticable at this late date.

F.B.

The University of Virginia
November, 1965.

CONTENTS

Elizabethan Revenge Tragedy
1587-1642

CHAPTER I

THE BACKGROUND OF REVENGE

I

BLOOD-REVENGE as a definite code appears sporadically in contemporary times; but it was universal among primitive peoples and strongly influenced their religion, law, and customs.[1] The modern theory of crime presupposes the existence of a State whose laws or regulations are broken, and punishment inflicted by this State for the breach of its rules. But in the earliest times there could be no crime because there was no State. Instead, a simple injury was inflicted by one individual on another or on a group of individuals bound together by the tie of relationship. For redress of this personal injury, in present times distinguished as a tort, the only possible action for the primitive individual was a direct revenge upon his injurer.[2] Since an act of violence was not a crime but merely a personal injury, the revenge for it in kind was the first manifestation of a consciousness of justice, for private revenge was the mightiest, the only possible form in which a wrong could be righted. Francis Bacon, with his usual acumen, recognized such a condition when he called revenge "a kind of wild justice."

In the first inception of revenge the injured person alone was concerned with the return of the injury. There was no question of right or duty but merely one of strength. If he were weak, he remained without vengeance and no one would procure it for him. With the growth of some sense of social consciousness there came a corresponding development from force to right in the theory of revenge. Finally, when the individual found himself an

[1] W. E. Wilda, *Das Strafrecht der Germanen* (Halle, 1842), p. 157, remarks, "In der Art und Weise der Uebung der Rache spricht sich der Charakter eines Volkes aus." See also, E. S. Tobien, *Die Blut-Rache nach altem Russischen Rechte, verglichen mit der Blut-Rache der Israeliten und Araber, der Griechen und Römer und der Germanen* (Dorpat, 1840), pp. 9-10.

[2] T. P. Ellis, *Welsh Tribal Law and Custom* (Oxford at the Clarendon Press, 1926), Vol. II, p. 67.

interlocking part of a family under the direct and terrible authority of a patriarch, the right to revenge was no longer a matter of choice but a binding obligation. Who offends a single member of the family now offends all. Two united families, sharing the possible spoils as a reward among their members, now oppose each other instead of two private men. If one of its members is murdered, the injured family need not seek out and punish the actual murderer. The solidarity of the family is so strongly felt that it suffices for any member to kill any other representative of the murderer's family. This is the true collective justice, which makes an obligation of a right, and which lies, enforcing the duty to revenge, at the base of the long-surviving historical vendetta.[3]

The vendetta may be divided into two chronological classes. First, the barbarous and unrestricted blood-feud among savage races which lack social machinery for the determination of blood-guilt. Second, the personal, restricted vendetta marked by the contraction of collective and hereditary punishment. Revenge is still extralegal because there are no laws dealing with it, and the duty to revenge lies with the near relatives of the slain man; but there is some power, whether of military autocracy or of public opinion, which prescribes bounds.[4] These bounds usually take the form of *talion,* the strict law of like for like, which popularized exact and standardized punishments for certain injuries and thus made the penalty, inflicted on the injurer alone, more suitable to the offense.[5]

At the time of the Anglo-Saxon migration to England the Angles, Saxons, and Jutes, among the most primitive of Germanic tribes in their law and social development, were just bridging the

---

[3] Raoul de la Grasserie, "De la genèse sociologique de la penalité," *Revue Internationale de la Sociologie* (Aug.-Sept. 1900), pp. 587-9, 612. For a further discussion, see Émile de Lavelaye, *De la Propriété et de ses Formes Primitives* (Paris, 1874), p. 197; J. Declareuil, "La Justice dans les Coutumes Primitives," *Nouvelle Revue Historique de Droit Français et Étranger*, Vol. XIII (March-April 1889), p. 163.

[4] H. J. Treston, *Poine. A Study in Ancient Greek Blood-Vengeance* (London: Longmans, Green & Co., 1923), pp. 1-2.

[5] For a sketch of the various laws of *talion* among early peoples, see Raoul de la Grasserie, *op. cit.,* pp. 601-11.

gap between the early and later forms of the vendetta.[6] The earliest extant English laws are based on the characteristic system of wergeld and contain no theory of state punishment. Acts of violence were still regarded as torts against individuals and families and the intensified Anglo-Saxon family spirit made the kinsmen responsible alone either to offer reparation for a murder or to risk the consequences. Comparably, if an agreement were reached, the injured family alone had the responsibility of collecting payment. The right of private warfare, known as *faehthe,* or feud, was inalienable to Anglo-Saxon freemen, since it distinguished them from the serfs.[7]

The feud was finally broken up not so much by Christianity as by the growth of a central power which made attempts to concern itself in what had always been considered private wrongs. This step came when the king demanded a share of the wergeld. In civil cases only, as early as the late seventh century, the king was supposed to have a share of the damages.[8] Later the king was paid a certain amount in criminal cases, and this requirement bolstered the idea that an offense against another subject was an offense against the king and state. The laws of Edward the Confessor disestablished the old kin-duties and instituted the *man-bote* payable to the king directly, although a small portion of the wergeld was reserved for the relatives. A further step limited the number of persons responsible for the wergeld and consequently the num-

6 W. E. Wilda, *op. cit.*, pp. 62-3. Tobien, *op. cit.*, p. 68, believes that the family solidarity which maintained the obligation to revenge in return for a share of the spoils, gradually fell into disuse in Germany from the end of the sixth century and was retained only by the Anglo-Saxons, among whom it survived longer than on the continent.

7 J. M. Kemble, *The Saxons in England* (London: Longmans, Green & Co., 1849), Vol. I, p. 267. See also John Thrupp, *The Anglo-Saxon Home* (London: Longmans, Green & Co., 1862), p. 141. The best outline of the code of Anglo-Saxon blood-revenge, as exhibited in the laws, is found in F. Liebermann, *Die Gesetze der Angelsachsen* (Halle, 1898-1916), Vol. II, pp. 320-2, under "Blutrache." For comments on the limits of the kindred in blood-revenge, see J. Thrupp, *op. cit.*, p. 144; B. S. Philpotts, *Kindred and Clan in the Middle Ages* (Cambridge, at the University Press, 1913), pp. 216-18; C. H. Pearson, *The Early and Middle Ages in England* (London: Bell & Daldy, 1861), p. 70.

8 *Hlothaere and Eadric* (685-686), cap. 11.

ber on whom vengeance could be taken for non-payment.[9] At last, in the mid-tenth century, the liability for a murder was fixed squarely on the shoulders of the slayer alone, and his kinsmen were allowed to repudiate the crime and their share of the wergeld.[10]

Progress was not always smooth. The intense individualism of the Danes and their more primitive civilization gave a temporary setback to the forward movement, and, although it has been stated that there is no evidence of legitimate blood-feud in England after the time of Edmund,[11] lingering traces seem to have continued into the reign of Henry I. Indeed, it was not until the time of Edward I that the law of wergeld was dead.[12] Private war, however, did not lose its legal sanction until the first half of the fourteenth century when the exaction of revenge by an individual began to be considered exclusively a crime against the state. And for many years individuals continued to value their own privileges far more than the common weal.[13]

William the Conqueror brought with him the Norman code of state justice which also depended on the help of the kinsmen for enforcement. He introduced to England the class of prosecutions called appeals by which the widow could prosecute the slayers of her husband, or a male heir the slayers of his ancestor. In the event of a conviction the king had no power to pardon; and to this extent the family rights of past ages were respected and the injury done was regarded as a private wrong. The legal procedure of the appeal, while abolishing the system of wergeld, retained

[9] *The Laws of Ine,* cap. 74, §2; *The Laws of Alfred,* cap. 30.

[10] *The Laws of II Edmund* (943-946), cap. 1, §§ 1, 3. See also T. P. Ellis, *op. cit.,* Vol. II, pp. 131-2, 135. E. Seebohm, *Tribal Custom in Anglo-Saxon Law* (London: Longmans, Green & Co., 1902), p. 357, on the evidence of the doubtful *Laws of Henry I* is not certain whether Edmund's innovation was adhered to.

[11] B. S. Philpotts, *Kindred and Clan in the Middle Ages,* p. 254.

[12] T. P. Ellis, *op. cit.,* Vol. II, p. 136.

[13] L. O. Pike, *A History of Crime in England* (London: Smith, Elder & Co., 1876), Vol. I, p. 170. J. W. Jeudwine, *Tort, Crime, and Police in Mediaeval Britain* (London: Williams & Norgate, 1917), pp. 84-5, places the great change in murder from tort to crime in the reign of Henry II when family solidarity at last gave way to monarchical supremacy.

the spirit of the old blood-revenge, for the nearest of kin had to take up the suit against the murderer and frequently to fight it out with him in the direct revenge of judicial combat. Trial by jury was an alternative, but it is' evident that most murderers preferred a judicial combat. The author of *The Mirror of Justices,* writing in the reign of Edward II, complains, "It is an abuse that justices drive a lawful man to put himself upon his country [i.e. by jury trial] when he offers to defend himself against an approver by body."[14]

Appeals were apparently the common and established means of prosecuting murder until the end of the fifteenth century. The whole procedure was so slipshod, however, that the murderer stood an even chance of escaping punishment completely.[15] To end the natural vices of the system Henry VII put forward the indictment, whereby the accused was to be tried at once merely on the presentation of information to the authorities.[16] This indict-

[14] *The Mirror of Justices,* ed. W. J. Wittaker (Selden Society, VII, 1893), p. 157.

[15] See L. O. Pike, *op. cit.,* Vol. I, pp. 290-2, for an account of the difficulties and delays which beset the appellant. Many of the cases for murder in the thirteenth and fourteenth centuries listed in *Select Cases from the Coroners' Rolls A.D. 1265-1413,* ed. Charles Gross (Selden Society, Vol. IX, 1896), tell a pitiful story of women relinquishing suits for murder through sheer inability to secure justice against stronger persons.

[16] Sir James Stephen, *A History of the Criminal Law of England* (London: Macmillan & Co., 1883), Vol. I, pp. 248-9. The difference between appeal and indictment was explained by Sir Thomas Smith, writing in 1583: "If any man hath killed my father, my sonne, my wife, my brother, or next kinsman, I haue choice to cause him to be indicted, by giuing information to the enquest of enquirie, (although he chaunce to escape the Constable or Iustices handes, and therefore not to bee apprehended) and therevpon to procure him to be outlawed, or else within a yeare and a day I may enter my appeale, that is mine accusation against him. If I began first to pursue him by information or denunciation to enditement, I am now no partie but the Prince, who for his dutie to God and his common wealth and subiectes, must see iustice executed against all malefactors and offenders against the peace, which is called Gods and his. . . . If I leaue that and will appeale, which is, profer my accusation against him who hath done to me this iniurie, the defendant hath this aduantage, to put himselfe to the Iurie, which is to that which before is said to haue that issue and triall by God and his countrie . . . or to demaund the triall by battle." *The Commonwealth of England and Maner of Government Thereof* (ed. 1589), sig. P₂ᵛ.

ment remained the legal method of prosecuting murderers in Elizabethan times, although the appeal was still known and in theory could be utilized. The appeal had been more or less a private matter and could be settled in a manner somewhat similar to the days of legalized private revenge: indeed, Sir Thomas Smith (1583) calls it "battle vpon his appeale & priuate reuenge."[17] But the indictment introduced almost in its entirety the system of state justice which operates today. The one remnant of the older times lay in the fact that the nearest of kin had to go to law with specific information and accusation before the state could move.[18]

2

In spite of the fact that justice was the sole prerogative of the Elizabethan state, with any encroachment on its newly won privilege liable to severe punishment, the spirit of revenge had scarcely declined in Elizabethan times: its form was merely different. Murder was still regarded as an injury done by the slayer to the nearest relatives, and the law tried to be as inflexible as possible in order to give the relatives justice. The rulers, of course, issued pardons, but usually only in cases of manslaughter.

Chief Justice Coke, the ultimate authority for Elizabethan law, defines murder as the act of a man of sound memory and of the age of discretion who unlawfully kills another within the realm with malice forethought, either expressed by the party, or implied by the law, so that the person wounded or hurt dies of the injury within a year and a day.[19] "Malice prepensed is, when one com-

[17] *The Commonwealth of England* (ed. 1589), sig. P₃ᵛ.

[18] Two customs—benefit of clergy and the privilege of sanctuary—were the only hindrances to the full penalties of the law. Benefit of clergy was forbidden in premeditated crimes by Henry VIII, who also, in 1540, exempted the privileges of sanctuary from murderers. For discussions of sanctuary in England, see J. C. Cox, *The Sanctuaries and Sanctuary Seekers of Mediaeval England* (London: Allen & Sons, 1911); N. M. Trenholme, *The Right of Sanctuary in England* (University of Missouri Studies, Vol. I, no. 5, 1903); I. D. Thornley, "The Destruction of Sanctuary," *Tudor Studies, Presented by the Board of Studies in History in the University of London to Albert Frederick Pollard,* ed. R. W. Seton-Watson (London: Longmans, Green & Co., 1924).

[19] *The Third Part of the Institutes of the Laws of England* (London, 1797), caps. 101, 105.

passeth to kill, wound, or beat another, and doth it *sedato animo*. This is said in law to be malice forethought, prepensed, *malitia praecogitata*. This malice is so odious in law, as though it be intended against one, it shall be extended towards another. *Si quis unum percusserit, cum alium percutere vellet, in felonia tenetur*."[20] Legally, therefore, Claudius in *Hamlet* is guilty of first-degree murder, and not of manslaughter, when Gertrude dies of the poison he has intended for Hamlet.

The accessory who gives the command is as guilty as the principal who commits the murder, but there are various fine distinctions. For one, the malice must be continuing until the mortal wound be given. Although there may have been feelings of malice between two persons who later met and were reconciled but afterward quarrelled again and one killed the other, the affair is one of manslaughter but not murder since the former malice did not continue. Thus if *A* commands *B* to kill *C* but before the act is done countermands the order and charges *B* not to kill *C*, *A* is not accessory if *B* afterwards kills *C*, for the malicious mind of the accessory must continue until the act is done.[21] Some such general situation is presented in D'Avenant's tragedy, *The Cruel Brother*.

If, for instance, *A* tells *B* of facts which operate as a motive to *B* for the murder of *C*, it would be an abuse of the language to say that *A* killed *C*, although no doubt he had been the remote cause of *C's* death. If *A* stopped short of counselling, procuring, or commanding *B* to kill *C*, he would not be an accessory before the fact, even if he had expected and hoped that the effect of what he had said would be to cause *B* to commit murder. Iago, for example, could probably not have been convicted as an accessory before the fact to Desdemona's murder, except for a single remark—"Do it not with poison, strangle her in her bed."[22]

Malice is the crux in determining murder, and is implied in the manner of the deed. One man kills another without provocation. According to the case, this might be simple malice, or malice prepense which carried the extreme sentence. Poisoning of a man so

---

[20] *ibid.*, cap. 7. [21] *ibid.*
[22] Stephen, *A History of the Criminal Law in England*, Vol. III, p. 8.

that he dies within a year implies malice in the eyes of the law and is therefore murder with malice prepense.[23] If a person has no malicious intention but joins with others who commit a murder, he is judged guilty only of manslaughter. Other manslaughters can also be voluntary but not judged murder with malice, as when they are occasioned by a sudden quarrel. In such a case the man is killed without premeditation and therefore without malice prepense.[24]

Private blood-revenge, because it necessarily arose from malice prepense, had no legal place in Elizabethan England. The only possible private retaliation at all countenanced was the instantaneous reaction to an injury, which was judged as manslaughter and a felony but which carried the possibility of royal pardon. The word "retaliation" is used advisedly, for the better minds allowed no "punishment" to be administered in his own behalf by a private man.[25] Private punishment, indeed, was not legal even in cases of injury for which the law provided no state punishment, as with opprobrious words and slight injuries to honor; although here Elizabethan sentiment was on the side of the revenger.

The right to punish their own wrongs was dear to many Elizabethans, who did not approve the interpretation of premeditated malice put by the law upon their revenges. James I took account of this attitude when he commanded "our louinge and faithfull Subiectes . . . vpon payne of our highe displeasure . . . that from this tyme forwarde they presume not vpon their owne

---

[23] Coke, *Third Institute,* cap. 7.

[24] "A just defence stands in these things. I. It must be done incontinent and forthwith so soone as ever violence is offered. For if there be a delay, and it come afterward, it loseth the name of a just defence, and becomes a revenge, arising of prepensed malice, as the lawyers use to speake." William Perkins, *The Whole Treatise of the Cases of Conscience* (ed. 1651), p. 293.

[25] Hobbes in 1651 argued that citizens of a commonwealth have covenanted to assist the sovereign in punishing others, and in so doing have laid down their ancient right of privately revenging injuries to themselves. "From the definition of Punishment, I inferre, First, that neither private revenges, nor injuries of private men, can properly be stiled Punishment; because they proceed not from publique Authority." *Leviathan,* ed. Waller (Cambridge at the University Press, 1904), pp. 223-4.

Imagination and construction of wronge . . . to aduenture in any sorte to ryghte (as they call it) or to reuenge (as the Lawe findes it) their owne quarrells."[26] The Elizabethans were conscious of the earlier periods of lawlessness when revenge was a right,[27] but Coke, speaking formally for the law, terms any and all private revenges "great misprisions," under no circumstances to be countenanced in the eyes of the courts.[28]

Blood-revenge for the murder of a close relative, therefore, falls in the same legal category as any other murder with malice aforethought. No evidence can be found that Elizabethan law allowed for motive or extenuating circumstances in any murder which was the result of such malice and premeditation as was owned by an avenger of blood. An unequivocal statement of that fact was written about the year 1612: "It is trewe that the lawe doth not att all distinguish of the nature of the provocation whether it wear slight or violent nor the manner of the facte whether the armor wear equall or onequall valueing life aboue all. In case of murder the lawe makes no distinction between him that enioyes the wife in reueng of iniurie or him that expectes hit by practise. For though we make the conditions none so equall yet the [law] allowes or admittes no wager for bloud."[29]

Elizabethan law felt itself capable of meting out justice to murderers, and therefore punished an avenger who took justice into his own hands just as heavily as the original murderer. The authorities, conscious of the Elizabethan inheritance of private justice from earlier ages, recognized that their own times still held the possibilities of serious turmoil; and they were determined that private revenge should not unleash a general disrespect for law.[30]

[26] "Treatise Against Duelling," Cotton MS., Titus C IV, fol. 407.

[27] See, for example, John Donne, "Paradoxes and Problems" [c. 1590-1601], Problem XI, *Complete Poetry and Selected Prose,* ed. Hayward (Bloomsbury: Nonesuch Press, 1929), p. 352.

[28] *Third Institute,* cap. 65.

[29] Cotton MS., Titus C IV, fol. 265. The treatise seems to have been written by Henry Howard Earl of Northampton. See F. T. Bowers, "Henry Howard Earl of Northampton and the Jacobean Duel," *Englische Studien,* Vol. LXXI (1937), pp. 350-5.

[30] For example, in 1615 one William Flodder was sentenced to a prison term

Perhaps the most eloquent statement of the legal position was made by Francis Bacon when prosecuting a duelling case in 1615:

"For the Mischief itself, it may please your lordships to take into consideration, that when revenge is once extorted out of the Magistrate's hands, contrary to God's ordinance, 'mihi vindicta, ego retribuam,' and every man shall bear the sword, not to defend but to assail; and private men begin once to presume to give law to themselves, and to right their own wrongs; no man can forsee the danger and inconveniencies that may arise and multiply thereupon. It may cause sudden storms in court, to the disturbance of his majesty, and unsafety of his person. It may grow from quarrels to bandying, and bandying to trooping, and so to tumult and commotion; from particular persons to dissension of families and alliances; yea to national quarrels."[31]

3

Though legal condemnation of private revenge came slowly in England, it was preceded by the denunciations of the clerics and moralists.[32] And after a system of state justice had finally been established, the religious and ethical protest against revenge increased until, in the God-fearing Elizabethan age, it exercised a force second to none in the constant war against the private lawlessness of the times.[33] The old Mosaic laws legitimizing blood-revenge in the Bible were either twisted so as to apply to

for threatening to revenge himself on one Elizabeth who had given evidence before the court which led to the condemnation and execution of his brother. See Sir Nathaniel Bacon, *Official Papers 1580-1620*, ed. Saunders (Camden Society, 1915), p. 32.

[31] *A Complete Collection of State Trials from the Earliest Period to the Year 1783*, ed. T. B. Howell (London, 1816), Vol. II, p. 1032.

[32] See the pious reflections in the entry for the year 979 in *The Anglo-Saxon Chronicle*, ed. B. Thorpe (London: Longmans, Green & Co., 1861), Vol. I, p. 232; see also *Old English Homilies and Homilectic Treatises of the Twelfth and Thirteenth Centuries, First Series*, ed. R. Morris (Early English Text Society, 1868), pp. 29, 79.

[33] For an excellent selection from the Elizabethan religious protest against revenge, see L. B. Campbell, "Theories of Revenge in Renaissance England," *Modern Philology*, Vol. XXVIII (1931), pp. 281-96.

state justice,[34] or were ignored, or contrasted to the new world created by Christ. The strongest expression of this overthrow of the Mosaic law as applied to life in England is given by Daniel Tuvil in 1609: "Ierusalem is new erected; among her Citizens, there is now no thirsting for reuenge. The law of Retribution is disanuld amongst them. It is not a *dictum est antiquis,* but a *dico vobis* which they follow. An eie no longer for an eie: a tooth no longer for a tooth."[35]

The chief argument against revenge may be quoted from Thomas Becon (1560), although it was the staple of every other moralist: "To desire to be revenged, when all vengeance pertaineth to God, as he saith, 'Vengeance is mine, and I will reward' . . . this to do ye are forbidden."[36] There was no gainsaying this direct command. "God would neuer haue assumed the power of reuenge as a parcell of his owne prerogatiue in case his purpos had bene to leaue all men to the reuenge of their owne particularities."[37]

With the word of God so expressly forbidding private revenge, it was only natural to believe damnation awaited those who disobeyed. Cleaver (1612) declares that the revenger "strips himselfe of Gods protection, he neither can pray for a blessing, nor haue a blessing; because he is out of Gods defence: he promiseth no shelter, neither do his Angels watch ouer him that is out of his wayes."[38] Bishop Hall (1612) predicts for the revenger a double death, of body and of soul.[39] The religious writers denounced the fact that men could "thinke that God is fauorable . . . when as they imagine, that the reuenge they pursue is iust, and that they

---

[34] See, for example, Thomas Nashe, "Christes Tears over Jerusalem" [1593], *Works,* ed. R. B. McKerrow (London: Sidgwick & Jackson, 1910), Vol. II, p. 24.

[35] *Essayes, Morall and Theologicall* (1609), sigs. K_{11}-K_{11}^v. For further expression, see Samuel Rowlands, "The Betraying of Christ" [1598], *Works* (Hunterian Club, 1880), Vol. I, pp. 43-4; Anthony Copley, *A Fig for Fortune* [1596] (Spenser Society, 1883), p. 54.

[36] *The Early Works,* ed. Rev. John Ayre (Parker Society, 1843), p. 323.

[37] Cotton MS., Titus C IV, fol. 39^v.

[38] *A Plaine and Familiar Exposition of the Ten Commandments* (ed. 1618), p. 267.

[39] "Second Sermon on the Impress of God," *Works,* ed. Phillip Wynter (Oxford University Press, 1863), Vol. V, p. 76.

haue beene vnworthilie abused."[40] No private revenge could ever partake of justice.[41] On a lower and more practical plane, it was argued that an act of revenge decreased rather than increased honor, since "the honour that is wonne by her, hath an ill ground. . . . Honour is a thinge too noble of it selfe, to depend of a superfluous humour, so base and vilanous, as the desire of vengeance is."[42]

Finally, moralists painted a gloomy picture of the mind of the man tormented by the lust for revenge, and of the tortures that awaited the successful revenger:

> O poor reuenge! behold, he thou hast slaine,
> Sleeping in rest, lies free from care and paine. . . .
> Whilst thou suruiuing feel'st the horrid smart
> Of many thousand tortures in thy hart.
> For say thou scape the rigour of the Law,
> Thy wounded conscience will haue many a flaw;
> Feares thou shalt passe by day, and then at night
> Dreames all of terrour thy scarr'd soule affright.
> Orphanes and Widowes curses thou shalt haue,
> To bring thee with confusion to thy graue.
> Which if in mercy God doe shield thee from,
> Iustice hath set this vnauoyded Doome,
> The plague of bloodshed on thy stocke shall lie,
> Till she be quit in thy posterity.
> Poore world, if these thy best contentments be,
> Seeke blood and vengeance you that list to me.[43]

---

[40] Grimestone, *A Table of Humane Passions, with their Causes and Effects. Written by ye Reuerend Father in God F. N. Coeffeteau, Bishop of Dardania . . . translated into English* (1621), pp. 321-2.

[41] Hall, "The Great Imposter," *Works*, ed. Wynter, Vol. V, p. 166.

[42] John Eliot, *Discourses of Warre and Single Combat, by B. de Loque* (1591), p. 55.

[43] George Wither, "Abuses Stript and Whipt" [1613], *Juvenilia* (Spenser Society, 1871), Vol. I, p. 85. See also Thomas Nashe, "Strange News," *Works*, ed. McKerrow, Vol. I, p. 333; Sir William Cecil, *Certaine Precepts, Or Directions, for the Well Ordering and Carriage of a Man's Life* (1617), p. 27; *The Rich Cabinet* (1616), fol. 4; Robert Burton, *The Anatomy of Melancholy*, ed. A. R. Shilleto (London: Bell & Sons, 1893), I, 298; John Eliot, *Discourses of Warre and*

4

So far attention has been paid only to the forces which were seeking to suppress private revenge, but it would be a grave error to neglect the stubborn, though not always articulate, resistance to reform.

The turbulent English nobles of the Middle Ages kept alive the spirit of violence and personal blood-revenge in times when the royal justice was more a name than a power.[44] Later, the Wars of the Roses loosed a full tide of vengeance for relatives slain in civil broils. At the battle of Wakefield occurred perhaps the most terrible example of the eagerness of a bloodthirsty revenger to exact the penalty on his helpless victim:

"He [the young Earl of Rutland] was by the sayd lord Clifford espied, folowed, and taken, and by reson of his apparell, demaunded what he was. The yõg gentelman dismaied, had not a word to speake, but kneled on his knees implorying mercy, and desiryng grace, both with holding vp his hãdes and making dolorous countinance, for his speche was gone for feare. Saue him sayde his Chappelein, for he is a princes sonne, and peraduenture may do you good hereafter. With that word, the lord Clifford marked him and sayde: by Gods blode, thy father slew myne, and so wil I do the and all thy kyn, and with that woord, stacke the erle to yᵉ hart with his dagger, and bad the Chappeleyn bere the erles mother & brother worde what he had done, and sayde."[45]

In Tudor times the mass violence which had marked the preceding ages was succeeded by an age in which violence became confined to the individual. The state had been regulated and laws

Single Combat (1591), pp. 54-5; Grimestone, *A Table of Humane Passions* (1621), pp. 573-4.

[44] See, for example, I. S. Leadam, *Select Cases Before the King's Council in the Star Chamber . . . A.D. 1477-1509* (Selden Society, XVI, 1903), p. xcv. For one particularly interesting case, in 1276, see *Calendar of Inquisitions Miscellaneous (Chancery) Preserved in the Public Record Office. Prepared under the Superintendence of the Deputy Keeper of the Records* (London: Public Record Office, 1916), no. 2197, 2140.

[45] *Chronicles of London,* ed. C. L. Kingsford (Oxford at the Clarendon Press, 1905), p. 172.

had been written on the books, but personal character, with its inheritance of fierceness and independence, had not changed. The idea of redress by private action was still very much alive, particularly among an aristocracy which prided itself on its individuality. Open assault and the duel were current practises, and for those too timid to take the law into their own hands there was no lack of private *bravi* ready to stab. A preacher (1585) inveighed from the pulpit: "For now a dayes the Courtier against his coequall . . . all and euerie one of these (I say) against another, (Yea for the least thing done amisse) doo on euerie hande breath out vengeance and recompence. Some doo it by bloodsheading in the streetes, as the Courtier."[46] Sir Thomas Smith (1583) truly wrote, "The nature of our Nation is free, hault, prodigal of life and bloud."[47]

The Elizabethan who attended public executions as an amusement was used to the sight of blood and would scarcely flinch from it on the stage. Rather, he would demand it, for he was keenly interested in murders for any other motive than simple robbery.[48] Murder to expedite a theft was easily understandable, and the offender was promptly hanged; yet murder for different motives excited the Elizabethan audience's curiosity. An essentially religious person, the Elizabethan regarded murder as the worst of all crimes—with death, to his Renaissance spirit, the ultimate disaster.[49] Characteristic English hatred of secrecy and

[46] Thomas Bankes, *A Verie Godly . . . Sermon against the bad spirits of Malignitie, malice, and vnmercifulness* (ed. 1586), sigs. D₃-D₃ᵛ.

[47] *The Commonwealth of England* (ed. 1589), sig. O₈.

[48] Dozens of pamphlets are preserved narrating in journalistic style the latest murders. This public interest in crime aroused the indignation of one A.Ar. in 1630: "It is indeede as if one attained or held honours by murders, treasons, adulteries, thefts, lies and the like; or by slobering them ouer, as som write of the smothered murder of Marques *Hambleton* and others." *The Practise of Princes* (1630), p. 21.

[49] "For he [James I] well obserued, no greater iniustice, no iniury more intolerable cã be done by man to man then murther. In all wrongs fortune hath recours, the losses of honor or goods may be repaired, satisffaction may be made, reconciliation may be procured, so long as the party iniuried is aliue, but when the person murthered is bereft of his life, what can restore it? what satisfaction can be giuen him? where shall the murtherer meete with him to be reconciled

treachery could, and did, excuse an open killing in hot blood, "For Actes done sodainly and without aduisement differ as much in kynde and qualitie from others that are done aduisedly and with prepensed malice in colde bloud, as reason doth from rage, chance from choice and necessitie from temeritie."[50] Premeditated, secret, unnatural murder, however, struck a chord of horror.

The English insistence on a semblance of fair play discountenanced the hiring of *bravi*. Queen Elizabeth herself frowned on bands of retainers, fearful that they might sow the seeds of revolution, and, to keep her kingdom peaceful, put down with an iron hand the squabbles of her touchy nobles.[51] Foreign ideas filtered in, however, and the Earl of Oxford, returning from travels abroad, was with great difficulty dissuaded from hiring *bravi* to revenge himself on Sidney.[52]

Points of honor and political grudges kept quarrels smouldering during Elizabeth's reign, but under James a fresh influence appeared following the sudden influx of Scotsmen into London. The strict application of state justice by the Tudors had done much to eradicate such motives as led to the murder of the young earl at the battle of Wakefield, but the Scots who came down with James had experienced no such weakening of the old tradition. Self-help and blood-revenge flourished practically unchecked in Scotland, where the powerful nobles played battledore and shuttlecock with the royal authority.[53] James himself asserted that in 1600 he had a

to him, vnlesse he be sent out of this world to follow his spirite, which by his wickednes he hath separated frō his body? Therfor of all iniuries, of all actes of iniustice, and of all things most to be looked into, murther is the greatest." George Eglisham, *The Forerunner of Revenge. Vpon the Duke of Buckingham for the poysoning of the most potent King Iames . . . and the Lord Marquis of Hamilton* (Frankfort, 1626), pp. 9-10.

[50] James I, "A Treatise against Duelling," Cotton MS., Titus C IV, fol. 414ᵛ.

[51] Sir John Hayward, *Annals of the First Four Years of the Reign of Queen Elizabeth*, ed. John Bruce (Camden Society, 1840), p. 93. See William Camden's comments on her treatment of the quarrel between Essex and Leicester in his *Annales, or The History of Elizabeth* (ed. 1635), p. 64.

[52] Lewis Einstein, *The Italian Renaissance in England* (Columbia University Press, 1902), p. 74.

[53] For duels, murders, and pitched battles in Scotland, see David Moysie, *Memoirs of the Affairs of Scotland MDLXXVII-MDCIII* (Edinburgh: Maitland

narrow escape from revengers of blood,[54] and the revengeful passion was not unknown to him.[55] The weak state of the law in Scotland forced men to take their own satisfaction when they failed to obtain revenge by legal means. Lord Uchiltrie, seeing how valueless were James's promises to prosecute vigorously a murderer of his kindred, rode to all his friends and asked them to sign a bond that they would assist his revenge. After he was captured he "affermit and confest his trauelling and obteaning of the samyn bond, alledging that he had great resoun so to doe, for he saw no vther appearance of reuendge to come; afferming oppinlie to his Maiestie at all tymes, that he wald embrace and refuse no friendship that wald assist and tak pairt in the reuendge of that murthour."[56]

The best example of the distinction the Scotsman drew between ordinary murder and what he considered a just slaying in private revenge, is found in the murder of the Regent Murray by Hamilton in January 1570. Murray had persecuted Hamilton, who was of the queen's party, and finally, after clapping him in jail, endeavored to confiscate his property. When the strain drove his wife insane, Hamilton broke prison, and, lying in wait, shot Murray as he rode through the streets. He escaped to France "and liued certaine yeares after, protesting many times that he had taken priuate reuenge on *Murray,* for that his patience could hold out no longer against the iniuries he had done him. . . . Neither could he be perswaded in *France* afterward, though he

Club, 1830), pp. 4, 7-9, 20-3, 35, 37-8, 41, 57, 65, 67, 69, 71, 85, 88-93, 110, 111.

[54] Camden, *Annales* (ed. 1635), p. 529, has an interesting account from the Elizabethan point of view: "So also was the Sword prepared at the same time in *Scotland* by the *Rethuens,* brethern, to take away his [James's] life; who boyling with reuenge for the putting to death of their father the Earle *Goury* by law in the Kings *nonage,* by a wile enticed the King to whom they were much bounden, into their house, most wickedly appointed him to the slaughter, and had indeed murdered him had not God . . . turned the wicked plot against the heads of the authors." For a modern analysis, see William Roughead, *The Riddle of the Ruthvens* (Edinburgh: Green & Sons, 1919).

[55] Thomas Birch, *Memoirs of the Reign of Queen Elizabeth* (London, 1754), Vol. I, p. 132.

[56] Moysie, *Memoirs,* pp. 92-3.

seemed a man forward to commit a villanous fact, to attempt the like against Admiral *Coligny,* saying many times that he had beene a iust reuenger of his owne griefe, whereof he repented him, but to a reuenger of another mans, he would neuer be drawn, neither by entreaty nor reward."[57]

The Elizabethans recognized to the full the quarrelsomeness of the Scot. "It is well knowne in *Scotland* how insatiable is the passion of Ire, and the appetite of Reuenge, for their deadly flod wil neuer be quenched, but with the blood of al their enemies and their adherents."[58] Peter Heylyn (1621) is even more definite: "The people haue one barbarous custome yet continuing, if any two be displeased they expect no law, but bang it out brauely, one and his kindred against the other and his; and thinke the king much in their common, if they grant him at a certaine day to keepe the peace. This fighting they call their *Feides.*"[59] The virus was transferred to London and by their example the Scots had a distinct effect in increasing the personal violence of the age among the English. In addition, the irritation of the English at the Scotch invasion of their city and the favoritism shown to them by the king, provoked such bad feeling between the two races that the anonymous (and scandalous) author of *The Secret History of the Reign of King James I,* written about 1615, comments, "Private quarrels nourished—but especially between the Scottish and the English, duels in every street maintained."[60]

The quarrelsomeness of the times was also extended to the law courts;[61] every satirist had something to say about the multitude of cases brought before the judges from a spirit of private vindictiveness.[62] When the legal decision was not that expected, retaliation and even murder could result. In 1616 John Bartram, being

[57] Camden, *Annales* (ed. 1635), pp. 119-20.

[58] Thomas Wright, *The Passions of the Minde in Generall* (ed. 1630), p. 72.

[59] *Microcosmus, or A little Description of the Great World* (1621), p. 266.

[60] *The Autobiography and Correspondence of Sir Simonds D'Ewes,* ed. J. O. Halliwell-Phillipps (London, 1845), Vol. II, p. 324.

[61] Philip Stubbes, *Anatomie of Abuses* (New Shakspere Society, 1877-9), p. 10.

[62] See especially, Samuel Rowlands, "Looke to it for Ile Stabbe Ye," *Works,* Vol. I, p. 45.

foiled in an unjust lawsuit by the judge, Sir John Tyndall, resolved to revenge himself, and, preparing carefully, assassinated him.[63]

The influence of the Scotch traditions of blood-revenge cannot be ignored in considering the attitude of the audiences at Elizabethan tragedies, but the Englishman was fully conscious of the workings of revenge in his own midst. Robert Anton (1617) writes, "Neuer more cholericke constitutions knowne, So practick in *reuenge,* as now are showne";[64] Wither (1626), enumerating the passions, assigns to Revenge a princedom as one who wishes to be sole commander.[65] And when revenge was mentioned, murder was always in mind. James I (1618) says plainly, "*Reuenge* and *Murder* come coupled together."[66] The Earl of Clarendon calls revenge the great patron of murder since the spilling of the first blood;[67] and Bishop Hall (1625) writes, "There are those, whose hands are white, and clean from bribes, from extortions; but *their feet are* yet *swift to shed blood* upon their own private revenge."[68] Cleaver (1612) exhorts men to take heed of revenge and God will keep them from murder.[69]

Since revenge was a serious matter, the Elizabethans' interest in it as a criminal passion led to various analyses of the subsidiary passions which excited it. Anger was often assigned as the first cause.[70] Grimestone in his study of the passions (1621) draws distinctions between anger and hatred which are important for a

[63] N.J., *A True Relation of . . . that horrible Murther committed by Iohn Bartram, Gent. vpon the body of Sir Iohn Tyndal. . . .* (1616).

[64] *Vices Anotimie* (1617), sig. H4[v].

[65] *Juvenilia,* Vol. I, p. 55.

[66] *The Peacemaker: or Great Brittaines Blessing* (1618), sig. E4.

[67] "The Difference . . . between . . . George Duke of Buckingham, and Robert Earl of Essex," *Reliquiæ Wottonianæ* (ed. 1672), p. 198.

[68] "The Estate of a Christian," *Works,* ed. Wynter, Vol. V, p. 304.

[69] *A Plaine and Familiar Exposition of the Ten Commandments* (ed. 1618), p. 270.

[70] "On Man," *Juvenilia,* Vol. I, p. 97. For other references to anger and revenge, see Thomas Becon, *Early Works,* ed. Ayre, p. 522; John Lane, *Tom Tel-Troths Message,* ed. F. J. Furnivall (New Shakspere Society, 1876), pp. 126-7; R. C., *The Times Whistle,* ed. J. M. Cowper (Early English Text Society, 1871), p. 95; Phineas Fletcher, *The Purple Island,* Canto VII, l. 55.

study of the villain-revengers of Elizabethan tragedy. Hatred, in the eyes of another, was to be defined as natural wrath which had endured too long and had turned to unnatural malice.[71] According to Grimestone, choler (or anger) comes from personal wrongs, but the person need not be touched to feel hatred; choler is felt for particular men, hatred may be for all humanity; choler can be cured by patience, but hatred is everlasting; choler wishes the victim to recognize the revenger, hatred desires only to watch the destruction of the victim without recognition; choler is full of pain, hatred is cold; choler has bounds in revenge, but hatred is boundless and always seeks the absolute ruin of its object.[72]

Jealousy was another prime mover of revenge and murder: "It sometimes bursteth out so farre, and exceedeth beyond her bounds so much, as it turneth it selfe into extream Hatred, and from thence falleth into a Frensie, and Madnesse, not alone against the partie it loueth, or his aduersary or Riuall, but as well against all such, who, as he thinkes, may be any way an obstacle or let, to hinder or crosse him in his dissigne and purpose, whereupon haue ensued most cruell reuengements, and most horrible and sauage murthers, beyond all common sense and reason; yea, many times against their owne reputations and Honours, and against their owne proper selfes, and lifes."[73]

Pride and ambition were also considered the forerunners of revenge and death: "For all vnbridled passions in man, and vpon which reason beares not a hard hand, are impetuous; but that of ambition is impetuously furious, and (when ioyned with reuenge-

[71] Gervase Babington, *Works* (ed. 1637), p. 22. See also Cleaver, *A Plaine and Familiar Exposition* (ed. 1618), p. 260; C. W., *The Crying Murther: Contayning the . . . Butchery of Mr. Trat* (1624), sig. C4ᵛ; Nathaniel Carpenter, *Achitophel, or The Picture of a wicked Politician* (ed. 1638), sig. C7ᵛ.

[72] *A Table of Humane Passions* (1621), pp. 196-200.

[73] Robert Tofte, *The Blazon of Jealousie* (1615), pp. 59-60. See also Phineas Fletcher, *The Purple Island*, Canto VII, l. 17; Thomas Carew, "Of Jealousy," *Poems*, ed. W. C. Hazlitt (Roxburghe Library, 1870), p. 78; *Politeuphia* (ed. 1598), fol. 21; John Kepers, *The Courtiers Academie. . . . Originally written in Italian by Count Haniball Romei* (1598?), p. 127.

ful disdaine) furiously outragious. Iniustice is the minister of disdaine, and reuenge is the executioner of iniustice."[74]

To judge by the number and the quality of the outbursts against it, envy was perhaps the greatest Elizabethan vice, and it may be considered one of the most powerful of the passions inducing revenge. Indeed, Burton (1621) believed revenge arose almost solely from emulation and envy;[75] another (1611) directly called it the fountain of murder.[76] The grudge deriving from envy was greater than that from direct injury, for a wronged man could forget or else pocket the injury, "but who is settled in enuie, leaues nothing vndone that maye aduance to reuenge."[77] Envy's hatred was so great that, in contrast to anger, no wrongs were necessary for a person to become the recipient of its malice; indeed, it was often directed against the most virtuous and peaceful of men.[78]

The envious man was not hesitant to shed blood even without provocation, but when, according to his lights, he was actually wronged, the injury became magnified tenfold, and "by secret ambushes, or by open hostilitie, he must carue himselfe a satisfaction. No plaister will heale his pricked finger, but his heartbloud that did it. . . . Malice is so madde that it will not spare friend, to wreake vengeance on foes."[79] John Norden (1597) pithily summed up the case: envy "carrieth no shape or resemblance, neither of valour, which consisteth in maintaining a iust quarrell, nor of reuenge, as it is truly reuenge: for that it seeketh to iniure

---

[74] Robert Dallington, *Aphorismes Civill and Militarie* (1613), p. 13. This quotation parallels the motives of such villains as Eleazar in *Lust's Dominion* and Brunnhalt in *Thierry and Theodoret*. See also Cotton MS., Titus C IV, fol. 92ᵛ; Joseph Hall, "Characters of Virtues and Vices," *Works,* ed. Wynter, Vol. VI, p. 122.

[75] *The Anatomy of Melancholy,* ed. Shilleto, Vol. I, p. 310.

[76] William Mason, *A Handful of Essaies* (1611), p. 124.

[77] Geoffrey Fenton, *Golden Epistles . . . gathered, as wel out of the remaynder of Gueuaraes woorkes, as other Authours* (ed. 1582), p. 244. See also *Politeuphia* (ed. 1598), fol. 23ᵛ.

[78] James I, *The Peacemaker* (1618), sigs. C₁ᵛ-C₂.

[79] Thomas Adams, *The Diuells Banket* (1614), pp. 77-8.

such as iniure not. He is a simple man that enuieth and cannot pretend matter to beare colour of lawfull reuenge."[80]

5

In spite of the preoccupation of the age with the subject of private revenge, not many narrations of Elizabethan revenges ending in murder have come down to us, with the exception of the numerous accounts of private duels. We do know that feuds between families, frequently resulting in blood, were not unknown in Elizabethan times, and James I (c. 1610) avowed his incessant care "to suppresse all factions and deadly feuds wch are the motives of greate mischiefe in great families."[81] These feuds were spoken of as "endless" and were caused by "contempt of all indifferent and equitable endes . . . as well betweene great families as priuat persons."[82] Saviolo commented that private quarrels between two or three persons not infrequently spread to whole families and ended in great hurt and bloodshed.[83] One of the arguments seriously advanced in favor of duelling (c. 1612) was "wher mani members of great howses or allies vnto those howses are like to make an euerlasting quarrel it were better with thē hasarde an euent of one battaile to make an ende of the matter and in this case the Duells may be warranted."[84] A glimpse of such a feud is given by the repentance, before his beheading in 1601, of Sir Charles Danvers, who craved the pardon of Lord Grey "to whom he professed hee had bene a great enemy, not for any wrong done to him by that Lord, but out of entire loue to *Southampton,* with whom the Lord *Grey* had beene at deadly feude."[85]

Private revenge among the nobles and gentlemen took almost exclusively the form of a duel, but the ill-famed Leicester was scandalously accused of endeavoring to revenge himself on Simier (who had revealed his marriage to the queen) by hiring one of

[80] *The Mirror of Honor* (1597), p. 24.
[81] Cotton MS., Titus C IV, fols. 398^v-399.   [82] *ibid.,* fol. 469^v.
[83] *Vincentio Saviolo his Practise* (1595), sig. R₃.
[84] Cotton MS., C IV, fol. 86.   [85] Camden, *Annales* (ed. 1635), p. 557.

her guards to murder him.[86] Felton's assassination of Buckingham in 1628 was almost universally attributed to motives of private revenge, in spite of his obstinate denials.[87] An accuser at his trial asserted that he was "of a stout and revengeful spirit, who having once received an injury from a gentleman, he cut off a piece of his little finger, and sent it with a challenge to the gentleman to fight with him, thereby to let him know that he valued not the exposing his whole body to hazard, so he might have an opportunity to be revenged."[88]

Masters had occasionally to fear the revenge of their servants. Fulke Greville was stabbed in the back by his servant in 1628 for not sufficiently rewarding him.[89] A servant in 1605 had been vowed the hand of his master's daughter and some land; but when this offer was replaced by vague promises, he swore revenge and succeeded in murdering his employer. The pamphleteer of the event romances vividly: "Thirtie pounds a yeare shall not satisfie him that should haue beene heire to fiue hundred, nor faire wordes tempt me from reuenge, which haue been wronged in my wife, yet I wil seeme calme, shew diligence, and creep againe into your loue, but as a serpent in your bosome, that when I seeme most kind, I will be subtile, and my reuenge most sudaine."[90] Chamberlain in 1623 records "a foul barbarous murder committed in Lombard Street by a 'prentice, upon two of his mistress's children, of six or seven years old, by cutting their throats, and then hanged himself. The reason is said to be some devilish revenge for ill

[86] Camden, op. cit., p. 205.   [87] Francis Osborne, Works (ed. 1673), p. 224.

[88] T. Howell, State Trials, Vol. III, pp. 370-1. D'Ewes gossips how Sir Henry Hungate had once basely revenged himself upon Felton and was ever afterward so afraid of a counter-revenge that he induced Buckingham to demote Felton, "and this caused him to work his revenge on the Duke's person, said some of the Duke's friends and followers." D'Ewes, however, believed Felton's protestations, and was most convinced that there was no motive of private revenge in the murder because Felton had asked mercy for Buckingham's soul at the moment he stabbed him. Autobiography, ed. Halliwell-Phillipps, Vol. I, pp. 382-4.

[89] Anthony à Wood, Athenæ Oxoniensis, col. 522.

[90] Two most vnnatural and bloodie Murthers: The one by Maister Cauerly . . . the other by Mistris Browne and her seruant Peter (1605), p. 22.

usage."[91] But there is no reason further to consider the long lists of such vulgar crimes which are common in any age.

The murder of Sir Thomas Overbury in 1613 was one of the most "Machiavellian" and complicated of all Elizabethan revenges. About the year 1601 Thomas Overbury, vacationing in Edinburgh, met young Robert Carr, an obscure page. The two became fast friends and journeyed to London together, where in 1606 Carr attracted the attention of James and rapidly became the royal favorite. Carr and Overbury retained their friendship to such an extreme that when Carr was created Lord Rochester in 1610, contemporary gossip made fun of Overbury's dominance over the favorite and thus indirectly over the king himself.

Early in 1611 Rochester fell under the spell of the young Countess of Essex whose reputation was already unsavory. Overbury remonstrated strongly, and Rochester was foolish enough to repeat Overbury's denunciations of her character to the countess. About this time the appearance in manuscript of *The Wife,* attributed to Overbury, increased the countess's anger, since she regarded it as an open exposure, by contrast, of her defects. Overbury fell into disfavor with the king through her machinations and, in April 1613, was thrown into the Tower. Rochester, disgusted by Overbury's arrogance and the gibes of his friends at Overbury's governance, made no effort to support the prisoner. The countess had Sir William Wade removed as governor of the Tower, and installed Sir Gervase Helwys, whom she believed corruptible, in his place. Mrs. Turner, an apothecary Franklin, and Richard Weston followed her orders and for some time attempted to poison Overbury, probably with doses of copper vitriol. Sir Gervase Helwys may perhaps be exempted from actual participation in the crime, although he had knowledge of it, and indeed protested at the trial that he did not inform the king because he believed that James knew what was going on.

The poison doses were sent to Overbury throughout the summer, but he remained alive, even though in great agony. The usual

[91] Thomas Birch, *The Court and Times of James the First* (London, 1848), Vol. II, p. 389.

explanation for the poison's inefficacy is that either the poisoners were too timid in their doses, or else they were cheated in their purchase of the poisons, a not unusual occurrence. The real reason may have been that Helwys diverted most of the poisoned food. At any rate, the countess's patience was exhausted by September of 1613, and Overbury was finally murdered by a poisoned clyster and hurriedly buried. Two months later Rochester, now Earl of Somerset, married the Countess of Essex. More than a year passed before suspicion was aroused by Somerset's enemies and the whole plot was discovered. The accomplices were executed, Somerset and his wife condemned by the court, but their lives were spared by royal intervention.

Contemporary opinion laid, correctly, the motive for the murder to the Countess of Essex's desire for revenge on Overbury for defaming her character in his attempts to obstruct her marriage with Rochester. Gossip was no more tender of her reputation than Overbury had been. Her divorce from the Earl of Essex was accompanied by highly scandalous allegations, and she was even believed to have consulted some time before with Doctor Forman and Doctor Savory, two conjurers, about poisoning her husband Essex, lest he discover her adultery with Rochester and revenge himself on them.[92]

The curious ineffectiveness of the poison which tortured but did not kill Overbury has already been remarked. Its slowness, however, was one of the strong points of the legal prosecution, which declared that murder was the most horrible of all crimes and of all murders that by poisoning the most detestable, but murder by lingering poison was the worst of all.[93] The Elizabethan was prepared to defend himself in open feud, "for by vigilancie and industrie meanes may be had to resist, or euite the most violent beast that euer nature bred, but from false and treacherous hartes, from poysoning murtherers what wit or wisedome can defend?"[94]

[92] D'Ewes, *Autobiography,* Vol. I, pp. 71, 88-9.

[93] *State Trials,* ed. Howell, Vol. II, pp. 911, 916. For comments on the intricacies of the plot, see D'Ewes, *Autobiography,* Vol. I, pp. 71, 73-4; Edward Parry, *The Overbury Mystery* (London: Fisher Unwin Ltd., 1925), pp. 304-11.

[94] George Eglisham, *The Forerunner of Revenge* (Frankfort, 1626), p. 10.

Simple poisons were frequently used in Elizabethan times among the common people, and especially among wives who for one reason or another wished to rid themselves of their husbands; indeed, Coke during the trial of Weston for the murder of Overbury, observed that adultery was most often the begetter of poisoning. Grudges between gentlemen were customarily settled by the sword, not by the cup. Whether the comparative absence of known poisonings in high life during the period was entirely due to the fact that poisons were not used, whether various poisonings were successfully hushed up (as the Overbury affair nearly was), or whether the poisons used by the wealthier persons defied the analysis of the doctors, must remain largely a matter of guesswork.

There is always the possibility that certain initiates in Italian poisons did employ strange potions which escaped the inexperienced English doctors. Certainly strange methods were believed in and many deaths were imputed in the gossip of the times to poison. On July 2, 1595, Edward Talbot complained before the Star Chamber against one Woode, who had "charged the plaintiff that he showld secretely intende the poyseninge of the Erle of Shrewseberye, his brother, by this defend[te]. . . . For the sayd Wood hathe suggested that more then three yeres, sythence this plaintiff wroughte secretely vnder hande with this defendante to poyson the sayd Erle by gloues."[95] According to scandalous gossip, the Earl of Leicester had poisoned the Earl of Essex, "so hee died in the way of an extreme Flux caused by an Italian *Recipe*, as all his friends are well assured: the maker whereof was a Surgion (as is believed) that then was newly come to my Lord from Italy. . . . Neither must marvaile though all these died in diverse manners of outward diseases, for this is the excellency of the *Italian* art . . . who can make a man die, in what manner or shew of sicknesse you will."[96] Leicester was also credited with the poisoning of his wife Lettice and of Lord Sheffield. The death of many a prominent man aroused whispers of poison, and it is not too much to say that the

---

[95] W. P. Baildon, *Les Reports del Cases in Camera Stella 1593 to 1609 from the original MS. of John Hawarde* (Privately Printed, 1894), pp. 13 *ff*.

[96] *Leycesters Commonwealth* (1641), p. 22.

Elizabethan courtier believed implicitly that death by poison was common in his circle. The uncommon number of diatribes against poison in Elizabethan literature of all sorts is not without significance; nor without significance is the fact that official Elizabethan law covered specifically the various subtle means by which it was believed poison could be administered: "*gustu* by taste, that is by eating, or drinking, being infused into his meat or drink: *amhelitu*, by taking in of breath, as by a poysonous perfume in a chamber, or other room: 3. *contactu*, by touching: and lastly *suppostu*, as by a glyster or the like."[97] The poisoning incidents in the tragedies were by no means so outlandish and beyond the experience or credulity of the audience as is usually believed.[98]

But the lurid details of suspected poisonings probably existed for the greater part only in the Elizabethans' imaginations. Two cases may be selected to illustrate revenges that could and did occur. The first illustrates the unromantic course of a quarrel between one Mallerie and one Hall, which first arose in 1573 when Hall repeated a friend's caution that Mallerie cheated at cards. Hot words ensued between Mallerie and Hall over the accusation, but there was no immediate action until Hall, angry at malicious reports that Mallerie had spread about London, assaulted him with a dagger but did no very great damage. Mallerie and his brother hatched various schemes of retaliation which they threatened darkly without putting into effect. Nevertheless, Hall's servants became angered and attacked and further wounded Mallerie. Hall asserted that he had not directed this second assault; nevertheless when Mallerie sued in court and had the servants jailed, Hall countered by arresting Mallerie for threats against his life.

Hall received no satisfaction from his suit but the jury awarded Mallerie £100 damages, with judgment stayed on Hall's appeal. A short time later Mallerie arrested Hall himself for the first per-

---

[97] Coke, *Third Institute*, cap. 7.

[98] For this matter, with further citation of cases, see F. T. Bowers, "The Audience and the Poisoner of Elizabethan Tragedy," *Journal of English and Germanic Philology*, Vol. XXXVI (1937), pp. 491-504.

sonal assault, and Hall again countered by arresting Mallerie for drawing a weapon against one of his servants. Both men were now at fever heat, and a personal encounter between them would have been inescapable had not Mallerie suddenly died. The case is interesting for the combination of private and legal revenge employed in quarrels where, though neither man was too anxious to fight, natural death alone finally prevented a murderous assault.[99]

The second case had a more serious conclusion. In 1607 the Lord Sanquire, who had followed James I from Scotland, was practising the foils with the fencing master Turner, and had the misfortune to lose his eye in the bout. Upon his recovery he went to France where the king, one day noticing the mutilation, inquired the reason and exclaimed in astonishment that the giver of the wound still lived. Sanquire was stung by the reproof and returned to England where some time after, in 1612, two of his hired ruffians, Carliel and Graye, murdered Turner. This murder caused considerable excitement, and James himself personally hurried and directed the capture of Sanquire and his two accomplices, who were all tried and executed. The trial was significant from the point of view of Sanquire's confession in which he asserted that no honorable man would have remitted such an injury and that there was no law to redress him:

"I must confess I ever kept a grudge in my soul against him, but had no purpose to take so high a revenge: yet in the course of my revenge, I considered not my wrongs upon terms of Christianity . . . but being trained up in the courts of princes and in arms, I stood upon the terms of honour. . . . Another aspersion is laid on me, that I was an ill-natured fellow, ever revengeful and delighted in blood. To the first I confess I was never willing to put up a wrong, where upon terms of honour I might right myself, nor never willing to pardon where I had the power to revenge."[100]

---

[99] F. A., *A letter . . . touching . . . a priuate quarell and vnkindnesse, betweene Arthur Hall, and Melchisedech Mallerie Gentlemen* (1576?). F. A. is actually Arthur Hall, who narrates the story in excuse of his actions.

[100] *State Trials,* ed. Howell, Vol. II, pp. 747-51.

Sanquire would probably have been pardoned by the king if he had killed Turner himself and without delay. As it was, the Italianate features of the long nursing of revenge and the use of accomplices—both brought out skilfully by his prosecutor Bacon as opposed to English sentiment and usage—procured for him an execution by hanging, since a nobleman's death was refused. Such a murderous, long-continued revenge was evidently considered unusual, for English practice confined itself in general to immediate assault or formal duel, or to a combination of personal assault and legal proceedings as with Hall and Mallerie, or else to court intrigue either such as Raleigh was supposed to have conducted to bring about Essex's downfall, or the machinations that laid Overbury open to James's displeasure and so made him vulnerable for slaughter.

6

When in January of 1603 the Sieur de Chevalier wrote that the English "doe not fight in single combate,"[101] he was at least half right; a few years later he could not have been farther from the truth. England in the sixteenth century had scarcely been free from bloody affrays, but these were mostly straightforward fights on the spot or surprise assaults without the formality of challenges and all the punctilio attached to the duel. With the success of the oppressive measures adopted by the authorities in France and Italy, the virus transferred itself to England in the latter years of Elizabeth's reign: the rapier supplanted the sturdier sword as the English weapon, honor grew more valuable than life, and the word "valiant" took on a new meaning. This private duel, though interdicted, became the most honorable and popular Elizabethan method of revenging injuries. And since Englishmen required instruction in managing their revenges according to the new imported etiquette, a number of books appeared which thinly masked their real purpose by pretending to give an historical account of

---

[101] Thomas Heighman, *The Ghosts of the Deceased Sieurs, de Villemor and de Fontaines. A most necessarie Discourse of Duells* (Cambridge, 1624), p. 34.

the judicial combat, long since in disuse, though actually instructing the reader in the code of the private duel.[102]

In general, Elizabeth kept a firm hand over her courtiers and, whenever possible, forcibly reconciled them or allowed them to suffer the harsh penalties of the law. In 1592, for instance, the Privy Council sent John Hollys and Jarvis Markham, who had disobeyed the queen's orders forbidding them to fight, to prison. For a similar act of disobedience to Elizabeth, John Stanhope was committed to prison for challenging Sir Charles Cavendish. In 1600 the Council sent a letter in the queen's name to the Earl of Southampton forbidding him to fight the Lord Grey de Wilton in the Low Countries as Southampton had purposed in leaving Ireland.[103]

The sudden extraordinary increase in duelling soon after the accession of James I has never been very definitely explained. It is true that James did not have Elizabeth's gift for controlling the court, that bribery could help a guilty gentleman, and that more knowledge of Italian and French practices had seeped into England. It may also be true that there was an added emphasis on court life and that courtiers in the midst of that precarious and competitive existence, each one jealous of his prerogatives, adopted a more highly sensitive code of honor. In a life where each strove to surpass his fellow in a sovereign's favor, personal honor had almost daily to be vindicated. The most trivial causes could excite bloodshed: "A crosse word is ground enough for a challenge. . . . We fall out for feathers; some lie dead in the Chanell, whiles they stood too much for the wall: others sacrifice their hearts blood for the loue of an Harlot. Not to pledge a health, is cause enough to loose health and life too."[104]

---

[102] For the irritation of the authorities at this device, see Northampton, "Duello Foiled," in *A Collection of Curious Discourses Written by Eminent Antiquaries,* ed. Thomas Hearne (London, 1771), Vol. II, p. 240; Francis Bacon in *State Trials,* ed. Howell, Vol. II, pp. 1035-6.

[103] *Acts of the Privy Council of England, New Series,* ed J. R. Dasent (Norwich, 1890-1907), Vol. XXIV, p. 125; Vol. XXX, p. 551.

[104] Thomas Adams, *The Diuells Banket* (1614), pp. 58-9; see also Francis Osborne, *Works* (ed. 1673), p. 28.

It is probable, however, that a great part of the growth in the duel can be traced to the Scots who invaded London, and who were, as has been said, nearer to barbarism than the English. The ill-feeling between the two nations frequently broke out between their partisans at court.[105]

To what extent duelling was in the air may be seen in an extract from a letter by John Chamberlain dated September 9, 1613:

"Though there be, in show, a settled peace in these parts of the world, yet the many private quarrels among great ones prognosticate troubled humours, which may breed dangerous diseases, if they be not purged or prevented.

"I doubt not but you have heard the success of the combat betwixt Edward Sackville and the Lord Bruce of Kinlos betwixt Antwerp and Lille, wherein they were both hurt, the Lord Bruce to the death. . . . Here is speech likewise that the Lord Norris and Sir Peregrine Willoughby are gone forth for the same purpose, and that the Lord Chandos and Lord Hay are upon the same terms; there was a quarrel kindling betwixt the Earls of Rutland and Montgomery, but it was quickly quenched by the king, being begun and ended in his presence. But there is more danger betwixt the Earl of Rutland and the Lord Danvers, though I heard yesterday it was already upon the point of compounding. But that which most men listen after is, what will fall out betwixt the Earl of Essex and Mr. Henry Howard, who is challenged and called to account by the earl for certain disgraceful speeches of him."[106]

The code of honor was carried to so high a pitch that "men so farre allow and commend, as they are not ashamed to say . . . that a man for cause of honour may arme himselfe against his country, the respect whereof is and euer was so holy; yea euē against his father, and with cursed hands violate his person, vnto whom (next after God) he must acknowledge his life and being, and what else soeuer he hath in this world."[107] Various "brain-

---

[105] For a terrible example, see Thomas Birch, *The Court and Times of James the First,* Vol. I, pp. 265-6.

[106] *ibid.,* Vol. I, p. 272.

[107] Lodowick Briskett, *A Discourse of Civill Life* (1606), p. 74.

lesse boutefeux" defended publicly "that what soeuer a man hath once affirmed be it true or false; nay thoughe he knowe in his owne conscience that the grounde is vniuste vppon wch he gaue the Lie, yet he must constantly mayntayne it, only because it came once out of his lippes."[108]

The stream of popular opinion upholding the duel was so strong that even persons who believed thoroughly in its unlawfulness were forced to conform to the practice or else to withdraw entirely from social intercourse lest they should be considered base cowards. Arguments in favor of the duel were listed: (1) If there were no duels, all persons would draw their swords who have an interest in the injured person's honor [i.e. collective revenge]; (2) The fear of damnation keeps men from indulging in unjust quarrels; (3) If an act is lawful for many, it is lawful for one: armies challenge one another and so should individuals; (4) Since laws value private honor no farther than concerns the public safety, the individual must revenge his own dishonor; (5) The laws of knighthood bind all men to revenge an injury; (6) Since no one shall judge of honor but him who has it, the judges of civil courts (who are base in their origin) are unfitted for the duty; (7) Soldiers are reasonable men, yet we condemn a custom which they have brought in and authorized; (9) Many murders are committed which are undiscovered by law; if private men were allowed to punish these with the sword, murders would decrease.[109] This last shows that the desire for personal blood-revenge was by no means dead in England.

By the year 1610 duelling had become a serious menace. In February of that year Sir John Finet wrote to the Earl of Northampton that worse would come unless "the blissed order intended bring not a speedy remedye."[110] The order referred to may have been the proclamation which James issued later in the year or his

[108] Cotton MS., Titus C IV, fol. 300. For illustrations of duelling and the code of honor, see F. T. Bowers, "Middleton's *Fair Quarrel* and the Duelling Code," *Journal of English and Germanic Philology,* Vol. XXXVI (1937), pp. 40-65.

[109] Cotton MS., Titus C IV, fols. 83-87^v.   [110] *ibid.,* fol. 482.

elaborate *Edict* of 1613, for which plans were certainly on foot as early as 1610. James followed these works with a more dissuasive tract in 1618 entitled *The Peacemaker*, but it was not in his power to stamp out the duel. Even Cromwell was obliged to issue a proclamation promising stricter penalties, and Charles II wrote two orders. The long list of eighteenth-century duelling books shows no abatement in the practice of illegal private revenge, and duels were fought well into the nineteenth century.

7

So far this illustrative material has concerned itself more with the general ideas of the age about private revenge and with the various methods employed by individuals, than with revenge tragedies themselves or the state of mind of their audiences. Discussion of the tragedies must be delayed, but it is time more particularly to examine the ideas of the audiences if we are ever fully to evaluate and understand the Elizabethan revenge tragedy of the whole period. What did these audiences think of the plays? How close were their sympathies with the revenge motives of the characters? How outlandish did the plays seem, or how familiar were the revenge situations to Elizabethan life? Were the tragedies as far removed from actual English as were *The Libation Bearers* of Aeschylus and the *Thyestes* of Seneca from their times? Partial answers have already been given to some of these questions, while others must wait upon the discussion of the plays; but it is possible at this point to examine the matter with some, if not a complete, particularity.[111]

The traditional critical view of the audience's reaction has been stated: "The notion that it was morally wrong for a son to avenge his father's murder—especially a murder conceived under such circumstances as represented in the play—was not entertained in Hamlet's time. . . . We must be careful not to import into the play modern conceptions of ethical propriety. To the people of his

---

[111] This section is condensed from F. T. Bowers, "The Audience and the Revenger of Elizabethan Tragedy," *Studies in Philology*, Vol. XXI (1934), pp. 160-75.

own time, and even to the audience of the Elizabethan age, Hamlet was called upon to perform a 'dread' [sacred] duty."[112] This assertion, so far as it relates to the Elizabethans, has been challenged by the theory that "there was a persistent condemnation of revenge in the ethical teaching of Shakespeare's England, a condemnation which was logically posited [on the biblical injunction, 'Vengeance is mine, I will repay, saith the Lord'] and logically defended."[113] According to this view the audience was prevented by its ethical and religious education from applauding the motives of the stage-revengers. The last conclusion is perhaps too rigid. While it is impossible to deny the immense force of the ethical condemnation of revenge by certain classes among the Elizabethans, yet the writings of the preachers, philosophers, and moralists of the age cannot be wholly depended upon to afford an accurate cross-section of the views of the dramatists or of the audience, both of whom were swayed by equally strong influences from another direction. To explain these influences is at present our concern.

In Thomas Lodge's novel, *A Margarite of America* (1596), Arsadachus is about to depart from his country when his father gives him this parting advice, "Be . . . in thy reuenges bolde, but not too bloody."[114] These words may well sum up the average Elizabethan's moderate conception of personal justice. John Norden (1597) admits on the one hand that revenge is a desire to requite an evil received by returning an evil, "which hath some colour to worke iniurie, for iniurie,"[115] while Bacon agrees with Sanquire on the other that murder for revenge of a serious injury was to be regarded with less horror than a slaying for jealousy or gain. Sir William Segar (1590) defended his book on honor from the imputation that it would incite men to needless revenge, by the argument that it was intended to prevent offenses, but for a man

---

[112] *Hamlet*, ed. J. Q. Adams (Boston: Houghton Mifflin Co., 1929), p. 211.

[113] L. B. Campbell, "Theories of Revenge in Renaissance England," *Modern Philology*, Vol. XXVIII (1931), p. 281.

[114] *Complete Works*, ed. E. Gosse (Hunterian Club, 1883), Vol. III, p. 18.

[115] *The Mirror of Honor* (1597), p. 24.

"being offended, [it] sheweth the order of reuenge and repulse, according vnto Christian knowledge." One of the occasions when he allows the worth of personal revenge—and it should be noted by dishonorable means—is when the offense has been given in a particularly dishonorable way: "for reuenge of such cowardlie and beastiall offences, it is allowable to vse any aduãtage or subtiltie . . . one aduantage requireth another, and one treason may be with another acquited."[116]

Retaliation for base injuries, then, was the first occasion on which certain writers tolerated revenge. There was a second occasion (highly important in a consideration of such revenge tragedies as *Hamlet, Antonio's Revenge, The Maid's Tragedy, Valentinian*, and *All's Lost by Lust*) when revenge was considered allowable. After justifying the use of force in self-defense, William Perkins (1606) whose books carried weight with every Elizabethan, argues that defense by force is lawful "when violence is offered, and the Magistrate absent; either for a time, and his stay be dangerous; or altogether, so as no helpe can be had of him, nor any hope of his comming. In this case, God puts the sword into the priuate mans hands."[117] Of practically the same import is the statement (*c.* 1612) condemning by God's law revenge of private passion "that Iustice can decide."[118]

Undoubtedly there seems to be a loophole here for the stage-revenger in a good cause who, like Hamlet, Antonio, and Maximus, may not be able to procure justice by law. Thus Bacon, in the midst of a condemnation of revenge, admits that "the most tolerable sort of revenge is for those wrongs which there is no law to punish; else a man's enemy is still before hand, and it is two for one.[119] Advocates of the duel extolled its virtues in maintaining law and order, and even went so far as to maintain that the priv-

---

[116] *The Book of Honour and Armes* (1590), pp. 19-20.

[117] *The Whole Treatise of the Cases of Conscience . . . by M. W. Perkins . . . published for the common good, by T. Pickering* (ed. 1651), p. 293.

[118] Cotton MS., Titus C IV, fol. 96.

[119] "Of Revenge," *Essays,* ed. M. A. Scott (New York: Charles Scribner's Sons, 1908), p. 20.

ilege of blood-revenge would strike more fear into the hearts of murderers than the cumbersome and often faulty processes of the law, which could not always discover and punish the slayer.[120] Segar (1590) considers the suit at law to be the true revenge for injuries offered in public, but for those in private without witnesses, and therefore without proof for law, it lies within the choice of the injured party either to revenge himself by challenge or by retaliation of like for like.[121]

There can be little question that many an Elizabethan gentleman disregarded without a qualm the ethical and religious opinion of his day which condemned private revenge, and felt obliged by the more powerful code of honor to revenge personally any injury offered him. The ordinary Englishman did not abjure revenge as such, especially when the duel was the means of action. It was only when the more treacherous and Italianate features were added (as in the murder of Overbury) or when accomplices were hired to revenge (as by Sanquire) that he considered revenge despicable. The frequency with which open assaults, even with disparity of numbers, and "honorable" duels were pardoned by the rulers of England in the seventeenth century indicates strongly that—no matter what the position of the law—it was the method and not the act itself which was largely called in question.

We come now to the third and most important justification of revenge: blood-revenge for murder. Legally the avenger of blood incurred the same penalties as any other murderer. Religiously, too, he was banned, since all revenge belonged to God. There is, however, much evidence of an Elizabethan sympathy for blood-revenge, which had survived from the tumultuous times not so long past. Thus Cornwallis (1601) inveighs against all private revenges, but specifically excepts murder, which he thinks needs punishment.[122] The influential fencing-master Saviolo writes (1595) that among the few injuries it is impossible not to revenge

[120] Cotton MS., Titus C IV, fol. 84ᵛ.

[121] *The Book of Honour and Armes* (1590), p. 39.

[122] *Essayes* (ed. 1632), sig. C₃ᵛ.

are treacherous rape and murder.[123] Treacherous murder would imply a lack of evidence for a legal conviction, and so the revenger would be justified by the sentiment for revenge in cases not covered by law or which could not be proved in the courts.

Although the Elizabethan had a strong native tradition of blood-revenge behind him, some of his ideas on the subject must inevitably have come from foreign sources. The correct revenge-code of the Italian gentleman given by Count Romei was known through Kepers's translation, *The Courtiers Academie* (*c.* 1598). In essence it was this: revenge may be undertaken on those who wrong our father, son, brother, friend, and so forth, if the injury was done in contempt of us and through no manifest fault of the injured one. The person injured, however, must be impotent to revenge himself, else there would be a loss of honor in allowing another to perform the revenge; thus the father is not bound to revenge his strong and able son, or the son his able father. The strong are always bound to revenge the weak, for it is considered that the offense is done as an injury to him who is able to revenge.[124] English practice coincided, since we find the statement (*c.* 1612), "It is dishonor to reuenge the fathers wronge if he be able to reueng it personally if he be not the son is bounde to it."[125]

The statement made by the extremely influential Gentillet that the civil law refused the inheritance to the heir of a murdered father unless he revenged the father's death,[126] is extremely interesting, since we find that the same opinion was held in England. Writing against duelling, an anonymous author (probably the Earl of Northampton) lists various current ideas (*c.* 1612) in favor of the duel and then refutes each item. Of importance is his mention of the prevalent idea that "the ciuile law denies the fathers inheritance to that son which will not reuenge the death of his father." The author answers, "The lawe meanes iudiciall and

[123] *Vincentio Saviolo his Practise* (1595), sig. P₁ᵛ.

[124] *The Courtiers Academie* (1598?), p. 103.

[125] Cotton MS., Titus C IV, fol. 294.

[126] Gentillet, *A Discourse upon the Meanes of Wel Governing . . . a Kingdome. . . . Against Nicholas Machiauel,* trans. Simon Patericke (1608), Part III, max. 11, p. 221.

ordinar meanes of which in like sort I aim for beside the bond of natur Iustice it self barres all particular agreements [that] stoppes mens mouthes from clamor in a cause of bloud qua sangine clamat."[127]

How this belief in the legal necessity for the son to revenge a murdered father may have had its origin and development has been noted elsewhere.[128] Of course, no such English law existed, but that there was no law is of little moment. What is of interest for the attitude of an Elizabethan audience towards a stage-revenger is the fact that it was popularly believed by Elizabethans to exist separately in England or else as a general law governing Western civilization. This idea, combined with the plea of the duellists for the right of blood-revenge, shows a very strong undercurrent favoring private justice for murder in Elizabethan times, a sympathy with (and native knowledge of) blood-revenge, and a persistent tradition by which the son, or heir, must take personal cognizance of the murder of his ancestor.

The Elizabethan audience's reaction to the revenge tragedies must be considered with an eye to this tradition as well as to their religious and ethical education. It would be far too much to assert that Elizabethans believed every murder should be privately revenged by the son as a sacred duty: this Greek and Roman, although scarcely Scandinavian, conception of a "sacred" duty was no part of any Elizabethan code except on the stage.[129] Nor, on the other hand, can the view be wholly accepted that every private revenger of blood was automatically considered by the man in the street as a criminal who must receive his reward in death. The truth lies somewhere between these two extremes. There is no

---

[127] Cotton MS., Titus C IV, fol. 241.

[128] See F. T. Bowers, "The Audience and the Revenger of Elizabethan Tragedy," *Studies in Philology*, Vol. XXXI (1934), pp. 171-4.

[129] The foundation of the classical belief in the sacredness of the duty lay in the fact that the ghost could not find rest until revenge for its murder was achieved. Neither the Scandinavians of Hamlet's time nor the Elizabethans conceived any such religious connection between the revenge and the welfare of the murdered man's spirit. In both countries the obligation to revenge was based purely on legal grounds.

question that the Elizabethans firmly believed the law of God to forbid private vengeance. Correspondingly, there was a very real tradition existing in favor of revenge under certain circumstances, and especially of the heir's legal duty to revenge his father, even though this could be satisfied (if the individual chose and if the legal evidence were so strong as to assure conviction) by bringing a legal appeal or indictment. Certainly the Elizabethan son was more personally concerned in such a murder than in later times under a system of complete state justice. Many thoughtful men refused to condemn revenge entered upon in cases where recourse to the law was impossible. There would be few Elizabethans who would condemn the son's blood-revenge on a treacherous murderer whom the law could not apprehend for lack of proper legal evidence.

Such being the case, the audience at the theaters seems to have made the customary compromise between a formal set of religious and moral ethics and an informal set of native convictions. Under these circumstances—and the evidence of the tragedies bears out the theory—the revenger of the drama started with the sympathy of the audience if his cause were good and if he acted according to the typically English notions of straightforward fair play. It was only, as with Hieronimo (although this example may seem the most debatable of the many available), when he turned to "Machiavellian" treacherous intrigues[130] that the audience began to veer against him. That the majority of stage-revengers—Hieronimo, Titus, Hoffman, Sciarrha, and Rosaura, to name only a few—met their death, may be attributed either to the fact that they turned from sympathetic, wronged heroes to bloody maniacs whose revenge might better have been left to God; or else that the strain of the horrible situation in which they found themselves so warped their characters that further existence in a normal world became impossible and death was the only solution.

---

[130] See Hieronimo's very important soliloquy, *The Spanish Tragedy*, ed. Boas, Act III, sc. xiii, ll. 1-44, and the discussion of his character, pp. 70, 77-82 below.

CHAPTER II

THE BACKGROUND OF THE TRAGEDIES

I

𝓣HE critical material about Seneca and his tragedies is so complete and accessible that an extended summary is unnecessary. Since, however, Senecan tragedy exercised for a time an important influence on the Elizabethan revenge play, a brief survey of the elements in his work which affected the Elizabethan playwrights must be attempted.

The three main themes of Seneca's tragedies were lessons on the inconstancy of fortune, as in *Troades* and in the tragic story of Oedipus; portrayals of great crimes and examples of the evil results of murder, as in *Thyestes, Medea*, and *Agamemnon*; and pleadings in favor of simplicity, of poverty, and of chastity, as in *Hercules Oetaeus* and *Hippolytus*. Of the three themes, that which treated murderers and their deeds is the most important,[1] and inevitably made the greatest impression upon the Elizabethans, particularly after the translation of Seneca into English between 1559 and 1581. Almost every one of the tragedies is built upon a "strong theme" which gave ample opportunity for blood and horrors. Seneca delighted to dramatize the great crimes of antiquity, as in *Medea, Thyestes,* and *Agamemnon,* or else such pathological cases as are found in *Hippolytus* and *Hercules Furens.* He took only those subjects which would yield to a psychological development and which permitted a detailed study of a passion: hate in *Thyestes,* jealousy in *Medea,* love in *Hippolytus.* Ambition, hate, and love are his favorite studies in passion,[2] and since the

---

[1] The theme of Fortune's inconstancy is often linked with that of murder, though in a subsidiary manner, while the Stoic philosophy of the third theme merely ornaments the rhetoric of the dialogue. See Léon Herrmann, *Le Théâtre de Sénèque* (Paris, 1924), p. 244.

[2] Ambition is incarnated in Eteocles and Polynices on *Phoenissae*. Hate is powerfully described in *Thyestes* (176-335) and also in *Agamemnon* (867-909, 953-1012). Besides the erotic love of Phaedra in *Hippolytus,* Seneca paints in *Medea* and *Hercules Oetaeus* the powerful passion of jealousy, which he regards as love mixed with hate, the most difficult passion to conquer since it is rooted fast in the

psychology of crime fascinated him, he drew with zest the portraits of Atreus, Medea, and Clytemnestra, those revengers beyond the pale of reason. The most atrocious crimes are described with realism, and vice is painted in its most vigorous colors.

Except in cases of fatal error, Seneca's criminals are fully responsible, for the will to crime was present.[3] Thyestes was guilty because of his rape and incest; both Medea and Clytemnestra were fully cognizant of their deeds. Aegisthus and Phaedra claim heredity as an excuse, but Seneca regards them as guilty since they used their criminal heredity merely as an excuse for yielding to their worst instincts. Seneca is convinced that man has liberty of choice between good and evil, and that he can cast aside a criminal inheritance. The will is all-powerful. Criminal heredity is a punishment, therefore, on the guilty ancestors and not an extenuating circumstance in favor of the descendants. Thus the fate of Eteocles and Polynices is the just consequence of the misdeeds of Oedipus and his ancestors, the adultery of Aegisthus of the incest of Thyestes; the evil doings of Atreus's sons will one day be the punishment of Atreus if he sets them a bad example. Amendment, however, is always possible if the guilty person repents and tries to lessen or end the wrong he has done. Death is always a last refuge and expiation. Seneca sympathizes with suicide when it saves honor or gives an escape from a life too full of pain; yet he feels it more courageous to combat misfortune than to succumb without a struggle.

heart and leads, almost inevitably, to crime. Pride is studied in *Medea* but its greatest development comes in the characters of his tyrants: Lycus in *Hercules Furens*, Atreus in *Thyestes*, Eteocles and Polynices in *Phoenissae*, Oedipus in *Oedipus*, and Pyrrhus in *Troades*. Anger is carefully analyzed with its accompanying passion revenge. Medea reflects that it is sweet to drag down others while one is perishing (426-8); she will have nothing less than an eye for an eye— Jason's sons for her brother and father (956-7); she exults in the torturing slowness of her revenge in killing the second son (1016-17). Medea, Deïanira, Atreus in their inordinate lust for revenge cast aside all honor in order to commit the most unspeakable crimes of which they are capable (*Medea*, 976-7; *Hercules Oetaeus*, 278-314; *Thyestes*, 176-204).

[3] Thus Hercules is innocent of the death of his children, for he is the victim of madness sent by Juno, and Oedipus is declared free from reproach by Jocasta

Horrors are piled on horrors, with the cruelty of the scenes augmented by the keen delight Seneca takes in the realistic descriptions of bloody actions and physical torture. Pity is felt, however, not only for the innocent but even for the guilty in the midst of the torments of their retribution or of their remorse. The unhappy Phaedra is at the last bemoaned, together with the blinded Oedipus, the repentant Deïanira, Theseus, and Hercules. Even the weary Thyestes evokes sympathy. The physical is often used to enforce this pity, just as it had been originally employed to raise the horror. Dramatic irony is frequent when the characters are portrayed as unaware of impending horrors already known to the audience.

Senecan tragedy strongly emphasizes blood-revenge for murder or flagrant injury, or else a serious revenge from motives of jealousy. In *Agamemnon* Clytemnestra revenges the death of her daughter Iphigenia on Agamemnon, but she is also driven by jealousy of Agamemnon's infidelities and by fear of the consequences of her own adultery. Aegisthus, the issue of the incest of Thyestes with his own daughter, is seeking blood-revenge for the murder of his half-brothers by Atreus and for the atrocities to which Thyestes has been subjected. Electra's first words are addressed to the child Orestes, whom she instantly visualizes as the revenger of blood for the murder of her father. The centaur, slain by Hercules in *Hercules Oetaeus*, in his death agony takes poison from his wound and gives it to Deïanira as a love potion for Hercules, and thus eventually secures the revenge for his death. Medea revenges herself on Jason for deserting her, and on Creon and his daughter for their parts in Jason's new marriage. Deïanira plans a sweeping revenge on Hercules for bringing a concubine into their household, but her actual revenge is involuntary, for she is unaware of the fatal properties of the centaur's gift. Juno in *Hercules Furens* revenges herself on Hercules because he is the child of her husband's illicit amours. Theseus in *Hippolytus* revenges himself on Hippolytus for the alleged rape. Atreus wreaks bloody ven-

and Antigone. Deïanira, an involuntary murderess, is absolved by her nurse and her son Hyllus.

geance on Thyestes for the rape of his wife and usurpation of his kingdom.

Since the revenge is personal, and in cases of true blood-revenge takes on the sense of a religious duty, it may be prompted by a ghost. The ghost of Thyestes as prologue to *Agamemnon* seems to speak directly to Aegisthus, urging him to remember his mother who had borne him for revenge. The ghost of Achilles in *Troades* is merely reported on the stage, but it instigates the last vengeance on the Trojans. The prologue ghost of Tantalus in *Thyestes,* goaded on by a Fury, unwillingly spreads his pestilential presence over the house of his descendants and thus starts the fatal action which will not end until Clytemnestra and Aegisthus fall by the hand of Orestes.

The revengers are occasionally spurred on by the hallucination that they see the ghosts of the dead. Medea, in her rage, first visualizes a horde of Furies and then the ghost of her mangled brother seeking punishment for his death. Octavia in the spurious *Octavia* sees the ghost of her murdered brother, although she is not a revenger, and in the same play the unavenged ghost of Agrippina rises to forecast the bloody ending of the marriage of her murderer son. Ghost confronts ghost when the shade of Agrippina seems to see the spirit of her husband, which attacks her for planning the murder of his son Britannicus and demands the death of the slayer Nero. Deïanira, after she has learned of her crime, sees Tisiphone rising to demand revenge, and rushes away to kill herself. Hercules in his madness sees Tisiphone and the Furies which were sent by Juno to lead him to destruction.

Revenge is collective as well as personal, in that it extends to all descendants of the injurer and to all his collateral kindred. Agamemnon expiates the crime of Atreus, Hercules the sin of Jove, and Polyxena the wrong done by Paris. The revenger may be satisfied to take vengeance not on the injurer himself but on his sons, as affording the greater torment. Hercules himself remains unharmed by Juno's revenge but in his madness kills his wife and children. Atreus is more than satisfied to leave Thyestes alive so that he may taste the dreadful banquet of his murdered sons.

When Medea realizes how deeply Jason loves his sons, she steels herself and slaughters them with the thought that they will expiate the deaths of her father and brother. The explanation for the rule of collective vengeance, in addition to its descent from primitive times, may well be Medea's line:

> cui prodest scelus
> is fecit.

The guiltless must fall with the guilty, for they cannot avoid profiting by the sin, and so have committed the sin too.

The revenger is warned to conceal and dissemble revenge lest the chance for vengeance be lost. Slow revenge provides the greatest enjoyment. Both Medea and Atreus cast aside all honor and yearn for unspeakable retaliation. Deïanira in her jealous rage calls for some unheard-of punishment for Hercules. With such sentiments, revenge overleaps the bounds of *talion* and may far surpass the injury.

> scelera non ulcisceris,
> nisi vincis.
>
> (*Thyestes*, 195-6)

No ordinary revenge develops but a harsh and terrible punishment. The banquet of human flesh, already served by Tantalus to the gods, and by Procne to Tereus, is brought before Thyestes. Jason's children are slowly killed before the father's tortured eyes and flung down to him from the parapet. The two crazed revengers hack at Agamemnon's corpse long after life has fled.

Innocent or deceived accomplices are sometimes used to help the revenge but never to consummate it. Medea sends her children to Creusa with the poisoned robe, and Atreus gives his own sons no inkling of his evil purpose when he orders them to invite Thyestes back to his country. Crimes are punished in hell or else by the kindred on earth. Suicide, as with Deïanira and Phaedra, may be an expiatory avengement of murder. Momentary hesitation may briefly halt the revenger.[4] Atreus, Medea, and Clytemnestra make

---

[4] *Medea*, 895-8, 926-32; *Agamemnon*, 239-43, 260-7, 273-4, 284, 286, 288-91.

free use of deceit to lure the victim to destruction. Actual insanity occurs only in *Hercules Furens*, where it is sent by Juno, but the revengers may claim to be imbued by the divine madness of the Furies, and may act so strangely as to cause concern to their attendants.[5] Insanity is never used for purposes of deception, although Deïanira, half-demented, bitterly accuses Hercules of having pretended madness in order to rid himself of his wife and children. Irony is ever-present both in situation and dialogue, and portents with supernatural warnings of disaster are customary before each tragic event. The plays abound in rhetorical reflections on life, death, and fate.

As most of Seneca's tragedies have revenge as the general motive for the catastrophe, so all unite in practically the same method of presentation. The Senecan drama starts with a monologue or dialogue which either casts back to previous events or anticipates those to come. The ghosts, which sometimes speak this prologue, take no part in the subsequent action, if the malign influence of the ghost of Tantalus be excepted. The whole of Act I is thus expository, since the play begins just after the crisis of the story and the drama is little more than the elaboration of the catastrophe. Act II consists of dialogue wherein the chief agent of the catastrophe plans the execution of his revenge. Act III brings the antagonists face to face and almost on equal terms, with the ascendant force of the chief agent growing swiftly. Act IV provides either a lull in the action or else a partial fulfilment of the catastrophe. In Act V the catastrophe is completed.

Thyestes may be taken as an example. In the first act the ghost of Tantalus lays the coming tragedy before the audience and reviews the previous story in order to explain the atmosphere of crime and vengeance. In the second act Atreus in conversation with his guard plans the scheme of his revenge. In Act III Atreus and Thyestes meet; the crown is offered to Thyestes and accepted. Act IV contains the partial fulfilment of the catastrophe in the slaughter of Thyestes's sons, and Act V completes the catastrophe with the hu-

[5] *Medea*, 401-7, 425-6, 670-9.

man banquet. From beginning to end, those plays of Seneca which are solely concerned with the dramatization of a revenge are welded into a complete and causal whole, with the catastrophe —the execution of the revenge—kept in mind from the start and led up to with little or no faltering in the course of the action.[6]

2

If one is to understand fully the dramatic motivation of the characters in the Elizabethan tragedy of revenge, some attention must be paid to the English opinion of the foreigners in whose countries the scenes are laid. Italian stories and characters, in especial, dominated the Elizabethan tragic stage and had a profound effect on the type of play produced.

The Italian was almost always regarded as a villain of a particularly jealous and revengeful nature, but there are a few references that put him in a better light. Thus Faunt in 1578 wrote to Anthony Bacon comparing the judiciousness of the Italian to the giddiness of the Frenchman.[7] In 1549 the historian William Thomas remarked that Italians were sober of speech and enemies of ill report. Although many discommend them for their touchy honor which deals out death for slander, "yet mine opinion doeth rather allow than blame theim. For the feare of suche daungers maketh men so ware of theyr toungues, that a man maie goe .xx. yeres through Italie without findyng reproche or villanie, vnlesse he prouoke it hym selfe."[8] In 1630 an obscure preacher dared to raise his voice in the faintest of protests against the sweeping condemnation of foreigners by the English:

"Such phrases are but hyperboles, involuing the most and not all; It is sufficient the denomination is after the greater part, Hee that makes Italy the Nursery of villaines, drunkennesse the badge of a Dutchman, and pride the shadowe of a Spaniard, sayes not

[6] H. E. Fansler, *The Evolution of Technic in Elizabethan Tragedy* (Chicago: Row, Peterson & Co., 1914), pp. 47-54.

[7] Birch, *Memoirs of the Reign of Queen Elizabeth*, Vol. I, p. 16; Vol. II, p. 329.

[8] *The Historie of Italie* (1549), fol. 4. For much the same opinion, see George Hall, *The Priuate Schoole of Defence* (1614), sigs. A4ᵛ-A5.

each in these places is so qualified, at the most, his words can bee screwed no higher then that the greater part is so."[9]

That "the greater part is so" expressed firmly the unalterable conviction of the average Elizabethan. Thomas Wright (1601) wrote: "Our people (for the most part) reueale and disclose themselues very familiarly and easily; the Spaniard and the Italian demurreth much . . . he wil shew a countenance of friendship although he intend reuenge, he can traine his purposes afarre off to vndermine where he pleaseth, he will praise where he hateth, and dispraise where he loueth for a further proiect; he can obserue his times better than we for his plots, and marke out fitter occasions to effectuate his intent."[10] Peter Heylyn recorded in 1621: "The people [of Italy] are for the most part graue, respectiue, and ingenious, excellent men (said a *Spaniolized Italian*) but for three things, in their lustes they are vnnaturall, 2 in their malice vnappeasable, 3 in their actions deceitfull, to which might be added, they will blaspheme sooner than sweare, and murther a man rather than slaunder him."[11]

The Elizabethan summed up the Italian in the person of Machiavelli, whose name was an English synonym for villain. "He that intends to expresse a dishonest man cals him a Machiavellian," roundly declared an anonymous writer about the year 1642.[12] The Elizabethan commoner regarded Machiavelli's works with horror: "*Sinnes* Text is from Hels *Scriptum est*: taken out of the Deuils Spell; either *Lucian* his olde *Testament,* or Machiauell his new."[13] Innumerable references accuse him of fostering every sort of vice,[14]

---

[9] E. B., *The Curse of Sacriledge. Preached in a Private Parish Church* (1630), p. 35.

[10] *The Passions of the Minde in Generall* (ed. 1630), sig. A7.

[11] *Microcosmus, or A little Description of the Great World* (1621), p. 90. See also Thomas Palmer, *An Essay of the Meanes how to make our Travailes . . .* (1606), p. 66; G. B. A. F., *A Discovery of the Great Subtiltie and wonderful wisedome of the Italians* (1591), sig. B3^v.

[12] *The Atheisticall Politition, or a Breife Discourse concerning Ni. Machiavell* (n.p.d.), sig. A1.

[13] Thomas Adams, *The Diuels Banket* (1614), p. 2.

[14] For example, see Samuel Rowlands, "The Knaves of Spades and Diamonds," *Works,* Vol. II, p. 25.

and his name expressed nothing but treachery, murder, and atheism to any Elizabethan.

The instant slaying of wife and adulterer on discovery was part of the early law of every land, but the number of instances and the cruelty exhibited in the process in Italy profoundly shocked the English and need some explanation. In Italy the husband's claim on the wife's fidelity was vastly different from that given by the firm foundation of courtship and betrothal in more northern countries. The young Italian bride quitted the convent or her father's house usually after the briefest acquaintance with her husband; and since the marriage was often one of convenience, the rights of the husband were largely conditional and he demanded chiefly the outward fulfilment of the contract without too much regard for the real affections.

The Renaissance spirit of vengeance on an erring wife was not so much sexual jealousy (although this is a broad statement) as the desire to spoil the triumphs of others, and to vindicate oneself publicly. Where the wife's infidelities exposed the Italian husband to the derision of outsiders he was justified by public opinion, and condoned by the law, in resorting to murder. The real motive behind his deed—personal vindication—is shown by the fact that not only husbands but also brothers and fathers of the guilty woman felt bound to take the same vengeance. A shocking example is found, for instance, in *The Chronicle of Perugia* for the year 1455 where a brother forces the seducer to tear out the sister's eyes, and then beats him in public.[15] When during the sixteenth century Italian life fell more and more under Spanish influence, real jealousy administered even more terrible punishments, but these must be distinguished from the retaliation for infidelity which existed before and which was founded on the spirit of the Renaissance itself. As Spanish influence declined, these excesses of jealousy decreased until towards the close of the

---

[15] Graziani, "Cronaca della Citta di Perugia dal 1309 al 1491," *Archivio Storico Italiano,* XVI (First Series, 1850), 629.

seventeenth century they were superseded by an indifference which recognized an official lover.[16]

The Elizabethans could not understand the peculiar qualities of the Italian marriage, where the husband thought more of the outward conditions of the contract than of the affections, and where (in the midst of what seemed like indifference) the outcome of any wifely infidelity which exposed the husband to derision was swiftly tragic. Thus the Italian adulteries and wife-murders seemed particularly cruel and heartless to the Englishman, who viewed the Italian marriage only in the light of his own, and Italians became notorious in England for their revengeful jealousy.[17] Fynes Moryson (1617) records: "Adulteries (as all furyes of Jelousy, or signes of making loue, to wiues, daughters and sisters) are commonly [by the Italians] prosecuted by priuate reuenge, and by murther, and the Princes and Judges, measuring their iust reuenge by their owne passions proper to that nation, make no great inquiry after such murthers besides that the reuenging party is wise inough to doe them secretly, or at least in disguised habbits."[18]

The custom of private revenge was not limited, however, to revenge for illicit love affairs. Not only was the vendetta, public or private, a legal custom, but murders committed in its prosecution were acknowledged as brave and praiseworthy acts.[19] The Italian was notorious for revenging the least injury, whether just

[16] Jacob Burckhardt, *The Civilization of the Renaissance in Italy,* trans. S. Middlemore (London: Swan Sonnenschein & Co., 1909), pp. 442-5.

[17] See *A Direction for Trauailers Taken out of Iustos Lipsius* (1592), sig. C_2^v; Cotton MS., Titus C IV, fols. 3^v-4; Francis Osborne, "Advice to a Son," *Works* (ed. 1673), p. 243; Thomas Palmer, *An Essay of the Meanes how to make our Travailes* (1606), p. 63; Robert Tofte, *The Blazon of Iealousie* (1615), pp. 21-2.

[18] *Shakespeare's Europe,* ed. Charles Hughes (London: Sheratt & Hughes, 1903), p. 160.

[19] "La vendetta privata . . . fino a che non potè sottentrarle la publica, fu un diritto legale; ed anche gran tempo dipoi rimase un dovere di onore." I. del Lungo, "Una Vendetta in Firenze Il Giorno di San Giovanni del 1295," *Archivio Storico Italiano,* Vol. XVIII (Fourth Series, 1886), p. 389.

or unjust, without resorting to the courts.[20] His pride was so great that the revenge was serious for even the slightest insult. "In their nature they are most impatient of any the least reproch or iniury. . . . And the greater men [revenge themselves] by treasonable murthers."[21] This revenge was always secret,[22] and, in cases of murder, collective.[23] Revenge was secured with a delight and pride in the dishonorable means, and occasionally with great disparity of numbers.[24]

The long endurance of the Italian revenger's enmity was proverbial in England, and precisely (as with Sanquire) one of the most deplored characteristics of revenge. Nashe wrote in 1592, "The Italian saith, a man must not take knowledge of iniurie till he be able to reuenge it";[25] and in 1593, "Nothing so long of memorie as a dog; these *Italians* are old dogs, & will carrie an iniurie a whole age in memorie: I haue hearde of a boxe on the eare that hath been reuenged thirtie yeare after."[26] It was this artistry in revenge, this waiting for the moment of weakness in the destined victim, even though years elapsed, this fanatic determination to revenge—but without risk—which the hotheaded and forthright Englishman could not understand. And not understanding, it fascinated and terrified him. The Italian niceties in revenge could draw forth only expressions of horror and loathing, such as Nashe's in 1592:

[20] See Thomas Palmer, *An Essay . . . of Travailes* (1606), pp. 64-5; *Florio's Second Frutes* (1591), p. 119; Thomas Nashe, "Pierce Penilesse," *Works,* Vol. I, pp. 176-7.

[21] *Shakespeare's Europe,* ed. Charles Hughes, p. 402.

[22] *The Traueiler of Jerome Turler* (1575), p. 41; Fynes Moryson, *An Itinerary* (1617), Part III, Book I, Chap. III, p. 48.

[23] Fynes Moryson (1617) relates as an unusual instance that on the discovery of the conspirators of the families of Pulci and Caponi who had banded to kill Duke Ferdinand of Florence, Ferdinand had the conspirators alone put to death but spared their innocent relatives. *Shakespeare's Europe,* pp. 95-6.

[24] *Shakespeare's Europe,* pp. 401-3, and *An Itinerary* (1617), Part III, Book I, Chap. II, p. 25. See also Sir Robert Dallington, *A Survey of the Great Dukes State of Tuscany* (1605), pp. 64-5.

[25] "Four Letters Confuted," *Works,* Vol. I, p. 309.

[26] "The Unfortunate Traveller," *Works,* Vol. II, p. 298. See also Dallington, *A Survey of the Great Dukes State* (1605), p. 65.

"Lastly, vnder hypocrisie all Machiauilisme, puritanisme, and outward glossing with a mans enimie, and protesting friendship to him that I hate, and meane to harme. . . . And finally all Italianate conueyances as to kill a man, and then mourne for him . . . to be a slaue to him that hath iniur'd me, and kisse his feete for opportunitie of reuenge, to be seuere in punishing offenders, that none might haue benefite of such meanes but my selfe, to vse men for my purpose and then cast them off, to seeke his destruction that knowes my secrets: and such as I haue imployed in any murther or stratagem, to set them priuilie together by the eares, to stab each other mutually, for fear of bewraying me: or if that faile to hire them to humor one another in such courses, as may bring them both to the gallowes. These and a thousand more such sleights hath hypocrisie learned by trauailing strange Countries."[27]

Further sensational features of Italianate vengeance were emphasized by Gentillet, from whose work most Elizabethans' knowledge of Machiavelli was gained: "According to the honour of his [Machiavelli's] Nation, vengeances, and enmities are perpetuall and irreconcilable; and indeed, there is nothing wherin they take greater delectation, pleasure, and contentment, than to execute a vengeance; insomuch as, whensoever they can haue their enemie at their pleasure, to be reuenged vpon him they murder him after some strange & barbarous fashion, and in murdering him, they put him in remembrance of the offence done vnto them, with many reproachfull words and iniuries to torment the soule and the bodie together; and sometimes wash their hands and their mouthes with his blood, and force him with hope of his life to giue himselfe to the diuell; and so they seeke in slaying the bodie to damne the soule, if they could."[28]

---

[27] "Pierce Penilesse," *Works*, Vol. I, p. 220.

[28] *A Discourse . . . Against Nicholas Machiavel* (1608), trans. Patericke, Part III, max. 6. This passage may well have influenced Nashe in writing Cutwolfe's speech at his execution in *The Unfortunate Traveller* (1593) and Esdras's magnificent valediction. *Works*, Vol. II, pp. 324-6.

Poison, a weapon at once secret and safe, was the traditional means of Italian vengeance.[29] The Italian history of Guicciardini, which was translated in 1579 by Geoffrey Fenton, gave to the Elizabethans many examples of Italian murders and atrocities besides such stories as the death of Bianca Capello by poison, which Fynes Moryson remarked "are famously knowne in . . . the mouths of liuing men." In Guicciardini they read of the duplicity of Caesar Borgia, who, to revenge the murder of his uncle by Liverot de Ferme, invited Ursini, Vitelloze, and de Ferme to a friendly banquet, and there killed the last two. From the same source they were acquainted with the scandal surrounding the supposed murder of his brother by Caesar Borgia and his supposed incestuous relations with his sister Lucretia. Further duplicity was found in the accounts of Hercules and then of Hippolito D'Este.[30] Such reports as those of the frightful atrocities committed by Ezzelino da Romano would profoundly affect their imagination,[31] as would the general gossip sent home by English travellers. According to contemporary ideas, Thomas Adams (1614) could with perfect justice describe the Devil's Banquet as consisting in part of *"Italian* waters *of Murder."*[32]

With such an opinion of Italy and the Italians, it was small wonder that the Elizabethans feared the Italianizing of England, and viewed with misgiving the fashionable vices picked up by English travellers. Italy for some time had been regarded as a corrupting influence by other countries,[33] but to the fear of moral

---

[29] "The Italyans aboue all other nations, most practise reuenge by treasons, and espetially are skillful in making and giuing poysons. . . . In our tyme, it seemes the Art of Poysoning is reputed in Italy worthy of Princes practise. For I could name a Prince among them, who hauing composed an exquisite poyson and counterpoyson, made proofe of them both vpon condemned men giuing the poyson to all, and the Counterpoyson only to some condemned for lesser Crymes, till he had found out the working of both to a minute of tyme, vpon divers complections and ages of men." Moryson, *Shakespeare's Europe,* pp. 405-7.

[30] *The historie of Guicciardin containing the warres of Italie* (1579), trans. Geoffrey Fenton, pp. 210, 133, 16, 257, 266.

[31] For a description, see Symonds, *The Renaissance in Italy* (London: Smith, Elder & Co., 1875), Vol. I, pp. 42-5.

[32] *The Diuells Banket* (1614), p. 24.

[33] "Gueuara, Chronocler to Charles the first, writeth, that from forraine Coun

corruption was added the English Protestant dread of Roman Catholicism.[34] Yet as much as the Elizabethans hated popery, they feared atheism more, and were perpetually afraid that native travellers to Italy would return with the widespread Italian atheistical ideas planted in their impressionable minds.[35] Atheism, sexual depravity, and murder were only a few of the vices to be learned in Italy according to the common report which Fynes Moryson quotes: "And because it is hard to learne vertues and more hard not to learne vices, or to depose them once learned; from hence they say it is, That so many homebred Angels, returne from *Italy* no better then Courtly Diuells."[36] Ascham's remark in *The Schoolmaster,* quoting "Inglese Italianato è un diablo incarnato," is famous.[37]

Italian deceit and hypocrisy were also feared, particularly since they were believed to have affected the English courtier profoundly. After commenting on the hereditary deceitfulness of the Italians, Thomas Palmer (1606) wrote regretfully, "I feare me, other Nations trauailing thither will say that we beginne to smell of that disease."[38] Joshua Sylvester in 1620 digressed from his translation of Du Bartas to warn England that he saw native plots like those of Italy:

tries, men commonly bring newes to prattle of, and strange customes to practise; and that few come out of Italy, that are not absolute and dissolute." *Wits theatre of the Little World* (1599), fols. 138ᵛ-139.

[34] Thomas White, *A Sermon Preached at Pawles Crosse on Sunday the ninth of December, 1576* (1578), p. 38; Roger Ascham, *The Whole Works,* ed. Giles (London, 1864-5), Vol. III, p. 157.

[35] *"Italy,* the Paradice of the earth and the Epicures heauen, how doth it forme our yong master. . . . From thence he brings the art of atheisme, the art of poysoning, the art of Sodomitrie. . . . It is nowe a priuie note amongst the better sort of men, when they would set a singular marke or brand vpon a notorious villaine, to say, he hath beene in *Italy."* Nashe, "The Unfortunate Traveller," *Works,* Vol. II, p. 301.

[36] *An Itinerary* (1617), Part III, Book I, Chap. I, p. 5. Moryson, however, with his wide experience did not always agree with the stay-at-homes. On p. 5 he added, "We must obserue vertues for imitation, and vices that wee may abhorre them," and on p. 7, "And let vs securely permit our men to passe into the heart of *Italy,* so they may be of ripe yeeres, and well instructed. Vpon my word they run no other danger, then the escaping the snares of the Inquisition."

[37] *Works,* ed. Giles, Vol. III, p. 156.   [38] *An Essay of Travailes* (1606), p. 66.

Strife-full *Ambition,* Florentizing States.[39]

Bishop Hall (1616) demanded: "What mischief have we amongst us that we have not borrowed. . . . Where learned we that devilish art and practice of duel, wherein men seek honour in blood, and are taught the ambition of being glorious butchers of men. . . . Where the art of dishonesty in practical Machiavelism, in false equivocations . . . with too many other evils wherewith foreign conversation hath endangered the infection of peace?"[40] The answer was, of course, Italy.

Finally, the Elizabethans were afraid of the influence of the Italian secret, deceitful revenge, which, they thought, was utterly foreign to English temperament and could be only a Continental vice.[41] Harrison in 1587 best summed up the Elizabethan attitude: "This . . . will turne to great ruine of our countrie, and that is, the vsuall sending of noblemens & meane gentlemens sonnes into Italie, from whence they bring home nothing but meere atheisme, infidelitie, vicious conversation, & ambitious and proud behauiour, whereby it commeth to passe that they returne far worsse men than they went out. A gentleman at this present is newlie come out of Italie who went thither an earnest protestant, but comming home he could saie after this maner: 'Faith & truth is to be kept, where no losse or hinderance of a further purpose is susteined by holding of the same; and forgiuenesse onelie to be shewed when full reuenge is made.' "[42]

The general opinion of the time in England held the French to be free in threats of revenge, but not especially liable to perform them. It was agreed they were deceitful and hypocritical even to

[39] *Du Bartas His Diuine Weekes and Workes* (ed. 1641), "The Second Day of the First Week," p. 16.

[40] "Quo Vadis? A Just Censure of Travel," *Works,* Vol. IX, pp. 556-7.

[41] See especially Daniel Tuvil, *Essayes, Morall and Theologicall* (1609), sigs. K_{12}^{v}-L_1.

[42] *A Description of England* (New Shakspere Society, 1876), pp. 129-30. The passage is not in the 1577 writing but was added in 1586 or 1587 when the work was enlarged, showing perhaps that the problem was more acute ten years later and needed comment.

their friends,[43] but in hatred they were either mere threateners[44] or else they were rash, returned wrongs immediately, and were easy to reconcile.[45] Fynes Moryson (1617) spoke emphatically of their quick remittance of hatred.[46]

Elizabethan opinion, for all practical purposes, made no distinction between the villainy and revengefulness of Italian and Spaniard, and the two were often linked in condemnation.[47] A quotation from Robert Johnson in 1601 will provide a sufficient example:

"The Spaniards are subtle, wrapping their drifts in close secresie, expressing suretie in their words, but keeping their intentions dissēbled vnder disguised assurance of amity, betraying the innocency of their friendes, in malice infinite, and so ouercarried with that passion, that for the most part they execute a reuenge farre aboue the nature of the offence: not giuing any suddain apparance of it, but waiting for opportunity so much redouble the blow, by how much it hath beene nourished with tract of time, and hung in suspence."[48]

Almost without dissent, the Germans were regarded as revengers,[49] "long in conceiving, long in retaining."[50] In connection with *Hamlet,* Moryson's account (1617) of the Danes is interesting: "For gentlemen [of Denmark] are not condemned to death,

---

[43] Thomas Palmer, *op. cit.,* p. 66.

[44] Jerome Turler, *The Traveiler* (1575), p. 41.

[45] Joseph Hall, "To My Lord, the Earl of Essex. Advice for his Travels," *Works,* Vol. VI, p. 154.

[46] *An Itinerary* (1617), Part III, Book I, Chap. III, p. 48. See also Cotton MS., Titus C IV, fol. 4.

[47] See especially, Thomas Wright, *The Passions of the Minde in Generall* (ed. 1630), sig. A7.

[48] "Of Histories," *Essaies, or, Rather Imperfect Offers* (ed. 1607), sig. D8ᵛ. For other comments in a similar vein, see Birch, *Memoirs of Elizabeth,* I, 89, 95, and *The Court and Times of James the First,* Vol. II, pp. 82-3; H. W., *A Pageant of Spanish Humours* (1599), sigs. B3-B3ᵛ; Robert Ashley, *A Comparison of the English and Spanish Nations* (1589), p. 19; Jerome Turler, *The Traveiler* (1575), p. 41; Robert Anton, *Vices Anotimie* (1617), sig. M2.

[49] Turler, *The Traveiler* (1575), p. 41; Moryson, *An Itinerary* (1617), Part III, Book I, Chap. III, p. 48.

[50] Joseph Hall, "To the Earl of Essex. Advice for his Travels," *Works,* Vol. VI, p. 154.

but only by the publique assembly of the States, and forfeite not their goods; and for mutuall wrongs and manslaughters among themselues, commonly they pursue them by priuate reuenge."[51]

The common internecine strife among the Turks was commented on by Richard Knolles in 1603,[52] and with the many books about the Turks written during the period English readers became well versed in the affairs and personal histories of the bloody rulers of the Ottoman Empire. A single tragic story, related by Sir Thomas Herbert in 1634, will suffice. Mirza, son of Shaw Abbas, Lord of Persia, was so victorious with the army and beloved by the people, that his father became jealous, recalled him from the military, and secretly had him blinded. Prince Mirza swore bloody revenge for the loss of his sight. Abbas in his declining years grew so fond of Mirza's young child, Fatyma, that he doted on her and called her his only solace. When Mirza realized this devotion, his long-brooding revenge flared and, to requite Abbas, he strangled his daughter and a day or two later ended his own life by poison.[53]

3

The Elizabethan's reading of the Italian *novelle* and their French translations and imitations, together with his own English adaptations, could only confirm his opinion of the Italians and the people of other nationalities whom he put upon his stage. To his knowledge of tragic murders in histories and, from hearsay, in travellers' reports, were added in these *novelle* scores of tragic stories taken from fact, and some from an imaginative reworking of traditional material.

Although certain of the tragic *novelle* were concerned purely with the pathetic, usually the tragedy resulted from a murder. One type of story stressed some brutal incident and its effect on the lover or beloved. Such was Boccaccio's tale of the wife of the

[51] *Shakespeare's Europe*, p. 180.

[52] *The Generall Historie of the Turkes* (ed. 1638), sig. A₅.

[53] *A Relation of Some Yeares Travaile . . . Into Afrique and the Greater Asia* (1634), pp. 99-104.

Sieur de Roussillon (fourth day, novel ix), whose husband gave her the heart of her murdered paramour to eat, and who committed suicide upon learning of her horrible meal. In somewhat the same manner Bandello writes of the murders of wives or paramours by jealous husbands or lovers. In one story (part II, novel viii) the husband forces the guilty wife to hang her lover with her own hands. Masuccio, too (novels xxii, xlv), has his quota of stories narrating the murder of unfaithful wives. Collectivity of revenge, as well as an infernal jealousy and brutality, is found in the first story of Fiorentino's eighth day, in which a husband invites the relatives of his guilty wife and her lover to an entertainment, and has them beaten to death by his servants. The wife is then tied to the dead body of her lover and left to starve. Another revenge is told in the ninth novel of the *Porretane* of Sabadino degli Arienti, where Malatesta elopes with Lelia and is inhumanly murdered by her enraged father. Lelia is flung into the death chamber and expires beside his body.

Stories were not lacking to illustrate the long memory and crafty brutality of Italian vengeance, nor was the motive of blood-revenge neglected, although blood-vengeance never took a prominent place in Italian tragic fiction. A typical narration is that from Bandello (part I, novel xlv) in which a slave revenges the murder of his master. The essence of a villainous Italian revenge is portrayed in Bandello (part IV, novel i), where Turchi, who wrongly believes himself cheated in money matters and injured in reputation by Deodati, lures him into a chair which immediately imprisons him. Turchi's hired accomplice then slays the helpless victim, and the two conceal the body. The account of Turchi's revengeful ideas illuminates the Elizabethan villainous revenger:

"This sinister humour of revenge having, then, entered his head, he resolved to kill Geronimo [Deodati] and do so memorable a wreak on him that it should be spoken of in all men's memory and above all to avenge himself on such wise that he might not be molested of justice and it should nevertheless abide in all men's minds that he had been the doer."[54]

Another base and terrible revenge is told in the eleventh novel of Anton-Francesco Doni. A noble cavalier has an enemy who prepares to revenge himself. One day when surrounded by only a few friends, the brave cavalier is overpowered by his enemy and a band of ruffians, and on promise of his life and the preservation of his friends, he is forced to sign a paper confessing himself a traitor, atheist, and heretic. Whereupon the villain assassinates the cavalier, thus robbing him not only of his life but also of his honor and his soul.

The more tragic stories of the Italian novelists were diffused through France and England during the sixteenth century by *Les Histoires Tragiques* (1559-1570) of Belleforest, which were later imitated in 1614 by *Les Histoires Tragiques de nostre Temps* of Rosset. Most of Belleforest's stories were translated from the Italian, although a few come from other sources like "De la mort du Comte de Barcelone, & comme son fils Geoffrey la vengea" (history lxxvi). The most important tale, however, was the story "Auec quelle ruse Amleth, qui depuis fut Roy Dannemarch, vengea la mort de son pere Horuendile, occis par Fengon son frere, & autre occurrence de son histoire," a narrative that was to have the most far-reaching effect on the Elizabethan drama.

A horribly contrived and Italianate story of revenge, of a type popular with the Elizabethan dramatists, was contained in Rosset's eleventh history, "De la cruelle Vengeance exercée par une Damoiselle, sur la personne du meurtrier de celuy qu'elle aymoit," in which Fleurie, to secure revenge for the murder of her lover, pretends that she will marry Clorizande, the murderer. She makes a secret assignation with him, and on his arrival he is entangled in ropes and securely bound. Fleurie then proceeds to cut off his nose and ears, to tear out his teeth and nails and to chop off his fingers; and at the end she cuts out his heart and throws it in the fire. On her return home she writes out the facts of the murder of her lover and of her vengeance, and swallows poison.

[54] *Novels,* trans. John Payne (Villon Society, 1890), Vol. VI, p. 179.

William Painter's *Palace of Pleasure* (1567-1568) first introduced the Italian and French *novelle* in translation to the general Elizabethan public. In Painter is found the ghastly story of the husband who killed his wife's lover and forced her to drink daily from his skull and to live with his skeleton (tome I, novel lvii). In another (tome I, novel lviii) the husband finds his wife guilty of adultery and secretly poisons her. The story of the Duchess of Malfi is told (tome II, novel xxiii), as is the tragic story of Tancred and Gismunda (tome I, novel xxxix); and finally we have the account of the murder of Mustapha by his father Solyman on the instigation of the jealous wife (tome II, novel xxiv).

In 1574 appeared George Turbervile's *Tragical Tales,* which narrated the revenge of Aretifilla on the tyrant Niocrates who had slain her husband (history II) as well as the story of the husband who forces his wife to eat her lover's heart (history iv). In Turbervile is also found the familiar story of Albovine (history v). The next translation to narrate real revenge stories was George Pettie's *Petite Pallace of Pettie His Pleasure* (1576), which contains the tale of Camma's revenge on Sinorix for the murder of her husband, and the classical tale of the revenge of Procne on Tereus. In 1577 Robert Smyth's *Straunge, lamentable, and Tragicall Hystories* retold from Belleforest and Bandello the story of the revenge of Mahomet the slave for the murder of his master. Thomas Lodge in *The Life and Death of William Longbeard* (1593) narrates the revenge of Julian on his sovereign who had debauched his daughter, a story used as the basis for William Rowley's tragedy *All's Lost by Lust.* In 1597 Thomas Beard included the story of Albovine in his *Theatre of Gods Judgements.*

Perhaps the most important collection of revenge stories which, though published late in the period, was used by dramatists as a source, is John Reynolds's *Triumph of Gods Revenge against Murther,* printed between 1621 and 1624. Book I, history i, tells of a jealous woman's revenge which slaughtered a whole family. In the same book history ii narrates the revenge of a woman on the man who murdered her lover; and history iv provides the source for Middleton's *Changeling.* The poisoning of an unfaithful husband by his wife is presented in book II, history vi, while history vii relates the story used later in Shirley's *Maid's Revenge*. Book II, history viii, tells of another revenge of a woman for her slain lover; history ix of the revenge of a daughter for the murder of her mother by her father-in-law. In book III, history xiii, an elderly wife poisons her maid for a suspected adultery with her husband, and then when the husband leaves her, has him assassinated in revenge. An insulted wife in book IV, history xix, spurs her husband to revenge her, and when he is killed in the attempt she has his slayer killed. Two younger sisters in book V, history xxi, poison their elder sister who has ruled them, and when the elder of the two remaining strives to gain control, the younger in revenge has her assassinated. In book VI, history xxix, a deserted woman kills her lover in revenge, and in history xxx there is another variation on the revenge of the wife for the murder of her lover.

These various collections of stories not only provided a perfect mine of material for the Elizabethan dramatist, but also trained the audience to accept the plot and characterization on the stage as dramatized truth, which confirmed the many prejudices from other sources concerning the general villainy and treacherous revengefulness of foreigners.

CHAPTER III

THE SPANISH TRAGEDY AND THE UR-HAMLET

I

𝒯HE tragedy of revenge has been classified as a definite, small subdivision of the Elizabethan tragedy of blood; and obviously, plays like *The Spanish Tragedy, Antonio's Revenge,* and *Hamlet* should be set apart as a specific type from Shakespeare's *Lear,* Marston's *Sophonisba,* and Nabbes's *Unfortunate Mother.* These represent the two extremes of the tragedy of blood: on the one hand a cluster of plays which treat, according to a moderately rigid dramatic formula, blood-revenge for murder as the central tragic fact; on the other, an amorphous group with no such definite characteristic, linked only by a delight in blood and sensationalism.

Since "tragedy of blood" is by necessity a generalized and all-inclusive term, it has been convenient to ticket certain subdivisions as revenge tragedy, villain tragedy, conqueror tragedy, and realistic or domestic tragedy. Thus set apart artificially, the revenge tragedy of the *Hamlet* school has been defined as "a distinct species of the tragedy of blood . . . a tragedy whose leading motive is revenge and whose main action deals with the progress of this revenge, leading to the deaths of the murderers and often the death of the avenger himself."[1] Until critics applied it too rigidly, such a distinction was very usefully employed for the small group of early dramas written almost exclusively under the influence of the Kydian formula for tragedy. But such a statement as that revenge tragedy died with Webster,[2] reveals a fundamental misunderstanding of what actually constitutes revenge tragedy and its place in Elizabethan drama.

[1] A. H. Thorndike, "The Relations of *Hamlet* to the Contemporary Revenge Play," *Publications of the Modern Language Association of America,* Vol. XVII (1902), p. 125.

[2] E. E. Stoll, *John Webster* (Cambridge: Harvard Cooperative Society, 1905), p. 118.

Between the two extremes of *Hamlet* and *Lear* lies a considerable body of tragedies wherein the exhibition of revengeful action is prominent and wherein the dramatists have depended upon revenge entirely for the motivation of their tragic catastrophes. Taken point by point, Shirley's *Cardinal* of 1642 is as strict a revenge tragedy as *The Spanish Tragedy*. Revenge is as much the leading motive and the force behind the action in Heminge's *Fatal Contract* as in Chettle's *Hoffman*. Massinger's *Duke of Milan* works out its tragic plot only by the use of a revenge for a serious injury. However, though many plays were only slight modifications of the Kyd formula, it is still difficult to classify them rigidly as revenge plays. The leading motive of *The Spanish Tragedy* is revenge, but the motive does not appear as a determinant in the plot until the middle of the play, since the characters must first be set in conflict to provide the murder which is to be revenged. Many later tragedies preserved Kyd's use of revenge as the cause of the catastrophe, but so far extended the preparative action at the expense of the resulting revengeful action that it becomes impossible to say that revenge is any longer the dominant motive.

For the average Elizabethan tragedy, "tragedy of blood" must stand as a general designation for the external characteristics of violence and blood, while "revenge tragedy," in its broader sense, defines the real dramatic motivation behind much of that blood and violence. But since this broader revenge tragedy developed by modifying a relatively pure type, the distinction of the original set form should be preserved for technical use, as formerly, by the term "tragedy of revenge."

The blood-revenge of the protagonist distinguishes the pure type of the Kydian "tragedy of revenge." This revenge constitutes the main action of the play in the sense that the audience is chiefly interested in the events which lead to the necessary revenge for murder, and then in the revenger's actions in accordance with his vow. The revenge must be the cause of the catastrophe, and its start must not be delayed beyond the crisis. "Revenge tragedy" customarily (but by no means necessarily) portrays the ghosts of the murdered urging revenge, a hesitation on the part of the avenger, a delay in proceeding to his vengeance, and his feigned or actual madness. The antagonist's counter-intrigue against the revenger may occupy a prominent position in the plot.

This definition holds only for the original type of *The Spanish Tragedy* and *Hamlet* in its purest form. The several types of the later modified revenge play require a broader definition. In the broader general type of the tragedy of revenge the catastrophe is brought about by a human or divine revenge for an unrighted wrong. The workings towards this revenge need not necessarily constitute the main plot, which may, instead, be concerned with developing the tragic situation which induces the revenge. Revenge, however, must be concerned in the catastrophe and must not enter the play solely as a fifth-act *deus ex machina* to resolve the plot without some antecedent interest in its action. To this generalized statement may be added an abstract of characteristics. The revenge may be conceived either by a hero or by a villain, who may be either protagonist or antagonist. The reason for revenge may range from blood-vengeance to jealousy, resentment of injury or insult (real or fancied), or self-preservation. The revenge must be carried out by the revenger himself or his interested accomplices. In some few plays, however, the theme of heavenly vengeance results in the destruction of the murderers or injurers either through their machinations against one another or through circumstances not consciously engineered by the revenger. When guilty the opponents of the revenger are usually killed or disgraced, and even the innocent do not always escape death. The revenger and his agents may fall at the moment of success, and sometimes even during the course of the vengeance. If the revenger is a villain he is always killed. Intrigue is customarily resorted to by one side or both sides; and since the revenge is serious, deaths are numerous and often bloody and horrible. Ghosts of the injured dead may appear to urge on the revenge or to utter forebodings, and a free use may be made of horrors. In extreme cases the interest through most of the play may be concentrated on the accumulation of various villainies and intrigues which at the last arouse the catastrophic revenge.

2

With the production of *The Spanish Tragedy* Elizabethan tragedy received its first great impetus. The immediate and long-lasting popularity of the play stamped it as a type, a form to be imitated. Thus it is of the highest significance that *The Spanish Tragedy* first popularized revenge as a tragic motive on the Elizabethan popular stage by using blood-vengeance as the core of its dramatic action.[3] True, earlier English tragedies, leaning heavily on Seneca, had utilized revenge to a certain extent for dramatic motivation. But in *Gorboduc* (1562) any incipient interest in the characters' motives of revenge is stifled under the emphasis on the political theme and the general classical decorum, and the ancient classical story of revenge in John Pikeryng's *Horestes* (1567) is so medievalized that it loses all significance except as a basis for comedy and pageantry. *Gismond of Salerne,* acted at the Inner Temple in 1567/8, borrows various revenge trappings from Seneca and the Italians but the pathetic love story usurps the main interest.

Elizabethan revenge tragedy properly begins with Thomas Kyd's extant masterpiece, *The Spanish Tragedy* (1587-1589) which presented revenge in kind—blood-revenge, the sacred duty of the father to avenge the murder of his son—and from that sensational theme derived its popularity. Sensational though the central motive proved, it was a universal one, appealing to all classes of people and to all time. As in the law-abiding Athens of Aeschylus, the Greek audience saw enacted in the Orestes trilogy

[3] In speaking in this manner of *The Spanish Tragedy* I am not forgetting my later thesis that the *Ur-Hamlet* preceded *The Spanish Tragedy*. Although it is true that the *Ur-Hamlet* influenced such plays as *Alphonsus, Emperor of Germany* and *Antonio's Revenge*, which may have appeared before the Shakespeare version of *Hamlet*, Shakespeare's play shortly outshone the Kydian work and was taken by later dramatists as their model. To all intents, therefore, *The Spanish Tragedy* was the earliest *main* line of influence, later combined with Shakespeare's *Hamlet*.

events of a more turbulent past but now outmoded, so the English spectators viewed dramatic action at once somewhat foreign to their present state of society yet still within their range of sympathy and understanding. The realism was clinched when the scene was laid in another country where, to their knowledge, the people were crueler and more revengeful, and where, as in Italy, the individualistic spirit still flourished among the nobility in despite of the law.

The Spanish Tragedy is far from a perfect working-out of a revenge theme. Kyd started to make a Senecan imitation adapted to the popular stage. Someone has been killed, and the slayer is to suffer the revenge of the ghost, presumably by becoming tangled in his own misdeeds as in *Hercules Furens,* or, as in *Thyestes,* through the malign influence of the supernatural chorus. Curiously, this Senecan ghost's reason for revenge is extraordinarily weak as seen through English eyes. The parallel with the ghost of Achilles in *Troades* which rises to demand vengeance for death in battle is obvious, but an English popular audience could not become excited over a ghost seeking vengeance for a fair death in the field.[4] No very personal interest can be aroused in the early action of the play if it proceeds solely from the point of view of an alien ghost, and with Horatio as the successful avenger of his friend.

The first human note is struck when Bel-Imperia resolves to use second love, in the person of Horatio, to revenge the death of her first lover. If this resolution had furnished the plot, the sequence of events would still have revolved about the ghost but with greater logic. Bel-Imperia is more closely connected with Andrea than Horatio, and some semblance of justification is added when Balthazar begins his suit, for the audience can visualize a forced marriage with the slayer of her lover, an impossible

---

[4] Andrea was killed by Balthazar in fair battle. True, a feeble effort is made to put Balthazar in a bad light by having his soldiers unhorse Andrea before he is slain (Act I, sc. iv, ll. 19-26), but that is not sufficient to justify a vengeance-seeking ghost. This demand and situation closely parallels the reported ghost of Achilles in Seneca's *Troades*; but it is a piece of Senecan ethics undigestible to English audiences.

situation. Furthermore, at the moment she was the logical revenger since women were noted for their revengefulness in Elizabethan life and the Italian *novelle*.[5] The whole first act is devoted
to the exposition and to the resolution of the beloved to revenge
the death of her lover. The rising action is begun when Bel-Imperia starts to charm Horatio, her chosen instrument for the
revenge, and some hint is given of an opposing force in the person
of her brother Lorenzo who has sided with Balthazar's suit.

Still the situation is dramatically almost impossible. Horatio
has no thought that Andrea's death requires vengeance; consequently, if he is intended for the revenger of blood, he will prove
no more than the weak tool of Bel-Imperia, who, by her insistence
in driving him to the deed, will become a villainess. And if Horatio is not to be made this anomalous revenger, Bel-Imperia's only
course would be so to set Balthazar and Horatio at odds over her
love that one or the other is killed. If Balthazar falls, the play is
no tragedy. If, on the other hand, Horatio is killed, his position
as Bel-Imperia's tool precludes the sympathy of the audience, and
forces Bel-Imperia herself to kill Balthazar, a course she might
have followed in the beginning without causing the death of an
innocent man. If Horatio is not conceived as a mere instrument
for the unscrupulous Bel-Imperia but as a real and requited lover,
his position as revenger for a preceding lover grows even more
anomalous, and the revenge for Andrea loses all ethical dignity.

The only solution lies in developing the strength of the opposing force. The second act, therefore, is given over entirely to
showing the ascendancy of Lorenzo. Necessarily the revenge
theme lies dormant while Kyd devotes himself to painting an
idyllic picture of the love of Horatio and Bel-Imperia, and its fatal
end. Bel-Imperia is ostensibly carrying out her avowed intention
to love Horatio and thus spite Balthazar, but since her passion for
Horatio (which has rapidly passed from pretense to reality) seems

[5] See especially, *Two horrible and inhumane Murders done in Lincolnshire, by
two Husbands vpon their Wiues. . . . Anno Dom. 1604, Thomas Cash, Iohn Dil-
worth* (1607); *Tell-Trothes New-yeares Gift*, ed. Furnivall (New Shakspere Society,
1876), p. 27; Thomas Nashe, "The Unfortunate Traveller," *Works*, ed.
McKerrow, II, 263; Phillip Stubbes, *Anatomie of Abuses*, p. 101.

to have replaced her desire to revenge Andrea, the central theme of revenge is dropped in the emphasis on the happy lovers. Balthazar now has a tangible reason for a revenge: first, because Horatio took him prisoner in battle, and second because Horatio has preempted his intended bride. With Lorenzo as the guiding spirit, the two slay Horatio. The deed is presumably the revenge of Balthazar, but Lorenzo's cold determination to brush aside all obstacles to his sister's royal marriage makes him the real murderer.

At this point the tragedy has strayed its farthest from the main theme as announced by the chorus composed of Revenge and the ghost of Andrea. This time, however, a real revenger of blood appears. Hieronimo does not know the murderers of his son, but he plans to dissemble until he learns and then to strike. At the finish of the second act, with Bel-Imperia imprisoned, and a new revenger for a new crime appearing, the play actually disregards the revenge for Andrea and settles down to dramatize a revenge among men for a crime already seen and appreciated by the audience, no longer a revenge for an unreasonable ghost. From this point the ghost and his theme, which was to be the core of the play, are superfluous; and, indeed, need never have been introduced.

The third act, which begins the second half of the play, works out two lines of action: the progress made by the revenger Hieronimo, and the efforts of the murderer Lorenzo to consolidate his position in order to escape detection. The difficulty of appropriate dramatic action for the revenger posed a nice problem for Kyd. A revenger with no knowledge and no possible clues to investigate is a static figure since action is impossible. Yet a revenger with complete knowledge would normally act at once, and the play would be over. Kyd solved the problem brilliantly. The note from Bel-Imperia which gives him the names of the murderers is so startling that Hieronimo suspects a trap, for he knows of no motive why Lorenzo and the foreign prince should have killed his son. He must therefore assure himself of the truth before he acts, and since Bel-Imperia has been removed from court a delay is unavoidable. At one stroke Kyd has given the necessary information to the revenger, and then tied his hands until the plot has further unfolded.

Hieronimo's projected investigation has provided him with some dramatic action, particularly when the course of his inquiries sets the opposing force once more in motion. Lorenzo, believing his secret revealed, endeavors to destroy all proof by ridding himself of his accomplices Serberine and Pedringano. Ironically, it is this deed which finally gives the revenger his necessary corroboration in the incriminating letter found on Pedringano's dead body. The doubts of Bel-Imperia's letter are now resolved; his delay ended, Hieronimo rushes to the king for justice. It is important to note that Hieronimo first endeavors to secure his legal rights before taking the law into his own hands. Again a problem in plotting occurs. Hieronimo with his proof will gain the king's ear; Bel-Imperia will second Pedringano's letter; the murderers will be executed. Another impossible dramatic situation looms, for there would be no conflict of forces and no tragedy except of the most accidental sort.

It is evident that the revenger must be made to delay once more. Fear of deception cannot be employed again, and clearly the only possible means is either to delay Hieronimo's interview with the king or else to introduce some motive that would lead the king to discredit him. Once again Kyd brilliantly solved the problem by introducing the motive of madness. Isabella, Hieronimo's wife, runs mad, and Hieronimo next appears so stunned by grief for her and for his son that his own wits have been unsettled. He answers a request for information so wildly that his questioners think him wholly insane. Realizing that his madness has made him impotent, he meditates suicide but thrusts the thought aside before the reviving sense of his duty to revenge. His distraction, however, keeps him from gaining the king's ear, and when he recovers his senses he realizes that he can never find legal justice but must act as the executioner himself.

At this point the reasons for delay, previously logical, break down. Hieronimo says simply that he will revenge Horatio's death, but

> not as the vulgare wits of men,
> With open, but ineuitable ils,
> As by a secret, yet a certaine meane,
> Which vnder kindeship wilbe cloked best.
> Wise men will take their opportunitie,
> Closely and safely fitting things to time.
> But in extreames aduantage hath no time;
> And therefore all times fit not for reuenge. . . .
>   *Remedium malorum iners est.*
> Nor ought auailes it me to menace them
> Who as a wintrie storme vpon a plaine,
> Will beare me downe with their nobilitie.
>
> (III, xiii, 21-38)

These are scarcely valid reasons for delay in the execution of his private justice, since he admits that open and inevitable ills exist (without the necessity for delay) by which he could overthrow his enemies. Of course, his intention to dissemble patiently and to wait until he can consummate his vengeance at the right time and place heightens the interest in the inevitable catastrophe. The speech, in its entirety, would nevertheless irretrievably weaken the logic of the plot and the conception of Hieronimo's character were it not that it marks the turning point from Hieronimo the hero to Hieronimo the villain.

The fourth and last act opens with Bel-Imperia, now entirely forgetful of Andrea, swearing that if Hieronimo neglects his duty to revenge Horatio she herself will kill the murderers. Hieronimo presumably has a plan in mind, for the manuscript of the tragedy is ready when Lorenzo asks for an entertainment. Isabella, tortured by the thought of the unrevenged death of her son, kills herself in a fit of madness. Hieronimo braces himself for his revenge, and the fatal play is enacted. Even with Lorenzo and Balthazar slain and Bel-Imperia a suicide, the Viceroy, Balthazar's father, interposes for Hieronimo. Then occurs a scene which is useless except as it leads to the final culmination of horrors and the eventual conception of Hieronimo as a dangerous, blood-thirsty maniac. Hieronimo from the stage has already rehearsed his reasons for the murders, but the king orders him captured and inexplicably tries to wring from him the causes (already explained) for the deed, and the names of the confederates (already revealed as Bel-Imperia alone). Without this senseless action Hieronimo would have had no opportunity to tear out his tongue or to stab the duke, Lorenzo's father. His own suicide closes the play.

An analysis of the play reveals the basic Kydian formula for the tragedy of revenge:[6]

(1) The fundamental motive for the tragic action is revenge, although the actual vengeance of Hieronimo is not conceived until midway in the play. This revenge is by a father for the murder of his son, and extends not only to the murderers but also to their innocent kindred. The revenger is aided by a revenger accomplice, and both commit suicide after achieving their vengeance.

(2) Hieronimo's revenge is called forth by the successful revenge, conceived for a supposed injury, of the villains on his son.

(3) The ghost of the slain Andrea watches the revenge on the person who killed him and on those who hindered his love, but the action of the latter half of the play does not spring from the motive of a revenge for him nor is this revenge directed chiefly at his slayer. Consequently the ghost has no real connection with the play. This loose use of a vengeance-seeking ghost was not repeated in later plays.

(4) An important dramatic device is the justifiable hesitation of the revenger, who requires much proof, and, on the failure of legal justice, supposedly lacks a suitable opportunity for straightforward action. Hieronimo finds his task difficult; he is burdened with doubt and human weakness and delayed by his madness. The letter from Bel-Imperia, Pedringano's posthumous confes-

[6] This analysis leans heavily upon A. H. Thorndike's admirable study, already mentioned, in *PMLA*, Vol. XVII (1902), pp. 142-8.

sion, the exhortations of Bel-Imperia and her offers of assistance, and the death of his wife, are all required to spur his resolution to the deed.

(5) Madness is an important dramatic device. Hieronimo is afflicted with passing fits of genuine madness brought on by his overwhelming grief and the overwhelming sense of his obligation and his helplessness to revenge which saps his will. It is not probable that in Kyd's original version Hieronimo ever pretended madness. There are two scenes in which his words are too glib and flighty (the reconciliation with Lorenzo and the plans for the play-within-a-play), but in both his nerves are under pressure owing to the rôle he is acting, and his wild talk shows the intense strain on a mind already somewhat weakened rather than a pretense to lure his opponents into false security.

(6) Intrigue used against and by the revenger is an important element. Lorenzo's machinations fill a considerable portion of the play. Hieronimo secures his revenge by elaborate trickery.

(7) The action is bloody and deaths are scattered through the play. Ten characters are killed, eight of these on-stage.

(8) The contrast and enforcement of the main situation are achieved by parallels. Andrea requires revenging, as does Horatio. Hieronimo's grief for his son is reenforced by the grief of the Viceroy for the supposed death of Balthazar and later for his actual slaying. More particularly, Hieronimo is paralleled by the petitioner whose son has been killed. His madness finds a counterpart in Isabella's, and his hesitation is contrasted to Bel-Imperia's desire for action.

(9) The accomplices on both sides are killed. Bel-Imperia falls a suicide, and the villain with keen irony destroys Serberine and Pedringano in order to protect himself.

(10) Lorenzo, the villain, is an almost complete Machiavellian, as full of villainous devices as he is free from scruples.

(11) The revenge is accomplished terribly, fittingly, with irony and deceit. Once his resolution is screwed to the point, the revenger becomes exceedingly cunning, dissembles with the murderers, and adroitly plans their downfall.

(12) Minor characteristics are: the exhibition of Horatio's body; the wearing of black; reading in a book before a philosophical soliloquy; a letter written in blood and a handkerchief dipped in blood and kept as a memento to revenge; the melancholy of the revenger, who struggles with the problems of revenge, fortune, justice, and death; the sentimental but desperately revengeful woman.

A specific source is customarily presupposed for *The Spanish Tragedy,* but it has never been found, and very probably no detailed source for the entire story ever existed;[7] for if this hypothetical source be disregarded, the roots of the play are found in Seneca's tragedies, the Italian and French *novelle,* possibly in the Renaissance Italian tragedy, and certainly in the old Teutonic story of Hamlet as told by Saxo Grammaticus and translated by Belleforest.

Senecan influence there is undoubtedly in the penning of the lines. The machinery of the ghost of Andrea and Revenge is also Senecan in construction, although the function of the two as chorus is not classical. The Spirit of Revenge is presumably influencing the actions of the characters in much the same fashion in which the ghost of Tantalus casts his malign influence over the house of Pelops in *Thyestes*. Such a pulling of the strings from without, therefore, is wholly Senecan, as is the parallel to *Thyestes* where a particular revenge enacted on the stage satisfies the debt to an unrelated crime from the past. Senecan, too, are the bloodshed and horrors, though typically Renaissance in their form. Seneca usually emphasizes one great passion; *The Spanish Tragedy* is a study of the overwhelming passion of revenge. Revenge either moderately forthright, as in *Agamemnon,* or else by secret, deceitful means, as in *Thyestes,* had already appeared in Seneca as a proper subject for tragedy.

[7] If Kyd actually drew upon some story, it must have been far less complex than the action of the play would indicate, since various important incidents can be traced to diverse sources. See F. T. Bowers, "Kyd's Pedringano: Sources and Parallels," *Harvard Studies and Notes,* Vol. XIII (1931).

To a certain extent, however, the debt to Seneca has been exaggerated. Actual insanity in Seneca is limited to the madness sent by Juno upon Hercules, a situation which has no possible parallel in *The Spanish Tragedy*. Somewhat closer to Kyd's conception are the divine "madnesses" of Medea and Deïanira, but the origin of Hieronimo's insanity does not actually come from the Roman tragedian. The hesitation of the revenger had appeared momentarily when Medea once falters in her resolve and when Clytemnestra requires the goading of Aegisthus. Neither of these plays, however, utilized the motive of hesitation to prolong the plot, as does Kyd, but instead merely to fillip the interest of the audience for a moment with the possibility that the revenge might be abandoned. The true source for Hieronimo's dramatically important hesitation is not there. Again, the suicides of Bel-Imperia and Hieronimo have no relation to the expiatory suicides of Seneca's characters who have caused the death of some beloved person. The most specific contribution of Seneca to the dramatic form of *The Spanish Tragedy* is the ghost; yet it has been noted how Kyd was gradually led away from the Senecan construction so that his supernatural chorus became superfluous and even intrusive. The interest in the play is on the revenge on Lorenzo (and only incidentally on Balthazar) for a Horatio murdered in plain view of the audience, not the revenge on Balthazar for the ghost of Andrea, with whom Hieronimo is entirely unconnected.

Yet the general influence of Seneca on the writing and the original conception of the play cannot be denied, for such an influence was unavoidable at the time. Classical tragedy had gained an enormous prestige in England because of the great value set on classical learning, of which tragedy was supposed to be the highest expression; and knowing little of the Greeks the Elizabethans came to regard Seneca as the most tragic, the most perfect of ancient writers. Senecan tragedy was dominant on the Continent; Seneca was read freely in the English schools and universities where his plays were acted, as were Latin imitations. His methods of treating tragic situations were akin to Elizabethan temperament, for the men of the time were well equipped to understand his philosophy, which held that man, the individual, was more than the puppet of medieval scholasticism and was, indeed, to some extent the master of his fate. Even the fatalistic Senecan passages found a ready echo in the breasts of Englishmen already afflicted with the melancholia which sometimes turned them to practising malcontents. Seneca's cosmopolitanism was near to the Elizabethans, who were starting an empire and were beginning to cast off their insular provincialism.

The crudity hidden beneath the superficial polish of the Elizabethans made them less sensitive to the fundamental emptiness of much of Seneca. They were delighted with his rhetoric, for they were still so intellectually young as to be impressed by bombast and flamboyance.[8] Introspection had become a national trait, and fed agreeably on the elaborate Senecan philosophizing, with its spice of stoicism suitable to a hard-bitten age. The long Senecan descriptions were suited for imitation on the bare English stage. Finally, Seneca's emphasis on sensationalism, on physical horrors to stimulate emotion, appealed to the English taste, for blood and horror on the stage could not be offensive to the spectators at cruel executions. Ghosts were accepted as fact, and forewarnings were everyday affairs, as with Ben Jonson's on the death of his son. Except for his classical subject-matter and his rigid classical form involving the use of choruses, there was no single element of Seneca that could not be accepted immediately by the spectator in the pit.

With such a tradition it was inevitable that *The Spanish Tragedy* should ring with Seneca in its rhetoric. Kyd, however, was no humble slave in his dramatic craftmanship. Admitting freely that it would be difficult to conceive *The Spanish Tragedy* without Seneca, we find, when details are sought for specific sources of plot and characterization, that the way leads beyond Seneca.[9]

[8] F. L. Lucas, *Seneca and Elizabethan Tragedy* (Cambridge at the University Press, 1922), p. 57.

[9] The question of Seneca's influence in Elizabethan Tragedy receives careful examination in Howard Baker's recently published *Induction to Tragedy* (Louisiana State University Press, 1939), which reaches conclusions substantially the same as those expressed above.

It is highly probable that Kyd, uninfluenced specifically save by Belleforest's story of Hamlet, drew his main inspiration for the working out first of Lorenzo's and then of Hieronimo's and Bel-Imperia's revenges not from Seneca but from the ethics and incidents in the Italian and French stories and from English ideas about the Italian character.[10]

So closely allied with the villainous characters of the Italian novels that the two cannot be separated is the Elizabethan's creation of the Italian villain based on Machiavelli's principles. Lorenzo in *The Spanish Tragedy* is the first of the long line of Elizabethan villains who owe their sole inspiration to Machiavelli. Although Lorenzo is not the protagonist of the play, he is so extremely active as the opposing force that he is almost as prominent as Hieronimo, and just as necessary to the extension of the dramatic action. Except that he is not a prince relying upon the doctrines of Machiavelli to rule and hold his state, every one of Lorenzo's actions reads like a exemplum of Machiavellian "policy." Even though the boundless Machiavellian ambition which produced the bloody Italian despot is absent, yet the ambition to raise his house by a royal marriage for his sister is the motivating spring of his murder of Horatio. His fundamental likeness to the Machiavellian comes in his ruthlessness toward all who stand in the way of his plans, in his perfect indifference to the sufferings he causes others, in his mania for secrecy and willingness to employ other men as catspaws, and in the tortuous and deceitful

[10] "The cases in which the English dramatists have woven individual features culled from this novel-literature [the Italian] into dramatic plots invented by themselves are innumerable. Particularly in the 'blood and vengeance' tragedies we can constantly realise how the poets' imaginations had been fired by those tales treating of a 'bellissima vendetta,' which Bandello especially relates with such grim enjoyment." Wilhelm Creizenach, *The English Drama in the Age of Shakespeare* (London: Sidgewick & Jackson, 1916), p. 95. See also p. 219: "The classic apparitions of ghosts were, of course, too valuable to be foregone, but it is in the tales of revenge carefully prepared with a refinement of cunning and cruelty that the dramatists seek most strenuously to emulate their Italian models."

That the scene is laid in Spain is of no importance, since no Elizabethan playwright strove overmuch for local color, and the contemporary Englishman lumped the Spaniard and the Italian together in the vicious and deceitful character of their revenges.

means he uses to attain his ends. Lorenzo is fundamentally cold-blooded and unsentimental, a practical man after Machiavelli's own heart.[11] What lends particular interest to his character is the weighty evidence for believing that he was partly drawn from scandalous accounts of the Earl of Leicester, who was naïvely believed by his enemies to be the foremost exponent in England of the hated Machiavellian doctrines.[12]

Although several are found in the French, the Italian *novelle* contain few stories of actual blood-revenge. Terrible revenges for other reasons are plentiful, however, and these influenced *The Spanish Tragedy* not only in incident but also in character and motivation. The type of revengeful woman exemplified by Bel-Imperia is a commonplace in Italian and French fiction, as is the brutal intriguing Lorenzo. In particular, his disposal of accomplices is partly drawn from the forty-fifth novel of the first part of Bandello. Balthazar, swearing revenge the moment he learns Horatio has won Bel-Imperia's love, fits the conception of touchy Italian pride which motivated so many tragic *novelle*. Above all, the atmosphere of the vendetta was unassailably Italian.

It is, indeed, the carrying-out of the vendetta tradition which turns Hieronimo from a hero to an Italianate villain. So long as he is pitiful in his grief for Horatio and in search of his murderers, so long the English audience would give him full sympathy. When, at last spurred to action by complete knowledge, he rushes to the king for legal justice, he would still be the hero whose actions, according to the best Elizabethan ethics, were those of an honorable man. But when Lorenzo foils him in his attempt at legal redress and he consciously gives up an open revenge in favor of a secret, treacherous device, according to English standards he inevitably becomes a villain. Indeed, so transparently weak is his sophistry and so open-eyed his turning from God's to the devil's means in the soliloquy opening Act III, scene

[11] For a full discussion, see C. V. Boyer, *The Villain as Hero in Elizabethan Tragedy* (New York: E. P. Dutton, 1914), pp. 31-9, 40-3, 241-5.

[12] F. T. Bowers, "Kyd's Pedringano: Sources and Parallels," *Harvard Studies and Notes*, Vol. XIII (1931), pp. 247-9.

xiii, that it is evident Kyd is deliberately veering his audience against Hieronimo.

Hieronimo begins,

Vindicta mihi,

and, pursuing this promise from the Bible,[13] consoles himself with the thought that Heaven never leaves murder unatoned; therefore he will await Heaven's decree. A quotation from Seneca then comes to his mind, and, swayed by the materialistic Senecan philosophy, he reflects that one crime opens the way for another, and he should repay wrong with wrong, for death ends both the resolute and the patient man and the end of destiny for each is merely the grave. Fortified by this un-Christian sophistry, he determines to anticipate Heaven's slow justice and to revenge for himself at his own appointed hour. Having decided to cast off Heaven, he cannot now expect a divinely awarded opportunity and so must carve the occasion for himself. He scorns acting

> as the vulgare wits of men,
> With open, but ineuitable ils,

(the only formula with which his "vulgar" audience could sympathize) and therefore, from his Machiavellian superiority to common humanity, he chooses a secret, albeit certain, plan,[14]

[13] Boas in his note to this passage (*Works of Thomas Kyd* [Oxford at the Clarendon Press, 1901], p. 408) describes this line as coming from the pseudo-Senecan *Octavia*: "Vindicta debetur mihi." However, the context of the following lines indicates that the reference is rather to the well-known "Vindicta mihi," "Vengeance is mine, saith the Lord" (*Romans* XII: 17, 19. See also *Deut.* XXIII: 25). See F. T. Bowers, *"A Note on the Spanish Tragedy,"* *Modern Language Notes,* Vol. LIII (1938), pp. 590-1.

[14] Here again, it seems, Boas makes too much difficulty over this line when he comments, "We should expect a contrast between the open and therefore by no means 'ineuitable ills' employed by vulgar wits, and the secret yet certain method which Hieronimo contemplates." Yet if the analysis of Hieronimo's change in character be correct, he is casting himself off from the ordinary run of humanity and their forthright though effective methods of retaliation, and knowingly entering on a villainous course with its deeper satisfaction. No one with a knowledge of Elizabethan duelling assassinations can deny that "open," the characteristically English method, did not invariably have an "inevitable" success. The contrast comes rather in the next line, where "secret" is juxtaposed to

which he will conceal under the cloak of pretended friendship with Lorenzo. Since his project is of so great weight, he cannot hasten the hour but must bide the proper time for his revenge; delay, and dissemble his true feelings, hoping by his feigned ignorance to deceive his wary opponents. He then weakly excuses his planned hypocrisy by arguing that, even if he revealed his true feelings, he is too helpless to prevail merely with threats against his enemies' high position. Therefore he must deceive until opportunity offers revenge.

Since the next scene with Bazulto shows Hieronimo led by his grief into a fresh fit of insanity, it might be held that he is not responsible for his actions, that his weakened mind has forced him into the winding channels of his soliloquy, and that the subsequent scenes of deceit leading to the final slaughter are the actions of an insane person holding himself so rigidly in check that his madness is not visible. Such a view might, to the Elizabethans, mitigate his deed,[15] but it would not release him from the consequences of his blood-guilt, since he would then be merely a villainous madman. Whether Kyd had enough psychological subtlety to portray Hieronimo's conversion according to this line of thought may well be a matter of opinion. A careful examination of the text leads to the view that, except for certain well defined scenes, Hieronimo is entirely sane in his revengeful plans —as sane certainly as Shakespeare's Hamlet when he stabs Claudius—although the actor may well have chosen to play him as unbalanced.

"certain,"—with the meaning that secrecy with its accompanying tortuosity of action could, by his plan, *still* become as certain as an open offensive would have proved.

[15]
> "Cruel *Orestes* bath'd his ruthlesse sword,
> Estrang'd from strangers, in his mothers blood,
> So little pittie did the child afford
> To *Her,* that was the parent of the brood;
> Yet some excuse for this *Orestes* had,
> Mad men exemption haue, and *He* was mad."
>
> Richard Brathwaite, *Natures Embassie* [1621]
> (Boston, Lincs.: Privately Printed, 1877), p. 119.

This change marked by the soliloquy from open to dissembling action was forced upon Hieronimo by the absolute necessity for Kyd to evolve a final reason for delay, and also, one may suspect, by Kyd's leaning toward the Italianate, the sensational, for the dramatic catastrophe. Once Hieronimo adopted the Italianate Machiavellian tactics, he immediately lost the absolute admiration of his audience. The English insistence on straightforward action by open assault or formal duel, which they would be inclined to view as manslaughter, refused to tolerate treacherous Italian plots. The Bible said, "Cursed is he that smiteth his neighbour secretly," and they heartily agreed. The Machiavellian breach of faith was not to be endured, for it led only to the total destruction of the breaker,[16] and Hieronimo's pretended reconciliation with Lorenzo, with its reminiscence of Judas's kiss, was branded with the brand of Cain and of Machiavelli.[17] With all allowance for the fact that, owing to Kyd's delight in wholesale slaughter, it was unlikely even an innocent Hieronimo would have survived the play, the fact that he was guilty of murder made it absolutely necessary for him to die. No slayer in Elizabethan drama escaped some penalty, and that penalty was usually death.

If the means by which Hieronimo ensnared and killed Lorenzo and Balthazar were not sufficient to label him a villain, the débâcle which ends the play (when, after promises of immunity if his cause has been just, he refuses all questions and wilfully stabs Lorenzo's father) certainly transported him beyond the pale. While collective revenge was understood in Elizabethan times, it was universally decried:

"Farre be the first from God, farther be this; to strike the godly sonne for the godlesse Sire, to punish innocencie for Iniquitie. . . . Man is so just, *Amagias* slew the men, that kill'd his Father: but their children he slew not, 2 *Chron.* 14. and mans law pro-

---

[16] See especially, Gentillet, trans. Patericke (1608), Part III, §21, p. 264; Daniel Tuvill, *Essayes Morall and Theologicall* (1609), pp. 133-5; Joseph Hall, "Heaven Upon Earth," *Works,* ed. Wynter, Vol. VI, p. 10.

[17] John Manningham, *Diary,* ed. J. Bruce (Camden Society, 1848), p. 115.

vides for it, that *factum unius* doe not *nocere alteri,* one mans
fact hurt another, saith old *Vlpian.*"[18]

The act would have been serious enough if Hieronimo had
wreaked his revenge on the duke alone, according to the primitive custom where, in a state of family solidarity, any member of
a family is as acceptable as the criminal; but when, after killing
Lorenzo, Hieronimo refuses a pardon and stabs the duke also,
he is departing so far from the English sense of justice as finally
to withdraw all sympathy.

Bearing on this question, the comments of John Bereblock on
a play *Progne* presented before the queen at Oxford in 1566 are
interesting. Progne truly had just cause to revenge her sister
Philomel, but Bereblock in his review of the plot writes: "It is
wonderful how she longed to seek vengeance for the blood of her
sister. She goes about therefore to avenge wrongs with wrongs,
and injuries with injuries; nor is it at all reverent to add crimes
to crimes already committed." Yet if her thoughts of revenge
were, in the first instance, wrong, the treacherous means by
which she achieved her revenge made her in Bereblock's eyes an
absolute villainess. "And that play was a notable portrayal of mankind in its evil deeds, and was for the spectators, as it were, a
clear moral of all those who indulge too much either in love
[Tereus] or in wrath [Progne]."[19]

Hieronimo's act is, therefore, either the culmination of his villainy (mad or sane), or else Kyd, swept away by a passion for
violence, wrote the scene with no motive in mind but the wish
to portray more bloody deeds. It is faintly possible that the duke's
death satisfies in some roundabout manner the justice demanded
by the ghost of Andrea—long since forgotten in the play's action
—for the duke had apparently discouraged with considerable
emphasis Andrea's love-affair with Bel-Imperia. It might be

[18] Richard Clerke, *Sermons* (1647), p. 392.

[19] W. Y. Durand, "*Palaemon and Arcyte, Progne, Marcus Geminus,* and the
Theatre in Which They Were Acted, as Described by John Bereblock (1566),"
Publications of the Modern Language Association of America, Vol. XX (1905),
pp. 515-16.

argued that Kyd was possibly following too closely his hypothetical source with its different morality, and so confused the
ethics of the play. But the theory that Kyd followed one main
source is very uncertain, and there is hardly a doubt that, mad or
sane, Hieronimo was a villain to the English audience at the end
and was forced to commit suicide to satisfy the stern doctrine
that murder, no matter what the motive, was never successful.

Bel-Imperia shares the blood-guilt with Hieronimo, but the
audience probably viewed her with a more lenient eye. Her suicide, thus, was not so necessary to satisfy morality as it was the
usual move of the woman in romantic fiction who refused to outlive her slain lover after seeing vengeance done. The women of
Elizabethan drama did not bear the guilt of blood, as did the men,
unless they were portrayed as unmistakable villainesses from their
position in the plot. That they, too, often perished after staining
their hands with blood or assisting in the revenge, is owing more
to their refusal to live after their slain lovers than to the demands
of contemporary ethics.[20] When the reason for their revenge is
not romantic, they customarily enter a convent to purge themselves.

[20] "If a woman therefore, replied Lady *Tarquina,* should committe a theft,
manslaughter, or faile in any other part of Iustice, should she not for such a fact be
infamous? And *Gualengo*: Although such offences, in men and women, are by
the laws equally punished, yet as often as in a woman they are not accompanied
with the act of dishonestie [unchastity] they make her not infamous." Kepers,
The Courtiers Academie (*c.* 1598), p. 126. See the story of Camma told by Pettie,
and the play *Gismond of Salerne.*

Legally, according to Coke, suicides were not accountable if they were suffering
from loss of memory at the moment "by the rage of sickness or infirmity or
otherwise" (*Third Institute,* cap. 8). Burton admits that suicide for noble reasons
is much admired by pagan classical authors, but refutes them with Christian
laws, excepting only "that in some cases, those hard censures of such as offer
violence to their own persons . . . are to be mitigated, as in such as are mad,
beside themselves for the time, or found to have been long melancholy, and
that in extremity, they know not what they do, deprived of reason, judgement,
all" (*The Anatomy of Melancholy* (Bohn Library, 1923), Vol. I, p. 504). Bel-
Imperia, as Gismond before her, by her clearly premeditated suicide cast herself
from the Christian to the pagan and romantic morality, but there is little doubt
that she, as well as later tragic heroines, was viewed sympathetically by an audience sentimentally close to pagan ethics.

The characters of Lorenzo, Hieronimo, and Bel-Imperia, the whole atmosphere of brutal and Machiavellian vendetta, together with part of the Pedringano incident, thus were the outgrowth of the Italian and French *novelle* and the Elizabethan's hostile view of Machiavelli and the Italian character. Of the most important influence from the *novelle*—the story of Hamlet—more will be said shortly.

There is no definite proof that Kyd had ever read an Italian tragedy. Indeed, with the exception of the translation of *Jocasta* from Dolce by Gascoigne and Kinwelmarsh, and some borrowings by the author of *Gismond of Salerne* from Dolce's *Didone* (not omitting the debt to the Italian of the academic *Progne* and *Roxana*), no direct relationship between Italian and English tragedy has been established.[21] Dubious parallels there are, to be sure, to indicate that early Elizabethan tragedy was perhaps following Italianate Seneca more than Seneca himself in the elaborate use of dumb shows, the rejection of the traditional Latin and Greek stories, and the extension of the scope of the action and of the list of characters. The motive of sexual love, the intensification of physical horrors and their performance on the stage, all had been paralleled in Italian tragedy; and in *Gismond of Salerne* and its later revision had been deliberately adopted from the Italian. With *The Spanish Tragedy* and *Locrine* the mingling of classical and popular traditions ended with the fixation of the English form of tragedy. The most suitable elements of Seneca were completely naturalized by incorporation with the main stream of popular drama, and henceforth Seneca or his Italian and French derivatives had really nothing more to teach.[22]

Moreover, even the few early parallels were all the work of men of the Inner Temple or of the universities, and, being learned performances, were no true indication of a diffused knowledge of the Italian tragic art. In Italy itself Neo-Senecan tragedy was not

[21] J. W. Cunliffe, "The Influence of Italian on Elizabethan Drama," *Modern Philology,* Vol. IV (1904), pp. 597-604.

[22] *The Poetical Works of Sir William Alexander*, ed. Kastner and Charlton (Manchester at the University Press, 1921), Vol. I, p. clxix.

a popular form, and there is no evidence that more than a handful of Englishmen were at all familiar with Italian tragedies. Certainly the typical sixteenth century Italian tragedies were not of a type to exercise any especial influence on *The Spanish Tragedy,* although certain rough parallels may be drawn. The Italian tragedy interested itself chiefly in the depiction of villainy and horrors. Horrors are emphasized in *The Spanish Tragedy* and Lorenzo is extremely important as a villain. The sources for Lorenzo's character, however, have been noted, and he bears little relation to the bloody tyrants of Italian tragedy. Furthermore, the horrors of *The Spanish Tragedy* are honest English horrors based on the copiousness with which blood is shed and the resulting emotional response of the audience, and have little to do with the unnaturalness of the crude Thyestean banquets and elaborate dissection and poisoning scenes of the Italian.

The most important point of similarity to Italian tragedy lies in the ghosts. In none of Seneca's plays does the ghost of the recent dead rise to demand vengeance for his own murder, as Andrea does, although such a demand is common in Italian tragedies like Cinthio's *Orbecche* (1541) and Decio da Orte's *Acripanda* (1591). The rather important parallel between the spirit of Revenge in *The Spanish Tragedy* and the spirit of Suspicion in Groto's *La Dalida* must be noticed, and there may possibly be an authentic borrowing here. For the rest, Seneca's tragedies, while bloody, are not the slaughter-houses of the Italian, where hardly a character remains alive. In this respect Italian tragedy is paralleled in Kyd.

Here the general resemblance ceases, for the action of Italian tragedy and *The Spanish Tragedy* is vitally dissimilar. No Italian play depends for its plot, like *The Spanish Tragedy,* upon blood-revenge for a person slain on the stage. The Italian usually revolves about a villain protagonist and a heroine, with lust ever in the foreground.[23] This villain is usually a tyrannous king, who is

---

[23] The best illustration of the increasing interest of Italian dramatists in the depiction of villainy is found in two tragedies of Albovine and Rosamund separated by sixty-six years. In the *Rosmunda* of Rucellai (1516) Rosmunda is an innocent

portrayed in some incident of his private life (like a love-affair where he is either the lover or the father of the lover) in which he exercises the powers of his kingship for a terrible revenge. "Tragic error" is expanded to include even the ordering of a Thyestean banquet.[24] There is little in common between such a type and *The Spanish Tragedy*. Possibly a detail or two in Kyd came from the Italian, but there is no argument for any general, thoroughgoing influence.

The chief foreign influence on *The Spanish Tragedy,* rivalling and probably even surpassing Seneca in the importance of its details, is the story of Hamlet which Kyd found in Belleforest, who had borrowed it from Saxo Grammaticus. To the Senecan, Italian, and French, is now added a primitive Teutonic influence on the nascent revenge tragedy.

Without going into the various arguments for and against, the belief may be stated that a play by Kyd, written on the subject of Hamlet's revenge, was in existence at some time before 1589. This play is not extant, and there is no reason to believe that it was ever printed. The first quarto of Shakespeare's *Hamlet* was entered on July 26, 1602, and published in 1603. This is a vulgarized memorial version, put together for pirated acting, of an original that is represented substantially by the second quarto of 1604/5, and it cannot be trusted to offer evidence about an earlier state of the play. Another text which must be considered is a German play, *Der Bestrafte Brudermord,* which bears obvious relations to the two quartos of *Hamlet.* Although the manuscript cannot be traced farther back than the early eighteenth century, the play is always thought to be of considerably earlier date.

pure woman who takes no part by word or deed in the assassination of Alboina; Almachilde is merely a disinterested lover who executes vengeance on the king from generous and patriotic motives while Rosmunda is in a fainting spell. In Antonio Cavallerino's *Rosimonda Regina* (1582), however, Rosmunda is guilty of both prostitution and assassination, and, with her lover, is a fair specimen of the character interest Italian dramatists took in illicit passion and its frequent twin, murder.

[24] Kastner and Charlton, *op. cit.,* Vol. I, pp. xc-xci.

In order to evaluate Kyd's *Ur-Hamlet* properly the major features of the plot and characterization must be surmised, and, if the connection with *The Spanish Tragedy* is to be of benefit, the date must be conjectured. The only clues to these questions can be sought in Shakespeare's *Hamlet* in its two quarto editions and in *Der Bestrafte Brudermord. Alphonsus, Emperor of Germany,* an anonymous tragedy of about 1597, may perhaps be included. A vast amount of learning and much ingenious conjecture have been brought to bear on the problem of the exact relation between the *Ur-Hamlet, Der Bestrafte Brudermord,* and *Hamlet.*[25] There is little reason here to venture into the conflicting theories of this criticism. For the purposes of this work it is postulated that *Der Bestrafte Brudermord* was drawn from the *Ur-Hamlet* either in its original form or in a somewhat revised version of 1594-1595, and that the *Ur-Hamlet* did not differ materially from the main outline of the story as represented in the German play and in the second quarto of Shakespeare.

Belleforest's account in *Les Histoires Tragiques,* from which Kyd drew, follows in the main the incidents as narrated by Saxo Grammaticus with the omission of the more primitive portions as in the details of the attempt to seduce Amleth, and with a considerable expansion of the speeches. Some few incidents are altered. Thus in Belleforest, Fengon has committed incest with Geruthe before the murder of Horwendille, and the murderer bolsters his excuses for the deed by the assertion that Horwen-

[25] See particularly Charlton Lewis, *The Genesis of Hamlet* (New York: Henry Holt & Co., 1907); Wilhelm Creizenach, " 'Der Bestrafte Brudermord' and its Relation to Shakespeare's 'Hamlet,' " *Modern Philology,* Vol. II (1904), pp. 249-60; M. B. Evans, " 'Der Bestrafte Brudermord' and Shakespeare's 'Hamlet,' " *Modern Philology,* Vol. II (1905), pp. 433-9; J. D. Wilson, *The Copy for 'Hamlet' 1603 and the 'Hamlet' Transcript 1593* (London: De la More Press, 1918); E. E. Stoll, *Hamlet: An Historical and Comparative Study* (Research Publications of the University of Minnesota, 1919); H. D. Gray, "Thomas Kyd and the First Quarto of Hamlet," *Publications of the Modern Language Association of America,* Vol. XLII (1927), pp. 721-35; G. B. Harrison, *The Tragicall Historie of Hamlet Prince of Denmarke 1603* (London: John Lane, 1923); E. K. Chambers, *William Shakespeare* (Oxford at the Clarendon Press, 1930); F. T. Bowers, *"Alphonsus, Emperor of Germany* and the *Ur-Hamlet," Modern Language Notes,* Vol. XLVIII (1933), pp. 101-8.

dille had threatened her life. Furthermore, he procures false witnesses to prove it, and so convinces the court. Belleforest, accordingly, paints Geruthe as a deep-dyed, lascivious villainess, and emphasizes her evil character by having her deliberately abandon Amleth to his fate. Still, the ground is prepared for her repentance when he (where Saxo is vague) makes clear that she knew nothing of the scheme to conceal the courtier under the quilt to overhear her conversation with Amleth. Whereas in Saxo the repentance of Geruthe comes only after Amleth's reproaches and is baldly described, in Belleforest the shock of the slaying brings her to remorse while Amleth is disposing of the body. Consequently, instead of being greeted at his return, as in Saxo, with reproaches for his folly, he finds her in a mood to listen to his harangue, and she afterwards promises to help him with his revenge. The course of Amleth's revenge follows that in Saxo except for the addition of a long speech after the slaying in which Amleth consigns Fengon to hell, there to tell his brother's spirit "que c'est son fils qui te faict faire ce message, à fin que soulagé par ceste memoire, son ombre s'appaise parmy les esprits bien-heureux, et me quitte de celle obligation qui m'astraignoit à pursuivre ceste vengeance sur mon sang."

The difference in spirit between the two narratives, however, is distinct. Saxo, telling his primitive tale, is never in doubt about the justness of the revenge, or, indeed, of any other revenge in his history. Belleforest, not at all influenced by the pagan Scandinavian tradition, is divided between his Renaissance French appreciation of a *bella vendetta* and the Christian doctrine that all revenge must be left to God. Moreover, he is apprehensive lest his tale of tyrannicide be censured as treasonable. At the start he grafts Christianity on revenge by asserting a moral purpose for his story and placing Amleth in the position of an agent of God, so that the long delay is explained in a sidenote as owing to "la tardiue vengeance de Dieu." After some quibbling over the ethics of feigning madness to procure revenge, Belleforest in Amleth's speech over the body of Fengon writes a final justification for the particular revenge, which is solely for the murder of a father, prefaced by the sidenote, "Vengeance juste, ou est ce que doit estre consideree." Amleth, after praising himself for his well considered and courageous plan of revenge, cries: "Si jamais la vengeance sembla avoir quelque face et forme de justice, il est hors de doute, que la pieté et affection qui nous lie à la souvenance de nos peres, pursuivis injustement, est celle qui nous dispence à cercher les moyens de ne laisser impunie une trahison, et effort outrageux et proditoire." Thus Belleforest follows Christian ethics on the one hand in denouncing private revenge for injuries, except that he is in perfect accord, on the other, with the pagan classical belief in the duty of the son to revenge the murder of a father. In his opinion such a crime exempts the revenger from following honorable means of revenge and justifies any mode of procedure, such as Amleth's trickery. Only king-killing is barred to the just revenger of a father's murder. Here Amleth's act is justified as no treason since Amleth is the rightful heir, and Fengon then, properly, his subject.

Kyd, with Belleforest's narrative for a source,[26] was forced to make wide changes to adapt the action to the stage and to the tragic form. First of all, to be suitably tragic the play must end with death to the avenger as well as to the victim, and they must drag down with them all other guilty persons concerned. As the first step, the incidents following Hamlet's revenge must be omitted, as well as those occurring during his first stay in Britain. At this stage the story would be: Hamlet's father has been killed and his mother incestuously married to the murderer, who now occupies the vacant office of prince-governor. Hamlet is bent on revenge and pretends madness in order to preserve his life. This madness is suspected by the prince-governor and his courtiers, who test him by tempting him with a young girl and eavesdropping at an interview with his mother, during which Hamlet kills

[26] M. J. Wolff, "Zum Urhamlet," Englische Studien, Vol. XLV (1912), pp. 16-18, suggests that Kyd may have known the Merope of Pomponio Torelli written in 1589, and lists ten resemblances of plotting between Merope and Hamlet. It seems more probable that the parallels between the two plays are accidental, since it seems practically certain that the Ur-Hamlet was written before 1589.

the spy. His mother repents and promises to aid Hamlet in his revenge. He declares he will meet trickery with trickery. The prince sends him to England with false messages intending his death which Hamlet discovers and rewrites to apply to his companions sent to guard him. He returns to Denmark to find the court celebrating his funeral feast, fires the hall and burns his enemies, and then kills the prince with his sword.

With this simple story Kyd begins the dramatization. At the very start, however, he confronts the most serious problem of the play. For there to be any play at all, the revenger must delay. The reasons for delay must also fulfil two requirements: they must be dramatic, and they must not prejudice the character of the revenger either by imputation of cowardice or of Machiavellism. The audience can have no sympathy for a craven in the most desperate situation that can well face a man. On the other hand, luring a victim to destruction by deceit is not the rôle of a hero, for it carried with it the imputation of Machiavellism. For this reason delay cannot be caused by a long and elaborate plot against the king. Belleforest was of little help. His Amleth delays, it is true, but only for the undramatic reason that he is awaiting the best opportunity.

Kyd, as is shown by *The Spanish Tragedy,* was a brilliant inventor of dramatic incident. He realized that the solution for his problem lay in the contrivance of positive obstacles through which Hamlet must cut for his revenge. And as the primary obstacle, Hamlet must find his path barred not by a hostile court in full possession of the fact of his father's murder, but by a court which had never dreamed that his father had been murdered. Since proof is completely lacking, Hamlet must act alone and in constant danger.

But if the murder is unrecognized, the problem arises how to introduce Hamlet to the truth. Kyd, the ever-spectacular, broke wide with tradition and introduced into the action of the play itself a ghost who acquaints his son with the true facts of his death. The classical drama had employed ghosts as omens of disaster and, as in *Agamemnon* and *Troades,* to demand vengeance; but, it must be emphasized, never as actors to reveal the murder to the unsuspecting revenger-to-be.

Amleth's pretense of madness in Belleforest is the real starting-point for the story, and, indeed, its most integral feature. It was the common Scandinavian practice for a murderer to endeavor to wipe out all possible revengers as well, and Amleth, rightly fearing for his life, pretends insanity only to preserve himself by lulling Fengon into the belief that no revenger for Horwendille will appear. The secrecy of the murder in the *Ur-Hamlet* automatically disposes of any reason for Hamlet's instant plan to play the madman, since Claudius, believing the murder unknown, can have no strong motive for slaying Hamlet also. Indeed, it turns out ironically that Hamlet's madness is the very thing that excites Claudius's fatal suspicions. Whether Kyd realized the logical uselessness of the device is impossible to determine. What we do know is that he retained Hamlet's feigned madness, for to discard it would have been to ruin the play.[27]

The Elizabethan audience would instantly recognize Hamlet's revenge as just, for a revenge for murder either by legal or extra-legal means was still felt as a bounden duty. That Hamlet cannot secure legal justice forces him to rely on personal justice; this distinction would be recognized by the audience which would thereupon approve his ends and await with interest his procedure. The feigning of madness was a clever trick but the audience would reserve judgment on Hamlet's character until it was shown he did not intend to use treachery and hypocrisy, or the hated Italianate devices, to secure vengeance.

As the first scenes close Kyd has provided for dramatic effects by the madness motif and has introduced the first step in the

---

[27] This feigning of madness for ulterior motives appears elsewhere in Saxo Grammaticus and was known to the Elizabethans from David's example in the Bible, from Livy's account of Brutus, and from various miscellaneous stories. As an example, Saviolo digresses from his advice on duelling to recount a tale he has read in the history of the last wars in Persia, in which Mahomet Bassa, general of the Turkish Empire, took a pension from a soldier who had deserved it and bestowed it on another. The soldier feigned madness until he secured an opportunity to murder Mahomet. *Vincentio Sauiolo his Practise* (1595), sig. Q₃.

necessary delay in Hamlet's search for an opportunity. The strict guard kept about Claudius discourages Hamlet as the play proceeds and his emotional frustration drives him to thoughts of suicide. It is impossible for him to make a direct assault on Claudius. Such a disclosure of his secret means the end of the play. From Hamlet's own point of view, it is a poor revenge which leads to the death of the revenger; since he wishes to ascend the throne himself, he must take proper precautions for his own safety, and so continue his delay. But this delay very shortly ceases to be dramatic, and additional reasons must be sought which yet will mark some sort of forward step. This problem was ingeniously solved by the doubt of the ghost, necessitating the play-within-a-play. Simultaneously the opposing action—which becomes of increasing importance as the play progresses—is started when Claudius takes steps to discover the reasons for Hamlet's madness. From this point the future action is indicated as a stirring duel of wits between Hamlet and the king.

The rising action, with Hamlet on the offensive, sweeps through the mousetrap play and into the prayer scene. The meeting of the two under such conditions is a daring though necessary move. Hamlet has lamented that he can never find the king without his guards. Yet the king must have some private life, and the audience may well begin to wonder why Hamlet cannot find an accidental opportunity. Kyd daringly presents this opportunity but under such circumstances that Hamlet cannot accept it. Probability of incident has been affirmed, a little crisis has developed and subsided, and the audience has been momentarily put upon edge. The religious scruples Hamlet advances combine ill with his bloodthirsty thoughts, but actions speak louder than words and the audience has been assured that Hamlet is no villain.

It is obvious from *The Spanish Tragedy* that Kyd had a fondness for balancing incident. The crisis of the tragedy has been cleverly formed from an elaboration of the relatively unimportant murder of the eavesdropper in Belleforest. Now the strength of the opposing action forces delay on Hamlet. The English voyage affords a period of rest, and on Hamlet's return he is met by a parallel revenger seeking his life. For this device Kyd is directly indebted to the maxims of Machiavelli which advised a prince to give the performance of cruel acts to another in order to escape the blame. One peg was best to drive out another, and enemies should be set at odds to destroy themselves.[28] The primitive revenge of the Belleforest story was unsuitable for the stage since it contained no real conflict, and also since it offered no means of drawing the play to a close with the death of Hamlet. Kyd therefore plans to create his catastrophe in the meeting of revenge and counter-revenge which will engulf all the principals in disaster.

The poisonings which end the play are interesting as showing how Kyd drew on the gossip of the period for a catastrophe which would involve the king. The backfiring of a poison upon the poisoner, the method by which Leonhardus is killed and the queen poisoned, is of considerable antiquity. Occurring as early as the ancient tale of Deïanira and the centaur's poison, it is also found in romances, as in the Tristram story, and was a standard piece of Renaissance gossip. Kyd may have drawn on a scandalous tale current about the Earl of Leicester (one of his alleged practices was used in *The Spanish Tragedy*) which recounted that Leicester prepared a poisoned draught for his wife Lettice which she was to drink whenever she felt faint. She, not suspecting its properties, gave him the drink a short time later when he returned from a fatiguing journey. But two other famous examples were at hand in the stories about the death of Pope Alexander VI and the accidental poisoning of her husband by Bianca Capello.[29]

Since, legally, the king was guilty of the murder of his wife as well as of Hamlet, his death was not only the culmination of a just revenge for a past murder but also a judgment for two present ones. Leonhardus, too, must die, for he has been the knowing agent in a murder by particularly treacherous means. He was not so culpable as the king, however, because his motive was purer

---

[28] See especially Gentillet, Part III, § 34, pp. 349-50.

[29] Francis Guicciardini, *The Historie of Guicciardin*, trans. Geoffrey Fenton (1579), p. 227; Fynes Moryson, *Shakespeare's Europe*, ed. Hughes, pp. 94-5, 406-7; G. F. Young, *The Medici* (London: John Murray, 1920), Vol. II, pp. 68, 334-5.

and he was merely the agent, not the principal on whom the chief guilt lay. It is significant that Hamlet, realizing the dupe the king has made of Leonhardus, forgives the unlucky revenger of Corambis. The queen, only doubtfully innocent of the murder of her first husband, is stained with the guilt of incest.

If, as seems probable, the catastrophe of *Der Bestrafte Brudermord* is roughly that of the *Ur-Hamlet,* the slaughter of Phantasmo by Hamlet is at first sight a particularly brutal and unnecessary piece of business; but Hamlet at the time does not know that he himself is doomed and in his royal capacity he is meting swift justice to an accessory before the fact to the poisoning of his mother.

The lengths to which Kyd went to maintain the audience's sympathy for his protagonist make Hamlet one of the least guilty of all Elizabethan stage revengers. Because he was no Machiavellian, Hamlet's sole actions toward revenge had consisted only in the play-within-a-play to establish the king's guilt, his refusal to murder a man at prayer, and the mistaken slaying of Corambis. His dissimulation had never overstepped the allowable bounds of "policy"[30] and if ever a revenger were blameless in his plots it is Hamlet.

It is probably true that Kyd's Hamlet was a more bloodthirsty person in his speeches than Shakespeare's. It is also true that a certain amount of brutality is shown in the stabbing of Phantasmo who might better have been left to his certain legal execution, as was usually the practice with guilty minor characters in later plays. But what puts Hamlet definitely over the borderline is the killing of Corambis. Kyd had probably taken some pains to make Corambis innocent of the plot laid by the king against

[30] William Perkins, *Cases of Conscience* (ed. 1651), pp. 284-5, discusses the methods of "policy" which may justly be used: "1. Nothing must (in policy) be said, done, or intended, to prejudice the truth of the Gospell. 2. Nothing is to be said, done, or intended against the honour or glory of God, either in word, in deed, or in shew. 3. Nothing must bee wrought or contrived against justice that is due to man. 4. All actions of policie, must be such as pertaine to our calling, and be within the limits and bounds thereof. . . . These Caveats observed, it is not unlawfull to use that which we commonly call Policie."

Hamlet, and his slaying, no matter what the circumstances of ironical mistaken identity, seals Hamlet's eventual doom, for the religious teaching of the day held that revenge by murder was never allowable: "That vengeance apperaineth vnto God only. . . . Therefore it followeth, that whosoeuer doth reuenge himselfe, committeth sacrilege. . . . That seeing the wrong that our neighbour doth, happeneth not without the prudence of God, it is not lawful for vs to resist and withstand it by oblique and sinister meanes, and such as displease God."[31] Hamlet cannot even plead manslaughter, for his intent was to kill the king, and it is still murder if he mistakes Corambis for his intended victim.

The Elizabethan audience always insisted on seeing eventual justice, and one who stained his hands with blood had to pay the penalty. That no revenger, no matter how just, ever wholly escapes the penalty for shedding blood even in error, is borne out by subsequent plays and is emphasized especially in Thomas Rawlins's *Rebellion*. Very likely Kyd would have killed off Hamlet anyway in order to end with a holocaust of pity and terror; but it seems probable that, as with later playwrights, he subscribed to the doctrine that a shedder of blood should not live.

One can imagine an Elizabethan sympathizer pointing out that Hamlet was justified since he could not appeal to legal justice. But the inevitable and unanswerable reply would come that Hamlet must therefore await God's justice. If he anticipates divine vengeance, he must pay the penalty: given his sympathetic characterization he is a hero, but he must die. But God sometimes uses human instruments as the agents for the heavenly vengeance. If Hamlet is such an agent, does he not operate under God's favor? That question was answered in such later plays as *The Atheist's Tragedy, The Maid's Tragedy,* and *The Unnatural Combat.* Heaven may be using Hamlet—and even Hieronimo—as its agent, but that does not remove guilt, for, as *The Maid's Tragedy* states,

[31] John Eliot, *Discourses of Warre and Single Combat, by B. de Loque* (1591), p. 52.

Unlooked-for sudden deaths from Heaven are sent;
But cursed is he that is their instrument.

This question outlines in sharp relief the fundamental problem facing every writer of a revenge tragedy whose protagonist is a hero. The audience is sympathetic to his revenger so long as he does not become an Italianate intriguer, and so long as he does not revenge. At the conclusion the audience admits its sentimental satisfaction with the act of personal justice but its ethical sense demands the penalty for the infraction of divine command.

It seems most probable that the *Ur-Hamlet* preceded *The Spanish Tragedy,* chiefly because the parallels between the two plays would originate more logically in the *Ur-Hamlet* to be copied in *The Spanish Tragedy.* A major parallel is the play-within-a-play. The idea for this device in the *Ur-Hamlet* without question came from current stories of the involuntary fear of criminals at the playhouse when viewing their crimes acted on the stage, and as such it has a vital and apposite part in the plot. Such an origin is not possible in *The Spanish Tragedy* where there is no source but a vague resemblance to the diversions of the Emperor Nero. The device for the final bloodshed in each play seems to have originated in the *Ur-Hamlet.* Hamlet's stabbing of Phantasmo was partially warranted as the disposal of the last of the conspirators, but in *The Spanish Tragedy* the unwarranted stabbing of the Duke of Castile seems merely a reminiscence of the earlier scene.

If the *Ur-Hamlet* came afterwards it is most surprising that the German play does not give any indication that Hamlet is actually insane, a part of Hieronimo's success which Kyd would have been sure to emphasize after its first proved popularity. This is not to say that Kyd's Hamlet could not have been slightly unbalanced on occasion. It seems very possible that Hieronimo's more complete emotional insanity, so extremely original if *The Spanish Tragedy* preceded the *Ur-Hamlet,* was an expansion of hints in Hamlet. Burton the Anatomist wrote, "Many lose their wits by *the sudden sight of some spectrum or divil, a thing very common in all ages,* saith *Lavater part* I. *cap.* 9. as *Orestes* did at the sight

of the *Furies,* which appeared to him in black."[32] Given the prece-
dent of Orestes and the popular belief, it seems almost inevitable
that Kyd with his dramatic genius portrayed Hamlet's feigned
madness as at times merging into real distraction, not only from
excessive grief and frustration but from the effect of the ghost's
appearance. On the evidence of *Der Bestrafte Brudermord,* as
well as the evidence of the relative unpopularity of the early
Hamlet, one may infer that this characterization was not emphasized as was Hieronimo's, and that it was not until he came to
write *The Spanish Tragedy* that Kyd realized the full latent possibilities in such a dramatic device. Even this emphasis was insufficient for Elizabethan taste, for another dramatist had to be
employed subsequently to expand the mad scenes.

The two chief breaks with Senecan tragedy in *The Spanish
Tragedy* involve the madness of the revenger and his delay. To
believe that Kyd conjured these important points out of his
imagination without a source,[33] wrote *The Spanish Tragedy,* and
then stumbled on them as an integral part of the Amleth story
in Belleforest and later wrote his *Hamlet,* is asking too much of
coincidence. The view must be accepted that Kyd at least knew
Belleforest's account before he wrote *The Spanish Tragedy.* But
if Kyd knew Belleforest's account beforehand, it is curious he
should abstract the two best dramatic features to create an original
plot instead of dramatizing Belleforest's story where they were
native. It must be emphasized that Kyd was forced to invent
certain dramatic conventions by the very exigencies of dramatizing the Amleth story, and that these are also found in *The Spanish Tragedy.* Merely to have known Belleforest cannot explain
them; they could have been evolved only by a person transferring
the Amleth material to the stage, and the lessons learned thereupon being transferred in turn to *The Spanish Tragedy.* Again,

---

[32] *The Anatomy of Melancholy* (Bohn Library, 1923), Vol. I, p. 387.

[33] The hypothetical source of *The Spanish Tragedy* never having been discovered,
cannot well be claimed to have first furnished both madness and delay. The coincidence would still be too startling. Furthermore, if the hypothesis be accepted that
the *Ur-Hamlet* preceded *The Spanish Tragedy,* there seems to be no reason to posit
a definite source for the full *Spanish Tragedy.*

the seeming lack of popularity of Kyd's *Hamlet,* with its superior plot and more intrinsic interest of character and situation, is difficult to explain unless it were a first crude attempt at tragedy which was bettered in *The Spanish Tragedy.*

Lastly, the Belleforest narrative as it stood, even without its tragic ending, bore a nearer relation to the standard elements of Seneca's dramas than *The Spanish Tragedy*: fratricide as in *Thyestes* with a parallel to the husband-murder in *Agamemnon*; cunning revenge as in *Agamemnon, Thyestes,* and *Medea*; and the conflict between revenge and the forces that would put it down as in *Medea.* Slight and obvious changes made the play even more Senecan, such as the creation of the confidant Horatio and the actual appearance of a speaking ghost demanding vengeance as in *Agamemnon.* The likeness of Belleforest's story to the Orestes legend, the first part of which was dramatized by Seneca, must have been apparent to Kyd. Horwendille was Agamemnon; Geruthe, Clytemnestra; the king, Aegisthus; Hamlet, Orestes. The revenge of a son for his father was nearer the classical tradition than Hieronimo's revenge for a son.

With these considerations the date of the *Ur-Hamlet* may be set with fair certainty as approximately 1587, with *The Spanish Tragedy* following in 1587-1588, prompted by the increasing interest in Spanish affairs at the threat of a Spanish invasion.[34] If

[34] Boas dates the *Ur-Hamlet* in 1587-1588, or shortly after *The Spanish Tragedy,* influenced by the theory that dramatization of the Hamlet story was prompted by the visit of English actors to the Court of Helsingör in 1586 but chiefly by their return in the latter part of 1587 or in 1588 (*Works of Thomas Kyd,* p. xlvi). The passage in *Der Bestrafte Brudermord* (Vol. III, p. 10) in which Hamlet, about to be sent to England, remarks that he should be ordered to Portugal instead, has been taken as a reference to an ill-fated English expedition in 1589. If this be true, it may well be a later addition, of course. Sarrazin gives 1588 as the latest possible date, and tends to Boas's ascription of 1587-1588 (*Thomas Kyd und Sein Kreis* [Berlin, 1892], pp. 95, 111). On p. 113 he notes a slight verbal parallel between *The Misfortunes of Arthur* (Feb. 1588), *Der Bestrafte Brudermord,* and Shakespeare's First Quarto, which if it is to be taken seriously would place the *Ur-Hamlet* in 1587. Sarrazin's views of the order of the two plays are complicated by his theory that *The Spanish Tragedy* as we know it is a reworking of earlier material. Evans finds the germ of Hieronimo's assumption of madness in the avowed purpose of Belleforest's Amleth, which he takes as proof that the *Ur-Hamlet* came first

one accepts the priority of the *Ur-Hamlet,* the material from which Kyd built *The Spanish Tragedy* becomes so evident that it is likely Kyd had few other sources than his earlier Hamlet play and various pieces of information about Spain and Spanish affairs. The story of a father's revenge for a son is merely the reversal of Hamlet's for his father. That it is prefaced by the Andrea story is only an indication that Kyd, realizing from his experience in *Hamlet* the difficulty of filling a play with the simple revenge theme, endeavored to avoid repetition by substituting a full account of the prior action. In addition, since Kyd was still to a certain extent under the influence of Seneca, the ghost of some previously murdered man was essential to start the action of revenge.

Hamlet's reasons for delay are only two: his doubt of the ghost, and his inability to conceive a plan for a safe revenge on a guarded enemy. There are indications that Hamlet becomes extremely discouraged and blames himself unjustly for his delay. Just as Hamlet doubts the ghost, so Hieronimo doubts Bel-Imperia's letter. As Hamlet is not certain that he has grounds for revenge until after the mousetrap play, so Hieronimo needs Pedringano's letter to fortify his conviction.

After a delay caused by Hieronimo's distraction arising from an over-burdening yet impotent sense of wrong, he is next balked by his failure to secure legal justice. Thereupon his character changes, for he attempts to excuse the treacherous acts which are to follow by the statement that he is otherwise unable to revenge himself on men in superior stations. This excuse is modelled on Hamlet's real problem, for Hamlet knows the king is suspicious, but Lorenzo does not realize that his guilt has been revealed to Hieronimo. Thus when Lorenzo thwarts Hieronimo's attempts to gain the king's ear, his sole motive is to hush the fact that Horatio has been murdered. It has been indicated how

(*MP*, Vol. II [1905], p. 445). T. W. Baldwin, "The Chronology of Kyd's Plays," *Modern Language Notes,* Vol. XL (1925), pp. 348-9, on the basis of rather dubious reasons argues for a date of 1582-1585 for *The Spanish Tragedy*, and 1589 for the *Ur-Hamlet.*

this excuse and the actions to which it led finally turned Hieronimo into villainous courses. His reconciliation with Lorenzo is a Machiavellian extension of Hamlet's with the king before the fencing match. His double-edged remarks are drawn from Hamlet's, which in turn came direct from Belleforest. The play scene utilizes Hamlet's mousetrap but with a gory conclusion, and finally the murder of Castile parallels senselessly that of Phantasmo.

The weak points in Hamlet's revenge have been strengthened. Hamlet, despite his firm purpose, is actually helpless except for the contrivance of the play to reveal the king's guilt, and so, without the saving genius of Shakespeare's philosophical characterization, tends to be too static a figure. Only the faith of the audience that a scheme for revenge will eventually come to him, and their confidence in his personal character—largely gained from the daring of his supposedly mad remarks—keep him a figure strong enough to balance the rising force of the opposing action. Since he is portrayed sympathetically throughout, he cannot be given too much to do, and yet he cannot be given too little. Circumstances force him unwittingly to slay an innocent man, but these are so arranged as not to alienate the sympathy of the audience, although the tragic error is recorded and must later receive payment. Fate provides the dénouement in *Hamlet*; conversely, in *The Spanish Tragedy* a change of character, through which the driving necessity for revenge corrupts the hero, affects the action more materially. The difference enabled Hieronimo to give the audience more positive action for its money, but by that action he became a faulty character.

As for the rest, Lorenzo is a villainous extension of the king: both are villains who oppose the revenger by Machiavellian sleights. Isabella's largely spectacular madness and suicide is based on Ofelia's, which was more essential to the plot. In like manner, Bazulto's demand for justice is only of emotional significance, whereas Leonhardus's is rooted in the action. Each of these minor parallels, owing to the derivative nature of the simpler story of *The Spanish Tragedy,* is not so closely linked to the main

CHAPTER IV

THE SCHOOL OF KYD

I

FOR some years Kyd's *Hamlet* and *The Spanish Tragedy* set the major pattern for tragedies which did not imitate the *Tamburlaine* of Marlowe. Shakespeare almost alone unshackled himself from the form, although in *Titus Andronicus* he experimented with it and in the final *Hamlet* achieved the apotheosis of the revenge play. Such plays as Robert Greene's *Alphonsus, King of Arragon* (1587) and the anonymous *Selimus* (1591-1594) lean heavily on Marlowe but also show that dramatists were learning the lesson Kyd had to teach: that there was no simpler method of motivating a conflict than by the revenge of a personal injury.

Hard on the heels of *The Spanish Tragedy* came *The Misfortunes of Arthur* (1588) by Thomas Hughes. Twenty years earlier the play would have been important. In 1588 it merely provides an example of the static nature of academic Senecan drama, for the tragedy makes little real advance in structure or theory over *Gorboduc,* from which it differentiates itself only in a more copious literal borrowing from Seneca and a freer use of horror in plot though not in staged action. The Senecan conception of hereditary expiation of a crime is called upon to explain the conflict of Arthur and Modred, who pay for the evil done by their ancestor Pendragon. In common with *Thyestes* and *Agamemnon* the revenge motif is furnished solely by the prologue ghost and not by the events unfolded in the plot, which details simply the crushing of the ambitious Modred and the fatal results to Arthur. The elements of a true revenge play which rest in the Pendragon story, as a consequence have no place in the action. The play was an ambitious attempt to transfer the pure Senecan technique to British history, and as such remains a warning against over-emphasis on the actual contribution of Seneca to the works of Kyd and his followers.

George Peele's *Battle of Alcazar* (1589) exhibits clearly the first fruits of Kyd's influence—combined with a direct debt to Seneca—an influence all the more remarkable since the play was called forth by the example of *Tamburlaine*. As with other chronicle-histories the chief interest in the piece lies in the bickerings, consultations, plans, and battles, but the influence of Kyd unites with these to add a vague sort of personal interest to the revenge (which purports to motivate the central plot) of Abdelmelec for the murder of his brother Abdelmunan. Not that the issue is clear-cut—the form of chronicle-history forbade that. Blood-revenge, though clearly conceived by Abdelmelec, is not the personal, hand-to-hand business of Kyd but rather an affair of armies. As a consequence the personal interest in revenge and counter-revenge is lost in the shuffle. Muly Mahamet, the murderer, is somehow killed in battle; not by the revenger's own hand but by his army. Furthermore, the interest is not only divided between a pair of revengers for the same deed, Abdelmelec and Muly Seth, but is also, after the start, entirely submerged in the struggle for a throne to which the original murder was a prelude. The appearances of the English hero Stukely add a contemporary interest but distract the attention.

Of greater moment, however, than a trio of ghosts out of Seneca who shriek "Vindicta!" or the various elaborate portents of disaster drawn from the same source, is the catastrophe borrowed from Kyd in which the culmination of the revenge causes the mutual destruction of revenger and counter-revenger. *The Battle of Alcazar* represents at least an attempt at presenting a well substantiated revenge of blood as a new dramatic motive in an unfamiliar form.

The anonymous author of *Locrine* (1591) proved more successful in a similar attempt. The play must be classed as chronicle-history, but into the historical treatment have been injected various foreign elements. First, the most obvious influence is that of Seneca as modified in *Gorboduc* and *The Misfortunes of Arthur* with their dumb shows, set speeches, and stories drawn from legendary British history. Next must be included the influence of *Tamburlaine,* which manifests itself chiefly in the attempts to raise the characters to a plane of grandeur by high speeches of bombast. Very vaguely to Kyd's influence may be ascribed the scenes of blood portrayed on the stage and the general dependence on blood-revenge to enliven a plot based on chronicle-history, although Kyd is of less importance than Seneca himself.

A play thus imitating three masters inevitably proved a *potpourri* in conception and execution. With the ponderousness of the academic tragedy it combines the loose plotting and comic-relief of chronicle-history, at defiance with the Senecan atmosphere of its basic conception, its miscellaneous trappings of ghosts, and its assorted rhetoric. Yet *Locrine* provides an excellent example of academic drama adapting itself to the popular stage, with its healthy desire to present all of life unrestricted by literary rules; and the confusion of the play indicates more a lack of training and of taste in its pioneering than a fundamentally bad conception of drama. That this adaptation of academic Seneca to popular taste produces a play vastly different from the type of *The Spanish Tragedy,* where Seneca is not the major influence, is of more than passing interest for a clearer conception of the real derivation of the revenge play.

It is obvious that the dramatist has recognized the value of a more personalized revenge to draw the threads of his plot together. The blood-revenge for Albanact motivates the battle which defeats the Huns; this battle brings about the meeting of Estrild and Locrine which in turn causes the quasi-blood-revenge of Thrasimachus and Guendoline. The incidents form a perfect chain—Locrine's death results from the slaying of Albanact—but in spite of this cause and effect, one revenge does not directly determine the other and so there is no conflict of revenge and counter-revenge to carry through the play.

Locrine is no revenge tragedy. The lesson the old *Hamlet* and *The Spanish Tragedy* had to teach was that the surest drama could be formed only by a personal revenge in kind clearly ex-

hibited on the stage. The chronicle-history form of *Locrine* pre-
cluded direct personal revenge, since disputes could be fought
out only by armies. Furthermore, the motives are somewhat confused or are unsuitable for blood-revenge. The author, in spite
of his revengeful ghosts crying "Vindicta" and his attempts to
make revenge as serious as possible, has actually written a clas-
sicized history play with undeveloped revenge elements. What he
has gained by his borrowings from Kyd has been a notion of
plotting by revenge which for *Locrine* resulted in a distinct advance over such plays as *The Battle of Alcazar* in well motivated
and causal complication of plot. What he has taken from Seneca
has been more a hindrance than a help.

2

The *Ur-Hamlet* and *The Spanish Tragedy* were perfect fusings
of a little Seneca with much of the Italianate and Teutonic. *The
Misfortunes of Arthur* was an attempt at pure Seneca in English;
The Battle of Alcazar and *Locrine* at Seneca made palatable for
the popular stage by infusions of Marlowe and Kyd. Each of the
last three plays, in its own way, was heading up a *cul de sac,* for
it was the Kydian form which was to rule the Elizabethan tragic
stage. But before the example of Kyd drew the complete imitation
of the dramatists of the day, another genius had prematurely, and
somewhat abortively, altered the form. Christopher Marlowe,
where the authors of *Alcazar* and *Locrine* had failed to unite
Seneca and chronicle-history, succeeded to a certain extent in
combining history with the Italianate elements of Kyd.

In the Kydian tragedy a murder is committed secretly, the name
of the murderer is given to the revenger by a medium which he
distrusts; delay results until additional facts corroborate the
ascription, but then the revenger is hampered by the counter-
designs of his enemy and all perish in the catastrophe. *The Jew of
Malta* is conceived on an entirely different plan. First, even taking into account the villain Barabas as the central figure, the
play actually revolves about the siege of Malta and its deliver-

ance, treated largely in the manner of chronicle-history; hence, the audience's attention is demanded for other matters than the revenge of Barabas, especially at the catastrophe which is unmotivated by revenge. Secondly, in Kyd's plays the revenge, once conceived, runs through the whole and reaches its culmination in the catastrophe, whereas Barabas's revenge ends to all practical purposes in the second scene of the third act. The rest of the play is given over to his attempts to save himself from the consequences of his revenge and to become master of Malta. In the last analysis we have a tragedy about the siege of Malta and the desperate intrigues of a revengeful Jew.

Since the success of the protagonist's revenge comes early in the rising action, the revenger differs from the Kydian hero. The overwhelming weight of a bounden duty is never felt, nor is there the mind-destroying self-accusation for delay and lack of opportunity. The field of character has been at once enlarged and narrowed. The enlargement furnishes the protagonist with all the varied traits of a Machiavellian, yet these same traits in turn limit the type since practically all Machiavellian villains are alike in their practises and differ only in their original motives. The motives, and the varying scenes of action, however, furnish more variety to Barabas and the protagonists of later villain plays than is possible for the comparatively simple type of the hero revenger. In this respect *The Jew of Malta* forecasts the more tumultuous and complicated tragedies of the Jacobean and Caroline dramatists.

This important change in the character of the protagonist and the structure of the play was the result of the carrying forward of Marlowe's particular construction, already found in *Tamburlaine* and *Doctor Faustus,* in which the hero became the chief unifying principle. The interest in character for itself which had already been foreshadowed in Hieronimo of *The Spanish Tragedy* reached its flowering in Marlowe, whose protagonists are interesting personalities in themselves, regardless of what they specifically do. This interest in a personality and in a specific dominating motive was at the basis of Marlowe's works and was transmitted as a legacy to future tragic writers.[1]

The Jew of Malta is first and foremost a play about a Jew whose overwhelming passion is for gold and the power that gold brings him. When his gold is forcibly wrested from him, he endeavors to retaliate and to secure power by another means— the rule of Malta. The failure of this last attempt brings about the tragic dénouement. Barabas is a Jew who has gained and kept his wealth by Machiavellian devices. A tragic conception involving considerable grandeur is possible in the first two acts which emphasize the original concept of wealth and power; but when this wealth has been confiscated and the Jew's Machiavellism comes to the fore in his schemes for retaliation, a degeneration is to be expected. The inspiration of Machiavelli may, indeed, be said to have kept the play from fulfilling its early promise. The general theories of Machiavelli, even as interpreted by the Elizabethans, were capable of building a character on as grand a scale as Marlowe's other heroes. But it is a curious fact that the actions the Elizabethans always associated with these theories and with the conception of the Machiavellian villain were composed of relatively petty and treacherous intrigues. Marlowe had already shown in *Faustus* that his choice of illustrative action was not always on so high a plane as his conception of character and central situation. The last three acts of *The Jew of Malta,* even in their present debased state, must confirm the weakness of the earlier play. Barabas's Machiavellism consists purely in deeds of wholesale slaughter, absurd in their conception, and in the usual deceits practised to rid the doer of witnesses to his crime.

The Jew of Malta in its search for a new type of superlative protagonist had turned to Machiavelli, and had missed its mark through the excess of treacherous incident which could be supported by no human characterization, even when the hysteria of the age in all matters touching Machiavelli is taken into account. By his desertion of Kyd's formula for the character of the protago-

[1] H. E. Fansler, *The Evolution of Technic in Elizabethan Tragedy* (Chicago: Row, Peterson & Co., 1914), p. 71.

nist, Marlowe was forced to adopt the unjustifiable Italianate revenge for a personal injury, a revenge which, instead of being a necessary and even legal duty, is a criminal passion. For the retribution of Heaven through a human agent is substituted the personal retaliation of angered spite. Barabas has a better reason for revenge than most villains of later dramas, for he could secure justice, which was what he originally wanted, in no other way than by private measures. Justice, however, in the return of his money, he does not seek; but instead, by planning the assassination of the Governor's son, he vents his anger on the Governor who had ruined him. His revenge is criminal, since it oversteps the ancient law of talion by revenging a material injury with a collective revenge and death.

The Machiavellian precepts which Barabas follows have been tabulated, and show that Marlowe went to Machiavelli and Gentillet direct for the springs of his action.[2] But in spite of these sources it is also certain that Kyd's Lorenzo was the prototype of Barabas and that the action of *The Jew of Malta* is merely an elaboration of similar action in *The Spanish Tragedy*. Once Abigail turns against Barabas, the play concerns itself almost exclusively with his attempts to dispose of all who have knowledge of the death of Lodowick and Mathias. Marlowe is merely inverting the plotting of *The Spanish Tragedy* by taking over the counter-action (Lorenzo's disposal of his accomplices) as the main line of incident for *The Jew of Malta*. There is, consequently, no real counter-revenge extending through the play, and the interest concentrates exclusively on Barabas.

The first step is the removal of Abigail so that her knowledge of the murder may die with her. Ithamore, the chief accomplice, is utilized, and Abigail is poisoned in the nunnery. There are indications that Barabas is using Ithamore only as an instrument later to be cast aside (as Lorenzo used Pedringano) in the best Machiavellian tradition, but these hints are never developed into positive action in the later scenes. The fourth act reveals that

[2] C. V. Boyer, *The Villain as Hero in Elizabethan Tragedy* (New York: E. P. Dutton & Co., 1914), pp. 45-51.

Abigail's secret has not perished, and more persons must be killed. Barabas's scheme is reminiscent of Lorenzo's. One friar is murdered, and the other friar is accused of his death and delivered to justice. So Pedringano slew Serberine and was imprisoned. Finally, as the accomplice Pedringano betrayed Lorenzo's secret, so Ithamore, the last person Barabas has failed to remove, is the means of his downfall. Ordinarily the discovery and punishment of his crime would have ended the tragedy, but since the chronicle-history is yet unfinished, Barabas (who has feigned death by a potion) is brought to life to play his final scenes of trickery in the surrender of Malta.

The Jew of Malta for much of its action and characterization owes an obvious debt to *The Spanish Tragedy,* yet it is obviously original. It is the first tragedy to develop Kyd's villain Lorenzo into the protagonist and thus to discard the theme of blood-revenge from a revenge plot. Barabas does not fall by the triumph of a force which has vigorously opposed his revenge throughout the play, but merely by an unpremeditated betrayal. This betrayal, catastrophic in the revenge plot, does not actually cause the catastrophe of the play itself, for the death of Barabas results from circumstances almost totally unconnected with his personal revenge on the Governor and its consequences.

The Jew of Malta in the last analysis is a play about a villain who overreaches, and so brings upon himself inevitable disaster. Revenge is of vital importance because it and its results motivate the actions of the protagonist throughout the major portion of the play; but other important motives are added for the larger picture of the character, and Barabas's lust for power, not his lust for revenge, causes the catastrophe. *The Jew of Malta* in its mixture of history and revenge, of action proceeding from revenge and action proceeding from ambition and pure villainy, presents a confused plot structure. Marlowe had his limitations as a working dramatist, and his theory of dramatic construction centered on a unifying hero could not overcome the fatal split between the grandeur of the character's conception and the pettiness of the illustrative action. The play undoubtedly had an

influence on later drama, but changes were made by later dramatists which were as important as those Marlowe had himself
made from *The Spanish Tragedy*.

3

The years from 1587-1588, which marked the production of the
Ur-Hamlet and *The Spanish Tragedy,* to 1607—the somewhat
uncertain date of *The Revenger's Tragedy*—were the golden era
of the true Kydian revenge tragedy. The later *Revenge of Bussy
D'Ambois* (1610) by George Chapman, *The Atheist's Tragedy*
(1607-1611) by Cyril Tourneur, and *Valentinian* (1610-1614) by
John Fletcher, each in its own way continued the tradition, although they were written in a time when the fashion for tragedy
had changed. But the twenty years after Kyd may be distinctly
set apart as the first period in the development of the Elizabethan
tragedy of revenge.

The need for a suitable variation of tragic story forced dramatists to tinker with Kyd's formula. Yet Kyd, however imperfect
his plays in detail and execution, had so perfectly comprehended
the form that for a time dramatists were loathe to change any
of its essentials and contented themselves with elaborating and
extending various of the details of Kyd's plotting and characterization. *Titus Andronicus* tried to surpass him in the portrayal of
blood and horrors. Marston extended the Italianate atmosphere
and characterization in *Antonio's Revenge*. Chettle's *Hoffman*
produced the first major innovation in Kydian plot construction
by creating the revenger of blood as a villain from the start. This
suggestion was carried forward in *The Revenger's Tragedy* in a
highly interesting and artistic manner.

In all the plays treated in this period there is a very definite
ethical background to the action, although no attempt is usually
made to align the dramas with contemporary life and its moral
and legal code. Only in this latter sense may these plays deserve
the frequently bestowed adjective "amoral," and even so the
atmosphere is not always so conscienceless as is supposed. Granted
that *Hoffman* and *The Revenger's Tragedy* portray a callous,

bloodthirsty vendetta—these are plays of a transition. In *Hamlet, The Spanish Tragedy, Antonio's Revenge,* and even in *Titus Andronicus,* the theme is of the problems of life and death and of the mystery of a soul in torment. The seriousness of the central situation, justice for murder, lends a corresponding depth of seriousness to its dramatic development. The dramatists may not preach, as Massinger does in *The Fatal Dowry,* but the interest with which they analyze their heroes—normal persons caught up by demands often too strong for their powers and forced into a course of action which warps and twists their characters and may lead even to the disintegration of insanity—indicates clearly that the playwrights were at least endeavoring to construct high tragedy. That their understandable love of the sensational occasionally led them astray and that they chose a particularly crude and melodramatic form for their attempt, are mere superficialities that have sometimes misled critics. The age of Elizabeth was not the age of Pericles, and each period and race must fashion from the materials at hand. Shakespeare's *Hamlet* is a living vindication of an Elizabethan treatment of a tragic situation which had engaged Aeschylus, Sophocles, and Euripides. And *Hamlet* differs from the revenge tragedies by other Elizabethan dramatists only in the measure that Shakespeare was above his fellows in genius.

Shakespeare's *Titus Andronicus* (1594), his first attempt at the type, gave little promise of his later *Hamlet.* The problem of an early *Titus Andronicus* play seems almost impossible of solution, but it is reasonable to suppose that a play existed about 1592 (not necessarily "tittus and Vespacia"), that in 1593-1594 Shakespeare revised it and gave it the form we now possess, and that some hints of this older play may perhaps be drawn from the Dutch and German versions, although not with the exactitude formerly believed.[3] Actually the plotting of these plays differs from Shake-

---

[3] A theory has been advanced (H. DeW. Fuller, "The Sources of *Titus Andronicus,*" *Publications of the Modern Language Association of America,* XVI [1901]) that Shakespeare combined and thoroughly rewrote two old plays on the subject

speare's in only one important action. The killing of Alarbus, which in Shakespeare provides a definite motive for Tamora's revenge, is absent from the German and Dutch plays.

Titus Andronicus is very similar in construction to *The Spanish Tragedy* and so deeply under its influence that, except for the omission of the supernatural, its outline conforms to that already given for Kyd's tragedy. As in the older play it is the revenge of the villains that calls forth in answer the blood-revenge of the protagonist. Although Shakespeare motivates Tamora's revenge by the murder of her son Alarbus and thus gives her better grounds than Lorenzo and Balthazar possessed, the earlier version of the play (if the foreign versions be accepted as indications of an early state) followed *The Spanish Tragedy* in the weakness of the villains' original motives.[4]

which are found mentioned in Henslowe's diary as "tittus and Vespacia," a new play in the spring of 1592, and "tittus and ondronicus," a new play in January of 1594, and that these are preserved respectively in a German version of 1620 and a Dutch of 1641. This interpretation has not gone unchallenged, and there is a very reasonable doubt whether "tittus and Vespacia" was an Andronicus play, although E. K. Chambers, *William Shakespeare,* Vol. I, p. 319, inclines to that view. An additional theory (G. P. Baker, " 'Tittus and Vespacia' and 'Titus and Ondronicus' in Henslowe's Diary," *PMLA,* Vol. XVI [1901], p. 71) that the old Andronicus play was introduced into Holland in 1590-1591 may possibly be right, but the ascription of "Tittus and Vespacia" (as an Andronicus play) to the early '80's and an introduction into Germany in 1586 is highly dubious. Such a dating presupposes not only that in each case Henslowe marked a play as new which had merely been retouched (a fairly common occurrence, but somewhat startling in the present coincidence) but also that two London companies acted practically the same play at the same time for several years. Finally, the recent discovery of the actual 1594 quarto of Shakespeare's *Titus Andronicus* entered in the Stationers' Register in February 1594, entirely ruins the argument for the non-Shakespearean authorship of the "tittus and ondronicus" entered by Henslowe in January 1594.

[4] The Dutch play of 1641, instead of the sacrifice of Alarbus, has the proposed sacrifice of Aran, the general of the Goths. Aran is, accordingly, the chief offended person and the instigator of the villainies while Thamera has no personal grudge against Titus. Thamera's sons, however, are led by Aran to believe that Titus killed their father (who was actually murdered by Thamera) with a poisoned sword, a ruse which persuades them to the rape of Rozelyna [Lavinia]. The incident of the sacrifice is missing in the German play of 1620, and Aetiopissa [Tamora] has no revenge motive against Titus. Instead, her intrigues to ruin him seem prompted merely by the desire to rid herself of the future danger that the honest and powerful Titus, disgusted with the excesses of the court, will lead a revolt. She, not

A second important change comes in the early disclosure of the faultiness of Titus's character. In the German version he is wholly good until the catastrophe; in the Dutch, Titus's cruel demand that Aran be slain is an incomplete omen of what is to come. Shakespeare avoided the sudden change in character that befell Hieronimo by emphasizing so strongly Titus's faults at the very beginning that the audience would not be too shocked at the conclusion. His consciousness of power makes Titus overbearingly proud and haughty. Although his demand that Alarbus be slain is justified by his religious beliefs, it is, as Tamora exclaims, a "cruel, irreligious piety." His murder of his son Mutius, though admirable according to the Roman patriarchal and stoic standards, is a misguided piece of callous, proud cruelty, calculated to remove from him the audience's personal sympathy and to leave him only the abstract admiration due his undoubted honesty. He is so egoistic, so sure the justice of his actions cannot be questioned, that, despite his share in the death of Alarbus, he expects Tamora's gratitude. Such a conception is infinitely more rounded than Hieronimo's, and, in combination with Titus's far more frightful sufferings, and the equally fiendish retaliations they provoke, undoubtedly prepares the audience for the final justice of his death.

In Shakespeare the revenge of the villains starts almost immediately when Tamora vows requital for the death of Alarbus. It is strengthened by the winning over of Saturninus, and reaches an early fruition in the second act rape of Lavinia. This deed is not originally accomplished by any set plan of Tamora's, but it is linked to her revenge when, reminded of Alarbus, she refuses Lavinia's pleas for pity. Whereas the villains of *The Spanish Tragedy* achieved their single revenge and stopped, the rape of Lavinia is merely incidental to the larger plans to strike at Titus

Morian [Aaron], is the chief villain. Shakespeare's change in Tamora's motive was thus a step towards more consistent and reasonable plotting woven about the person of an opposing villainess, even though it left Aaron a somewhat anomalous figure in the play.

through his sons. It must be noted that Aaron, not Tamora, contrives the plans although her help is indispensable.

The revenge has been almost completed by the end of the second act and Titus made practically helpless. The revengers have one more scheme, however, and in the third act Titus is tricked into the loss of his hand. For an act and a half he has received blow after blow. His son-in-law Bassianus has been killed, his sons are accused and condemned for the murder, his daughter has been ravished and mutilated, his pleas have been unheard, his son Lucius banished, and finally he has lost his hand in a vain attempt to save the lives of two more sons. Such a chain of incidents was missing from *The Spanish Tragedy* where the revenger is never personally injured and has only the death of his son to revenge. But they are a necessary part of the plot of *Titus Andronicus* to fill the action (covered in Kyd by the love of Horatio and Bel-Imperia and the events occasioned by the capture of Balthazar) until the protagonist starts his vengeance. In *Titus* the turning-point comes at the end of the third act when the final indignity affects Titus's mind, and his sudden laugh foreshadows his madness. For the moment incipient insanity sharpens his wits. He solemnly swears revenge and plans the invasion of the Goths under Lucius as the first step.

The succeeding scenes face the same problem as in *Hamlet* and *The Spanish Tragedy*: the revenger must discover the identity of his foes but must be prevented from instant vengeance. Kyd had solved the problem differently in both his plays. In the *Ur-Hamlet* the counter-action had gone steadily forward against the revenger and, barring the prayer scene, no occasion had presented itself until finally the counter-action designed to kill Hamlet had back-fired and in the midst of disaster presented Hamlet with his long-awaited opportunity to revenge. In *The Spanish Tragedy* the revenger was delayed by lack of knowledge as to the identity of his opponents, and when that ignorance was resolved had made a thwarted attempt to secure revenge. Foiled in that, and hampered by the weakening of his will in fits of madness, he was forced to

bide his time. Opportunity finally came, he conceived a plan to en-
snare his foes, and carried it to a successful completion.

The plotting of both plays is drawn upon to prepare for
the catastrophe of *Titus Andronicus*. Titus is yet ignorant of the
assailants of Lavinia, although he knows his other foes. The
revelation of this information follows without the delay of Kyd's
plays so that Titus by the first scene of the fourth act, immediately after his vow of revenge, has all the information he needs.
One avenue for delay is closed, and others must be sought. Therefore the opposing action, having rested satisfied as in *The Spanish
Tragedy,* is once more set in motion, as in *Hamlet,* by the new
knowledge of danger from the revenger. This information is
given the villains, however, by incidents arising from the revenger's delay through his madness, as in *The Spanish Tragedy*.
Titus for a time does nothing personally to revenge his wrongs.
In fits of madness he relieves his feelings by sending ominous
tokens to the sons of Tamora and to Saturninus. One of these
tokens seems about to start the counter-action, when the enraged
recipient, Saturninus, orders Titus to be dragged before his court,
but actually the news of Lucius's rebellion is the eventual cause
of Tamora's final trickery.

In the old play, if we may judge from the German version,
Tamora's scheme involved the assassination of Titus and Lucius,
a plan which owes much to *Hamlet,* while in the Dutch, Tamora
merely tries to turn Titus's mind against Lucius and to dispose
in that way of the menace of the invasion. Shakespeare's Tamora,
trusting to her wiles to reconcile all parties and save Rome, desires only to know what plans are afoot. The plotting of *The
Spanish Tragedy* now comes to the fore. Titus has no plan until
Tamora's move presents him with an opportunity which he seizes
as the means for revenge. Just as Hieronimo's complaisance tricks
Lorenzo into taking part in the play, so Titus by his feigning of
harmless madness lures the villains to his house and secures possession of Tamora's sons. The difference must be noted, however,
that the offer to present the play is not made to Hieronimo by his

antagonists and that, as in *Titus,* there is no plot against himself concealed in the opportunity.

The dénouement of *Titus Andronicus* follows *Hamlet* only so far as the chance to revenge is offered by the opponents' final counter-plot, which was set in motion to dispose of a new danger after they had thought their previous plots successful. The two differ, however, since the new plot against Titus is not aimed directly at his life. Madness is given a new and unique dramatic importance, for the villains' final device is based on the assumption that the revenger is mad. Such a situation had already been partially suggested in the Hamlet-Ofelia scene, but in *Titus Andronicus* the trick is given a far greater importance by its position in leading to the catastrophe. That Titus, although unbalanced, is not absolutely insane and so can detect the motives of the villains, spells their downfall. The feigning of madness which was absent in *The Spanish Tragedy* and never quite legitimately motivated in *Hamlet,* is here an essential part of the plot to bring on the dénouement and is therefore more closely and ironically bound to the revenge.

For this reason the catastrophe of *Titus Andronicus* differs from the essential plan of Kyd's two plays. Hamlet is unaware of the plot behind the fencing-match, while Titus sees through the device of the banquet and is able to plan his revenge beforehand. Hieronimo's revenge is perhaps more premeditated than Titus's, since his plans, although dependent on the request for entertainment, are not forced upon him, as in *Titus,* in order to wreck the villains' plot to nullify his revenge. In *Titus* it is the weakness of Tamora's overconfident device which brings about her downfall. Since her plot was not laid against his life, Titus is killed by Saturninus in just such an unpremeditated fashion as Hamlet stabbed the king. The deaths in the catastrophe lack, thus, the premeditation of *The Spanish Tragedy* or even the ironic miscarrying of *Hamlet.* Two murders, indeed, are carefully planned: the slaying of Lavinia and the murder of Tamora after her ghastly meal. The other two are portrayed in a hugger-mugger fashion.

Saturninus stabs Titus, and Lucius, an unwitting accomplice to Titus's revenge, stabs Saturninus in retaliation. Since Lucius and Marcus had no part in Titus's revenge, they are spared. Aaron, the remaining accomplice of the villains, is taken away to execution, and the play ends quietly with the election of Lucius to the throne.

The chief variations in *Titus* from Kyd's plays are (1) the adequate but undeveloped motivation of blood-revenge as a cause for the villains' machinations; (2) the increased importance and complexity of the villains' actions before the start of the protagonist's revenge; (3) the number of faults in the revenger's character, which, though balanced by obvious virtues, make necessary a tragic ending for his bloodstained life; (4) the more logical and ironic use of the revenger's madness; (5) the change in the manner of bringing about the catastrophe, although the plotting here suffers from haste; (6) the inclusion of an important villainous character who is only loosely connected with the main plot.

This character, Aaron, illustrates clearly the influence of Marlowe's Barabas in his delight in villainy for its own sake. He is thus placed before the audience as a creature of "motiveless malignity"[5] a conception heightened by his place in Shakespeare's plot. Aaron himself is never personally injured, and whatever grudge he holds against the Andronici can result only from his original defeat and capture, a motive not touched upon. After the rape of Lavinia, which first inspired his villainous aid, his plans seem governed simply by the desire to preserve their new positions in Rome against the inevitable revenger for the deed; but it soon becomes obvious that the plot he envisages will fall in with Tamora's revenge and may even lead to further advance-

---

[5] Some confusion results when, in reproving Tamora for interrupting his preparations, Aaron cries:

> Vengeance is in my heart, death in my hand,
> Blood and revenge are hammering in my head.

The whole passage (II.iii.30-9) reveals a characterization which may possibly go back to the old play where, as in the Dutch version, Aaron himself was the offended person.

ment at court. His natural love of villainy is thus turned to the uses of his mistress.

As the moving spirit and actor of Tamora's revenge he deals successive blows to Titus, but when Titus's message to Chiron and Demetrius reveals to Aaron that the group is discovered, he keeps that knowledge to himself. Shortly afterwards the saving of his child diverts his attention so that he is no longer an important factor in the plot except as his inexplicable failure to warn the conspirators, and his absence from the scene, fosters the fatal scheme for which they die.

If Aaron had been merely a clever, villainous accomplice,[6] his part in the play would have been more closely connected with the main plot and its important dénouement. But as it is, he plays his rôle, drops out, and has nothing to do with the direction of the ending. Indeed, the clear-cut outlines of the play are blurred because it is really he who has devised the methods of revenge, and is abetted instead of commanded by Tamora, the chief person injured. The blurring is carried still further when the villain's part is so absorbed by Aaron that blood-revenge for Alarbus, the prime motivation of Tamora's revenge, disappears from her thoughts shortly after the start and is never mentioned by her sons. The incidents arise not from the originally announced clear-cut motive, the thirst of Tamora for revenge for blood, but rather from Aaron's natural villainy finding in Titus a fit subject on which to spend itself. The conflict is drawn between Titus and Aaron, and the catastrophe loses force when Aaron is not included in its workings.

[6] Just as the execration in which Jews were held in Elizabethan England dictated the choice of Barabas as Marlowe's great villain, so the notorious villainy and revengefulness of the Moors, who by their color were commonly associated with Satan, lent force to the choice of Aaron's ancestry. See Belleforest, history XXXI: "Il n'ignorait point que le More se tueroit plustot, qu'il ne se vēgeast d'vne iniure receuë. De cecy fait foy l'Abbé de sainct Simplician, à Milan, lequel ayant seulement donné vn soufflet à vn sien More, la nuict ensuiuant, le Barbare, qui auoit seruy monsieur l'Abbé plus de trente ans, luy couppa la gorge, lors qu'il estoit au plus profond de son sommeil . . . il [the Moor] vaut mieux mourir en se vengeāt que viure auec ce continuel elancemēt de coeur, ayant tousiours ceste iniure deuant les yeux, sans en auoir pris condigne vengeance."

The imitation of the Marlovian protagonist villain Barabas (himself sprung from Lorenzo, the villain of the counter-plot) as a quasi-accomplice in a Kydian revenge tragedy, meant first the deepening of Aaron's villainy and second his inevitable extension beyond the limits of an accomplice's part. By this extension the balance of forces was disordered, the natural villain Tamora was forced into the background and the normal conflict between injurer and revenger was so modified that the justness and symmetry of the plot was disturbed. Shakespeare's *Titus Andronicus,* then, must be considered as an experimental play, uniting in an imperfect form two wholly dissimilar methods of plotting and theories of tragedy. That it had a later influence, perhaps even exceeding Marlowe's, on the revenge tragedy with a villain as protagonist, may be seen in the examples of *Alphonsus, Emperor of Germany* (1594-1597) and *Lust's Dominion* (1600?). Otherwise, Kyd's influence was transmitted through Marston, and the first considerable variation of the Kydian formula, actuated (among other reasons) by the increasing interest in villainy as illustrated in *Titus Andronicus,* came about not so much as a result of Marlowe's influence as through the change in character, found in Chettle's *Hoffman* (1601-1602), of the Kydian protagonist revenger of blood from hero to absolute villain.

John Marston's *Antonio's Revenge,* produced in 1599,[7] carries on the pure Kydian tradition untouched by the influence of Marlowe. The incidents of the plot form a patchwork of borrowings from *Hamlet, The Spanish Tragedy,* and *Titus Andronicus,*[8] and there is a considerable debt in the structure itself. As in

[7] D. J. McGinn, "A New Date for *Antonio's Revenge,*" *PMLA*, Vol. LIII (1938), pp. 129-37, puts forward some very plausible arguments for a date in the winter of 1600-1601, following Shakespeare's first production of *Hamlet*. See also, his *Shakespeare's Influence on the Drama of his Age Studied in Hamlet* (Rutgers University Press, 1938), pp. 14-15.

[8] Outside of the larger matters of plot, various small reminiscent incidents may be mentioned. Antonio's premonitory nosebleed is paralleled in the early *Hamlet*. The sudden laughter of Pandulfo after the death of his son is imitated from *Titus Andronicus,* as is the strong emphasis on the lyrical laments of the victims of the villain's revenge. Antonio appears wearing black and carrying a book as do

Hamlet the murders have been committed before the play opens, and the action of the villain is almost from the start directed against the life of the hero. A ghost is also used to expose the author of the murders, although its appearance is delayed until the third act. The difficulty of prolonging the hero's revenge through the whole play, which faced Kyd in *Hamlet,* Marston escapes by this delay, but he falls on the other horn of the dilemma, discovered by Kyd in *The Spanish Tragedy* and Shakespeare in *Titus Andronicus,* that of devising suitable action before the revenge was started.

Marston's solution combined the methods of all three plays. As in *Hamlet* the villain is seeking the hero's life instead of merely thwarting him. This more serious counter-action is begun sooner than in *Hamlet* and follows the plotting of *Titus Andronicus* by which the villain usurps the stage and deals blow after blow to an ignorant and passive hero. An extra fullness of plot is gained by creating a pair of revengers for two different murders, and also by the addition of much extraneous matter, as in *The Spanish Tragedy*. These additions to the plot in *Antonio's Revenge* are concerned with Piero's wooing of Maria, the love of Antonio and Mellida, and the plots laid against Mellida's reputation.

Following the ghost's revelation Marston adopts three means of piecing out his story. First, his revenger delays partly from excessive grief which saps his powers of action as in *The Spanish*

Hieronimo and Hamlet, and like Hieronimo he is once brought upon the stage in his nightgown. Antonio's reproaches to his mother are copied from *Hamlet.* The voices of the ghosts understage, the elaborate oath of the revengers, the belief of the mother in the madness of her revenger son, the appearance of the injured ghost demanding vengeance of his son, and a second appearance before the mother, come also from *Hamlet,* as does the inspiration for Antonio's wild speech and his playing the fool. The fifth act is reminiscent of *The Spanish Tragedy* in the ghost prologue and spectator ghost. Piero's tongue is torn out like Hieronimo's, and the letters found on the murdered accomplice Strotzo have a hand in betraying Piero, as Pedringano's brought about Lorenzo's downfall. The exposure of the limbs of his child before Piero recalls the Thyestean banquet of *Titus Andronicus.* Kydian parallelism is copied in the death of Julio in payment for the murder of Andrugio and Feliche, and in the revenge for his son by Pandulfo which joins that by Antonio for his father. Lastly, Antonio's mind is momentarily unbalanced by the weight of his duty, in spite of an earlier jeer at the theatricality of insanity.

Tragedy, and, more originally, in part from a fixed desire to provide a more lingering torment for his victim. Hieronimo's vague
talk about the proper time and place for his revenge, and Hamlet's
bloody but futile ravings, are here replaced by a revenger who
delays from choice and not necessity. Such a motive is not con-
ducive to much illustrative action, and after its possibilities have
been largely exhausted with the murder of young Julio, Marston
brings forward emotional delay from grief. Secondly, more prominence is given to the story of the revenger's mother and her relations with the villain than in *Hamlet.* Lastly, the abortive plot of
the villain for Antonio's downfall by striking at him through his
love for Mellida adds to the crowded action and the delay. Indeed, the disposal of accomplices, which had necessarily so important a place in the action of *The Spanish Tragedy,* is here rushed
through perfunctorily lest it overshadow in interest the trial of
Mellida. The comic scenes with Balurdo help to fill the action,
but Marston was no artist in comic relief. Balurdo's first scene
with Antonio undeniably gives body and wit to the play, but
after that he is a mere excrescence despite the feeble efforts to
link him to the plot.

Granted the whole central situation of *Antonio's Revenge* parallels *Hamlet,* with the murderer of the hero's father wooing the
mother, plotting against the son, and finally falling by the son's
revenge with the tacit aid of the mother. Granted the extreme
borrowings of incident from Kyd and Shakespeare skilfully combined to give a greater unity and dramatic actability. Yet Marston
added much that was new to the form. First and foremost, he
set his tragedy in the turbulent Italian Renaissance court of an
imaginary Sforza and painted a full-fledged Italian despotic villain of the Renaissance. Machiavellian deeds in this play have
their proper background, and in many ways Marston's Piero is the
best villain yet exhibited. He is more human, he has more real
blood in his veins; for most of the time he is decidedly not a
caricature like Barabas or Aaron, who were abstract villains.
Piero bears the strongest resemblance to the intellectual Lorenzo,
with a dash of warmth that Lorenzo sadly needed. His motives

are baser than Lorenzo's, for lust has entered in, and his jocularity, his aching for praise and appreciation help keep him near to normally villainous mankind. Piero not only plans, he also performs; while Lorenzo, except for his unavoidable part in the murder of Horatio, makes a fetish of secrecy and merely pulls the strings. Piero's heartiness, his occasional naïveté, his bold effrontery are highly interesting. The ironic gusto of the conversation with his accomplice Strotzo about the false confession which will implicate Antonio and free Mellida, furnishes considerable amusement. Although he insists that his accomplices be ignoble, for "Poison from roses who could e'er abstract?" he becomes realistically impatient when they fail in appreciation of his shrewdness or try to rise above the obsequiousness he demands.

The Renaissance petty tyrant was ambitious and notoriously a schemer for the extension of his state. Piero's plots have, realistically, a political as well as a personal cast. On the first side, Mellida is not to be wasted on Antonio but is to be married where he, Piero, will benefit. On the second, his revenge has been long brewing, ever since the marriage of Andrugio and Maria years before, but he has successfully dissembled it,

> For tyrants haue this propertie 'boue other,
> They meane reuenge, yet their reuenge cã smother.[9]

This dissimulation automatically gave the keynote of his character to the Elizabethan audience.[10] The pretense of friendship has been an effort to his proud soul, and the moment of action finds him exultant:

> Sweet wrong, I clap thy thoughts!
> O let me hug thy bosom, rub thy breast,
> In hope of what may hap.
>   (II.i.9-11)

---

[9] *Brathwaite's Natures Embassie,* p. 122.

[10] "Deuilish is that disposition, which to wait an opportunity of reuenge, will seeme, to rake vp its malice in the cinders of obliuion; but when the time serues will not stick to giue fire to the whole heap of its hell-bred mischief." Robert Chamberlain, *Nocturnall Lucubrations* (1638), pp. 19-20.

The first stratagem after the murder of Andrugio is the defamation of Mellida (made possible by the murder of Feliche) and the subsequent accusation that Antonio has killed his own father. Such "policy" had been discussed by Machiavelli (*The Prince*, VII) and mentioned by Gentillet (III, 2) so that the Elizabethans were familiar with the Machiavellian methods of disposing of an enemy by discrediting him.[11] Piero's device, which he hoped would cause Antonio's downfall, instead led to his own ruin, for the wanton murder of Feliche eventually raised two revengers, Pandulfo and Alberto, who at a critical moment joined with Antonio. Piero, then, has committed a tactical error, according to Machiavelli, in being too free with bloodshed.[12] Although he has followed one sound maxim, "A Prince which would have any man to die, must seeke out some apparent colour thereof," he has neglected another, "When you have once injured, there never forgive." Piero's fatal error lay in underrating Pandulfo, and it was Pandulfo who turned the scales against him.

Piero remains credible throughout much of the play until he suffers from Marston's inevitable heightening process. As a crafty and egotistical Machiavellian he is a success in every detail; but when Marston strains the character to excess in emulation of the other great villains, Piero becomes a mere hobgoblin to frighten children. Thus in the fourth act, afire with ambition, he climbs to rank absurdity:

> Young Galeatzo! Ay, a proper man;
> Florence, a goodly city; it shall be so,

[11] See *The Times Whistle,* ed. Cowper, p. 49; *Leycesters Commonwealth* (1641), p. 149; "Save a thief from the Gallows, and he'l hang thee if he can: or, The merciful Father and the merciless Son," *The Roxburghe Ballads,* Vol. III, p. 28.

[12] "*Machiavel* doth accuse as imprudent, all such *Princes . . . that knew not when to stop that issue of Blood, which may at first be necessary to keep such Titles in . . .* nothing more obvious to probability, than the raising of some *Spirits* (amongst the number of Enemies, such a continued practice will in all reason produce) as can never rest satisfied without *Revenge . . .* as no *purvyance can sheild* the person of a *Prince* from: who, whilst his prudence, like the *Philosophers eyes,* are fixed upon higher and more remote *dangers, he falls into some nearer Trap he never dreamt of."* Francis Osborne, "Advice to a Son, the second part," *Works* (ed. 1673), pp. 223-4.

I'll marry her [Mellida] to him instantly.
Then Genoa mine, by my Maria's match,
Which I'll solemnize ere next setting sun:
Thus Venice, Florence, Genoa, strongly leagued.
Excellent, excellent! I'll conquer Rome,
Pop out the light of bright religion;
And then, helter skelter, all cock sure.

(IV.i.260-68)

It was this straining for effect which was at once Marston's strength and his weakness. It produced the grisly scenes, the eeriness of the night episodes, the horror of the blood-spattered Antonio, the whole display of the pageantry of terror and the panoply of death which thrilled an Elizabethan audience. At its worst, Marston's bent led him to futile extravagances of passion and the empty inflation of character so marked in the later Piero. His flair for strong scenes produced melodrama, stirring no doubt on the Elizabethan stage but cold in the study.

Precisely because of its melodramatic leaning, *Antonio's Revenge* does not escape the fatal inconsistency inherent in the early type of the revenge play. The murder of Julio is a purely gratuitous piece of business brought in merely to make the audience shudder.[13] Piero is near and unarmed; the time is ripe to strike. Instead Antonio mutters:

No, not so.
This shall be sought for; I'll force him feed on life
Till he shall loath it. This shall be the close
Of vengeance' strain.[14]

(III.i.136-39)

[13] This incident, although somewhat reminiscent of the prayer scene in *Hamlet,* was probably an adaptation of the murder of Thyestes's sons by Atreus, without the clear-cut motivation present in Seneca.

[14] Such a sentiment was close to the Italianate theory of the proper revenge. Margaret of Navarre explains: "Thus man's greatest misery is to wish for death and not be able to obtain it. The greatest ill which can befall a criminal is not to be put to death, but to be made to suffer so much that he longs for death while his sufferings, though continual, are of such a nature as not to be capable of abridging his life." *The Heptameron,* fourth day, novel XXXI, trans. W. Kelley (London, n.d.), p. 48.

Piero, indeed, tastes to the full the tortures of Antonio's threat when he is finally entrapped. But such a delay, and for such reasons, particularly when united to the outrageous murder of Julio, should have stamped Antonio as a villain who must suffer death at the end. That Marston continued to treat Antonio as a guiltless hero, must be laid to the obvious influence which the morality of Seneca exercised on the play.

Of far more importance than the large number of Senecan quotations and echoes in the mouths of the characters is this imposition of the Roman callousness on the conventional English ethical view of the limits to which a revenger could go and the methods he should pursue. No other matter in the play illustrates so well the direct influence of Seneca on Marston. By every English tenet, Antonio is a cruel and bloodthirsty villain who has overstepped the bounds of revenge. Yet by Marston's Senecan morality Antonio is a dutiful son sacrificing the blood of the murderer's kindred to appease the ghost of his slain father, and he remains a hero to the end. It is curious that Marston who with Webster and Tourneur was one of the most Italianate of Elizabethan dramatists in the sense that he more correctly portrayed the Italian scene and character as the Italians themselves would have recognized it, was at the same time one of the most Senecan.

In 1445 *The Chronicle of Perugia* records, "Then Monsignore appointed peacemakers, two men per ward, to whom it was given in charge to make peace and bring together those who had been enemies; and under commandment of Monsignore many murders were blotted out and old enmities healed; and many citizens took the cowl."[15] Antonio's retirement to a monastery after his murder of Piero, it would seem, implies no more sense of moral guilt than did the ancient classical idea of exile to wash away blood-pollution. Rather, as the extract from the Italian chronicle appears to indicate, Antonio, in pursuance of a previous vow, refuses the dukedom and retires with no sense of moral guilt from a world in which there is nothing but empty glory left for him.

[15] Francesco Matarazzo, *Chronicles of the City of Perugia 1492-1503*, trans. E. S. Morgan (London: J. M. Dent & Co., 1905), p. 10.

Linked with a possible tinge of the idea of blood-pollution is the stronger medieval Christian theme of loathing for the vanities of the world, to which Pandulfo's speech gives the key:

> We know the world, and did we know no more,
> We would not live to know; but since constraint
> Of holy bands forceth us to keep this lodge
> Of dirt's corruption, till dread power calls
> Our soul's appearance, we will live enclosed
> In holy verge of some religious order,
> Most constant votaries.
>
> (V.ii.146-52)

The theme is that the conspirators have nothing left for which to live, and are prevented from a Stoic suicide (entirely divorced from any sense of expiation for murder) only by the canons of the Church.[16] They have lived enough to see the vanities of the world at their true value and to despise them and to wish to escape the world. Superficially, Marston's close is not unique, yet actually the morality is so different from the expiatory catastrophe of all other Elizabethan revenge tragedies that *Antonio's Revenge* will always have a certain importance in the history of the type.

Hoffman, by Henry Chettle, appeared before 1602. The main action comprises the revenge of a son for the death of a father, a revenge that extends to the slayers' kindred. Ghosts have no part in the play, but the skeleton of Hoffman's father is preserved, like Horatio's body and the bloody handkerchief, as a memento of vengeance. There is the customary hesitation on the part of the revenger, but since the delay is caused solely by the lustful pas-

---

[16] Creizenach, *The English Drama in the Age of Shakespeare,* p. 103, thinks that the retirement to a monastery in *Antonio's Revenge* and in Chapman's *Revenge of Bussy D'Ambois* of "the survivors of an overwhelming tragic catastrophe" was actuated by "a delicate appreciation for the poetic element in some Catholic institutions which perished under the régime of the Reformation," and points out Shakespeare's delight in the monk in *Much Ado* and the hermit in *As You Like It,* both of whom were not in the sources. Marston, in fact, later took Anglican orders, but such a criticism is probably giving Marston credit for too great a sentimental refinement.

sion he conceives for the mother of one of his victims, he is totally free from any frustrating sense of wrong which had halted the Kydian revenger on the threshold of his duty. As a consequence Hoffman is impeded neither by oppressive melancholy nor by insanity, and madness is portrayed, as in *Hamlet,* only in the daughter of a victim. Deceit, trickery, and dissimulation are freely used by Hoffman and by his opponents, and Hoffman disposes of his accomplices in the time-honored fashion. Among minor characteristics may be mentioned the strong irony, the scenes at a tomb, the wearing of black, the premonitions of disaster, the ritualistic swearing to revenge, the use of poison, and the delight in the portrayal of unbalanced minds.

The early form of revenge tragedy was incapable of much variation, and in *The Spanish Tragedy, Hamlet, Titus Andronicus,* and *Antonio's Revenge* its possibilities had been nearly exhausted. Every means of ingenuity had been racked, both in embroidering the incidents and in experimenting with characters, to vary what was at bottom the same dramatic situation. It is apparent that the Elizabethan dramatists had progressively discovered their chief hope for variation to lie in the elaboration of the character of the villain and in his extension to an even more important place in the plot. From Lorenzo to Piero the Kydian villain had been increasing in prominence even to the extent of occasionally overshadowing the hero. Such offshoots of the type as Barabas, Alphonsus of Germany, and Eleazar had indeed usurped the place of the protagonist, but Barabas had been an extended Lorenzo, Alphonsus a Tiberius, and Eleazar an Aaron, and in each play Kyd's central situation had been voluntarily relinquished.

With one bold step Chettle did just the opposite by taking the Kydian hero revenger and carrying him to his logical conclusion as a villain, still as the central figure of a true tragedy of revenge. Besides the need for variation in the formula which lay behind this move, we must also reckon with the classical influence. Hoffman, after his murder of Otho, cries:

Come, image of bare death, ioyne side, to side,
With my long iniur'd fathers naked bones;
He was the prologue to a Tragedy,
That if my destinies deny me not,
Shall passe those of Thyestes, Tereus,
Jocasta, or Duke Jasons ielous wife.

(I.383-88)

In endeavoring to rival the classical tragic stories, particularly those of Thyestes, Tereus, and Medea, Chettle was forced to fill his play with strong and bloody incidents. Only a villain revenger could fully serve his purpose, and one with the strongest possible motive—vengeance for blood. While the character of Hoffman had to a certain extent been anticipated in Laertes of *Hamlet* and Alexander of *Alphonsus, Emperor of Germany,* his installation as the protagonist was a master stroke.

Moreover, the transition was inevitable. The development of the tragedies of revenge before and after *Hoffman* indicates clearly that the Elizabethan audiences were growing increasingly chary of accepting the bloody heroes as good and admirable men. Since some time has already been spent on this point, it will suffice here to note that in the character of Hoffman may be perceived most readily the dramatic transition from the virtues of the revengers to their vices. Earlier revengers had all had good causes, but Hoffman's was tainted from the beginning. His father had been legally executed as a pirate, and in spite of the fact that Hoffman vigorously defends his father's deeds in the light of the wrongs he had received, his action in seeking a personal revenge on the legal judges of his father strikes at the very root of the judicial system and could not be condoned. No man had secretly murdered his father; he had been executed in accordance with the law and was thus a malefactor who, according to Elizabethan tenets, should not be revenged: "for otherwise to reuenge his cause who is iustly offended, were no other, but to faile in iustice, & therefore I say by manifest fault."[17]

---

[17] Kepers, *The Courtiers Academie* (c. 1598), p. 103.

Even if Hoffman were convinced of the justness of his cause, the audience, hearing his bloody plans, could not agree that his intention was also just:

"Their intention also must be rightfull, not that they fight for ambition to get the authority, or for couetousnesse to get riches, or for malice to be reuenged of grutches, or for cruelty to murder men: For if their intention be wicked, though their cause be iust, they sinne in manslaughter, and for their wicked intention God suffereth them to be ouercome in a rightfull cause."[18]

Hoffman, however, had wrongfully convinced himself that his cause, and his intention also, were both rightful:

"But without all these signes and presages men thinke that God is fauorable, when as they thinke they fight for a good cause . . . yea, when as they imagine, that the reuenge they pursue is iust, and that they haue beene vnworthily abused. The reason is, for that Choler which is always enflamed by the iniurye receiued, and not by that which wee doe vnto others, makes men hardy, perswading themselues, that God assists them that are wronged and vniustly persecuted."[19]

Hoffman's last sin was that he did not keep a mean in his revenge but let it degenerate into wanton collective slaughter. He is, therefore, in the direct line of such revengers as Hieronimo, Titus, and perhaps the earliest Hamlet, who by their too great bloodiness or Machiavellism had turned away the sympathy of the audience.

No revenge begins more quickly than in *Hoffman*: within the first two hundred and twenty lines the first victim of Hoffman's vengeance has fallen. From that point the plotting follows the only logical course. Hoffman must carry the battle to his adversaries, and as his cold-blooded and insatiable revenge mows down one person after another, his inherent villainy comes ever to the fore. Chettle is disdainful of earlier hero revengers with their hesitant action and unbalanced rant of blood, and burlesques them in the character Jerome.

[18] Thomas Lodge, "The Diuell Conjured," *Works* (Hunterian Club, 1883), p. 86.

[19] John Eliot, *A Discourse of Warre and Single Combat* (1591), pp. 51-3.

Although Hoffman, in his rôle, makes every endeavor to win sympathy at the start of the play, Chettle allows the audience no illusions about the real ethics of Hoffman's action. The villainous accomplice Lorrique, analyzing the situation, says:

> I am halfe a Monarke: halfe a fiend
> Blood I begun in and in blood must end
> Yet this Clois [Hoffman] is an honest villaine, has
> Conscience in his killing of men: he kils
> None but his fathers enemies, and there issue,
> 'Tis admirable, 'tis excellent, 'tis well
> 'Tis meritorious, where? in heauen? no, hell.
>
> (II.618-24)

This speech marks the difference between the protagonist villain stemming from the Kydian hero and villains like Barabas, Aaron, and Eleazar who have sprung from the Kydian antagonist villain. These last had always been conscious of their villainy—that they were damned souls—and gloried in their evil deeds because they were evil. Of such breed is Lorrique. Yet Hoffman, developed from the Kydian hero, is fiendishly exultant as each of his enemies falls, but always believes that his cause is pure. His moral sense is atrophied, and it is only after the fatal moment when he hesitates over his prey and falls a victim to lust that his motives follow those of the conventional villain instead of the revenger of blood.

Chettle has tidily made use of the conventional situations of revenge tragedy. Hoffman's lust provides the counter-revengers with their lever for his undoing. Madness from shock at the murder of a loved one, dramatically unnecessary in *Hamlet* except as an added spur to Leonhardus, is here vitally linked to the plot when the mad Lucybella discovers vital evidence which invites the first suspicions of Hoffman. The downfall of the villain through the posthumous evidence left by his destroyed accomplice is varied to actual betrayal by the accomplice whom he kills too late. Chettle has also used the opportunities for comedy first exploited in the Phantasmo of the old *Hamlet* and developed in

Marston's Balurdo, as well as the comic aspects of madness treated in *Hamlet* and *The Spanish Tragedy*. Finally, he has raised to the highest importance the emphasis on deceit and trickery in the revenger's intrigue.

Hoffman is a play of considerable historical interest because of Chettle's creation of his protagonist villain not through the line of Lorenzo, Barabas, and Aaron, but through the logical development of vices inherent in the heroes of earlier revenge tragedy. The play represents the first major variation within the Kydian form, and had considerable influence on later dramas. Of Chettle's most important innovation—a revenger in disguise—more will be said directly.

Marston's *Malcontent* (1604), although a comedy, has so much of the technique of the revenge tragedy and, more important, was such a vital influence on later revenge plays, that a brief consideration is necessary.

The play contains an intriguing, unsuspected revenger, a variation on the device of the disposal of accomplices, emphasis on the torture of the victim's mind, the lust of the supposed murderer for the wife of the supposed victim, and, finally, the deceit of the masque in which the revengers secure their opportunity. So far *Hamlet* and *Antonio's Revenge* are the models and there is nothing new.

Where *The Malcontent* had its first great influence was in its popularization of Chettle's device of the disguised revenger introduced when the rightful Duke Malevole returns in disguise to revenge himself on the usurper. In *The Spanish Tragedy* Lorenzo acknowledges Hieronimo as his opponent but is not aware that, in return, Hieronimo is aware of Lorenzo's guilt. The character of Hamlet as revenger is not long concealed from the king. Titus's opponents know him as the revenger, although they are tricked by his madness into disregarding their danger. The relation of villain and revenger in *Antonio's Revenge* follows roughly that in *The Spanish Tragedy* except that Piero holds more complete control of the situation than does Lorenzo. Antonio, therefore, instead of dissembling like Hieronimo to deceive his opponent, is forced to circulate a report of his own death and then to re-enter the court in disguise to secure his revenge. Where the balance of power was more nearly equal, the revenger needed no more protection than the assumption of ignorance or of madness; but where he is in positive and active danger, as in *Antonio's Revenge,* this cloak to his motives had perforce to be altered to a complete transformation of his outer appearance in order for him to approach his enemy without suffering instant death. Chettle took the hint from *Antonio's Revenge,* and in *Hoffman* the revenger moves disguised in the midst of his enemies throughout the whole play. Although Marston had originated the device, it is likely that in *The Malcontent* he borrowed its extended application from *Hoffman.*

So far the matter is clear, but when we examine the strands of the plot and characterization we find that *The Malcontent* has evolved a new formula. Instead of the elementary scheme of revenge and counter-intrigue, or (as in *Hoffman*) counter-revenge, there is a tangled web of revenges. There is the revenge of the disguised Malevole on Pietro for the usurpation of his throne. His tactics are not aimed at Pietro's life but consist of torturing his mind, and as a part of this scheme he directs Pietro's revenge against the adulterer Mendoza. Mendoza in the meantime has conceived revenge on Ferneze for supplanting him in the affections of Pietro's wife, and manages to direct Pietro's suspicions away from himself to settle them on Ferneze. To this revenge Mendoza adds a burning desire for vengeance on the wife for slighting him and, curiously, on Pietro for his mistrust. The revenge on his master opens such fresh vistas before him that he becomes ambitious of displacing Pietro on the throne.

Thus Marston first taught the lesson of dramatic complication by a multiplicity of revenges working against one another. Unfortunately, it was a dangerous lesson, for the central situation, even in *The Malcontent,* is likely to be lost in the whirl of largely extraneous intrigue. As an example, there would be little essential difference in the action of *The Malcontent* were Malevole really the disinterested character he pretends to be in his disguise and not the banished rightful claimant working to recover his seat.

Finally, Mendoza had an important influence on later villains. His character, which is in the line of Lorenzo and Piero, is crude and inconsistent. That is of no moment. What lends him his eminence is his position in the plot as an ambitious villainous favorite who intrigues to oust his villain master. This type, first popularized by Marston, became the favorite protagonist for later writers of villain plays.

With *The Revenger's Tragedy*, usually attributed to Cyril Tourneur and doubtfully dated 1606-1607, we come to one of the last of the great tragedies composed under the specific influence of the Kydian formula. Almost twenty years, however, had passed since the first performance of *The Spanish Tragedy*, and in that time other playwrights had been subtly varying the pure tradition. Two of these authors, Chettle and Marston, exercised, indeed, a more important guidance over Tourneur than did Kyd.

Chettle, in his endeavor to please the developing taste for a highly colored villain, had instituted an important change in the form by endowing his villainous protagonist with the revenge motives of a Kydian hero. The audience, however, had never been in doubt about Hoffman's real character. But with Vindici in *The Revenger's Tragedy* there is that doubt, directly caused by the curious moral atrophy of the play. In spite of the assertion sometimes made that his revenge is no longer a solemn duty justified as a code and approved by the audience, but springs from a malicious desire for retaliation,[20] Vindici's wrongs as first portrayed to the audience are as real as any hero revenger's. His betrothed has been poisoned after she had repulsed the duke's lustful advances. Owing to the seriousness of the Elizabethan betrothal, Vindici is seeking revenge for the murder of a woman who was, in effect, his wife. To supplement this central motive Tourneur adds the traditional revenge for a father, although in a

[20] Boyer, *The Villain as Hero*, p. 145.

very feeble manner, for Vindici's father is supposed merely to have died from discontent at his disgrace by the duke.[21]

Last, and quite important for the audience's sympathy, Vindici is seen in the light of a moral purger of a corrupt court. The rape of Antonio's wife did not touch him except as Antonio was his brother's friend. Yet this revenge for Antonio, long quiescent after the first solemn oath, plays an extremely important part in the catastrophe, for the device of the masque in which Vindici slays Lussurioso is aided by two lords who are, presumably, the friends of Antonio. Vindici is not content with the death of the duke, his logical victim, but must scourge from the court all his vicious progeny and set up a new and righteous succession. He has no ambitions to usurp the ducal seat, and he believes himself to be a good man and a virtuous revenger. Deciding on the trial of his mother and sister, he says,

> Tho I durst almost for good,
> Venture my lands in heauen vpon their good.
>
> (I.iii)

Here, then, is presented to the audience a revenger with entirely adequate motives of blood-revenge, one who is a purifier of the state and, unlike the traditional villain, firmly believes in his own salvation.

That Tourneur has actually formed Vindici as a villain and so at the last exposes him, is a triumph in objective character-por-trayal—a very rare occurrence on the Elizabethan stage. Every previous thoroughgoing villain had known he was a villain, and was excessively anxious to make that fact clear to the audience: thus he was a completely self-conscious individual who had no illusions about himself and was anxious that the audience should have none. Chettle's Hoffman marked the first change towards

---

[21] Vindici is serious about the worth of this motive, for when the duke lies dying Hippolito cries:

> And let this comfort thee. Our Lord and Father
> Fell sick upon the infection of thy frounes
> And dyed in sadnesse; be that thy hope of life.
>
> (III. v)

objectivity, but the transformation was incomplete because Lorrique, in the capacity of chorus, exposed Hoffman's true character. With Tourneur the objectivity is complete. The spectators were forced to decide for themselves as to Vindici's true character and to trace, step by step if they were analytical, his self-deluded downfall.

Indeed, the action of the play and the characters are so feverish and abnormal that the audience may well have been carried along unthinkingly until the common sense horror of Antonio at the revengers' deeds came like a shock of cold water both to the listeners and to Vindici. Not until the startling anticlimax does the cold reason of a normal person with whom the audience can identify itself enter the play. The moment Antonio speaks, the spectators are oriented and the true horror of the smirking admissions of Vindici and his brother is realized. This lack of a normal character to act as a touchstone accounts in a great measure for the at least partial acceptance of the lurid deeds of the revenger, particularly when the playwright's own views are so completely hidden. In fact, one might be tempted to believe that Vindici would have remained a hero if Tourneur had not felt the lure of an unexpected climax.[22] But as it is, the unique situation where the revengers of blood are hustled off to prison and execution like common criminals, removes all possible glamour clinging to a revenger.

Tourneur, then, took over the villain revenger from Chettle but changed him into a far more artistic being by a strict objective characterization. There are other reminiscences, also, which show his influence. Vindici preserves the skull of his beloved as Hoffman the skeleton of his father, and thunder rolls as a portent. The last lesson involves a total change in the revenger's code. Hieronimo and Titus had been openly boastful and exultant once their

[22] In his liking for the unexpected and the strained situation, Tourneur fairly anticipates the methods of Fletcher. The whole situation of the testing of the mother, with the daughter's pretended acquiescence, while undoubtedly derived from *The Malcontent,* is handled in just the manner Fletcher employed to titillate a jaded audience with strong situations.

revenge was consummated. The reason was simple: their revenge had been aimed at only a few persons and had been concentrated in one single action. Hoffman and Vindici, however, are in a society where every man's hand would be against them if they were known. Furthermore, they have not one but several revenges to perform; therefore they must strike secretly and then preserve themselves for their further revenges.

Although the character of the protagonist is indebted to *Hoffman,* perhaps the strongest influence on *The Revenger's Tragedy* came from Marston's *Malcontent,* itself not uninfluenced by Chettle. All three plays contain the central situation of a revenger living disguised in the midst of his enemies and endeavoring to secure his revenge by setting them one against another or by fobbing off his own deeds on one of his enemies for punishment. As in *The Malcontent,* the disguised revenger is hired as an accomplice by his enemy, and so secures his chance for revenge. Part of the duty of each is to attempt for his master the seduction of a woman of his own family. Both revengers create the initial discord in the ranks of their enemies by reports of adulteries in their households. Lastly, both protagonists are malcontents, and an important part of the revenge is completed by the use of a masque.

Marston's *Antonio's Revenge* has also left its mark. The brutal and long drawn out revenge on the duke parallels the torture of Piero. Most important, however, is the communal character of the revenge where the revenger is aided by his friends and by supporters of vengeance for another man—Pandulfo in *Antonio's Revenge* and Antonio in *The Revenger's Tragedy.* Owing to this alliance of revengers, the protagonist does not die in the final slaughter. Ironically, in *The Revenger's Tragedy* the alliance itself afterwards ruined the revenger. Tourneur has not hesitated to take striking incidents from other plays. The meditative speech on a skull comes from *Hamlet* and perhaps the solemn swearing to revenge over crossed swords; the stabbing of a body thought to be alive is from *The Jew of Malta*; and, lastly, murder by poisoned lips is found in *Soliman and Perseda.*

Both Chettle and Marston had worked with the complete plot as the unit, but with Tourneur, as later with Fletcher, the scene was the unit and the plot is composed of a series of strong, brilliant situations, each occupying a single scene, somewhat loosely strung together. Complicated intrigue on the parts of all the characters against one another is elaborated from *The Malcontent* and completely displaces the simple dual conflict of the Kydian plot already revolutionized by Chettle. But what Tourneur gains in brilliance of scene he relinquishes in coherence. There are so many intrigues that the revenger loses control and is lost in the maze. The opposing forces are stronger than he, and he is frequently of no purpose in the plot. By turning his revenger protagonist into a villain, Chettle had centered in him the audience's increasing interest in villainy which had already in other plays caused the enlargement of the villain's part at the expense of the revenging hero's. But Tourneur created so many villains, each struggling against the others but none against Vindici, that Vindici is too often submerged, and the play lacks on occasion a controlling protagonist.

The fact, also, that Vindici has no one clear-cut opponent against whom he can direct every scheme, adds to the confusion. Presumably the duke is his chief victim, but most of Vindici's revengeful plans center on Lussurioso, who has injured him so slightly in comparison that Vindici seems to wander from his true revenge. At no time does he hold the reins tightly. He has waited nine unexplained years[23] without opportunity for vengeance and has at last come to court hoping that circumstances will somehow prove favorable. His enemies are so powerful that the most he can do is to try to set them to destroying each other. But the

[23] This long wait for vengeance before the opening of the play gradually became a semi-convention, as in Massinger's *Duke of Milan*. Presumably the audience was to be impressed with the revenger's tenacity of purpose and fierceness of resolve. Seldom is this period of inactivity well motivated, for the revenger's ultimate course of action could as well have been adopted at the beginning as at the end. Since only rather villainous revengers are presented as waiting such a period, the suspicion is well founded that the information is given to illustrate their over-bloodthirsty characters. No normal, sympathetic person by Elizabethan standards would harbor his wrath for such a time and withstand the promptings of religion for forgiveness.

solidarity of the court has disintegrated before his arrival, and the villains do not need his help to be at each other's throats: most of their internecine warfare occurs without Vindici's instigation or even his knowledge. His direct plot against Lussurioso is laid aside as early as the second scene of Act II when he refuses a golden opportunity as did Hamlet and Antonio. Thereupon he transfers his attentions to the duke and thus does succeed in his revenge on the original injurer.

After this murder of the duke in the fifth scene of Act III, the action is continued by the strife among the duke's ambitious sons. The brothers determine to work revenge for the death of their younger brother on Lussurioso, but this action proves abortive when the revengers are before them in the masque and the brothers are themselves destroyed. Vindici evolves an elaborate plan to murder Lussurioso over the body of his father, but the unexpected presence of witnesses causes it to be abandoned. After Spurio has determined to kill Lussurioso, and Ambitioso to kill Spurio once the deed is done, the fatal masque is presented. The revengers achieve their purpose in slaying Lussurioso but there is no indication that the destruction of Spurio and the other brothers is anything more than an unexpected accident in the general tussle.

Hoffman, at least, conceived a far-reaching plan, and carried it through to the result he wished. It is he who pulls the strings and motivates each action. But *The Revenger's Tragedy* is full of uncompleted situations for which the ground has been laid. In *Hoffman* clarity was achieved and the interest of the audience held by watching the cause and effect, the inception and the result, of Hoffman's schemes, even though the basic law of drama—conflict—was missing from a major part of the action because of Hoffman's disguise. Tourneur has so constructed his play that the conflict chiefly occurs among the foes of the revenger without the revenger's instigation. Vindici, therefore, is not so firmly placed in the plot as Hoffman or Malevole; in addition, the continual promises of actions which never come off, the maze of intrigue and counter-intrigue, serve in the light of cold analysis virtually to disintegrate the plot. Where Tourneur saves himself is in his emphasis on scene and strong situation. The testing of Gratiana, the murder of the duke, the ghastly even though theatrically arranged irony, the unfathomed lust and brutality of the characters—these make the play.

The Revenger's Tragedy stands practically at the crossroads of Elizabethan tragedy. Henceforth with few exceptions the taste of the next period into which the tragic drama was entering led to the portrayal of extreme villainy, already foreshadowed, where the villains are the protagonists and the depiction of horror and tortuous intrigue is of such prime importance that revenge, while still the leading motive of the plot, does not carry the main interest of the audience except as a means to an end. *The Revenger's Tragedy,* while obviously linked to the past, is the distinct forerunner of the new school of true horror tragedies which were to break temporarily with the narrower tradition of the Kydian revenge play.

4

To all intents and purposes *The Revenger's Tragedy* closes the first period in the history of Elizabethan revenge tragedy, a span of years devoted almost exclusively to plays modelled on the double form of the type created by Kyd in *Hamlet* and *The Spanish Tragedy.* But the chronology of a literary form does not always lend itself to neat ticketing within definite limits of date. Within the second period, which had thrown off the bonds of Kyd, there were produced three major tragedies which turn back to the Kydian form for inspiration. These were Tourneur's *Atheist's Tragedy* (1607-1611), Chapman's *Revenge of Bussy D'Ambois* (1610), and Fletcher's *Valentinian* (1610-1614). It must be remembered that the huge stock company, the Elizabethan theater, was always in the process of reviving old plays or continuing their production without any real withdrawal from the repertory. Consequently, while the fashion for new plays changed to a great extent after 1607, the popular tragedies of the Kydian period, and especially Shakespeare's *Hamlet,* were still being acted along with the more fashionable dramas. Tourneur, Chapman, and Fletcher, therefore, in writing tragedies according to the model of the earlier school were not in any true sense revivers, nor were they penning solitary anachronisms. That the plays of all three are distinct criticisms of the defects of Kyd's formula shows plainly that the type was still of current interest and account.

The Atheist's Tragedy may be dated 1607-1611. The title indicates that a villain is the protagonist. Various villain atheists had already trod the stage before Tourneur's D'Amville, for to the Elizabethan audience anyone who was not a Christian was automatically an atheist. Thus not only Barabas, Aaron, and Eleazar shared the additional villainy of atheism, but also such Machiavellians as Piero, for the popular concept of Machiavellism held that it denied religion. D'Amville, however, is a renegade Christian, an apostate, and as such was awarded the fullest possible terror and loathing by an age to which atheist was a word of fear and unutterable detestation. Thomas Adams (1612) says roundly, "Wee doe (not say but) liue, as if it was better to be *a liuing Dog, then a dead Lion:* which I would yeeld true among Beastes; but among men, a dead Beast is better then a liuing Atheist."[24] An atheist, released from the fear of Hell and divine retribution, could feel no restraint put upon his actions, and so could commit the most atrocious crimes with a clear conscience.[25]

By thus drawing D'Amville as a professed atheist, Tourneur has endeavored to create the greatest villain of the stage up to his

[24] *The Gallants Burden* (1616), p. 31.

[25] Thomas Lupton, *A Dreame of the Deuil and Diues* (1584), sigs. E₂-E₂ᵛ. See also Thomas Becon, "A Pleasant New Nosegay," *The Early Works,* ed. Ayre, p. 191. In his "Character of An Atheist" (1615), John Stephens the Younger writes: "He will instantly discover what he beleives; being bolde enough to speake plainly (if thou canst apprehend) that vertue, innocence, and crafty dealing are alike rewarded: That wicked and religious men have no difference but the Name: That wronges may lawfully (if without danger apparent) bee repelled with worse wronges." See "Essayes and Characters," *Book of Characters* (1857), ed. Halliwell-Phillipps, p. 179.

time. To D'Amville's atheism Tourneur adds the sin of avarice, heartily loathed by the Elizabethan, and rounds out the portrait by gilding the lily with a touch of incest. That his bogey man has not remained a thrilling figure is unquestionably due to Tourneur's own excessive and somewhat naïve awe at his creation. D'Amville's atheistical reasonings are with justice regarded by modern critics as puerile in the extreme. It is only in the picture of D'Amville with mind unbalanced by his misfortunes that any subtle touches of realistic psychology are apparent. His ravings are exceptionally well done, and his mystification at the fortitude of Charlemont and Castabella when faced with the scaffold is a sound dramatic and psychological touch.[26] Otherwise, D'Amville is a standardized Elizabethan villain atrociously inflated.

The Atheist's Tragedy is, however, a rather unusual villain-play, for the counter-action comprises a complete story of a revenge for a father's blood directed against the villain protagonist.[27] The trappings of this revenge are decidedly of the old Kydian school and are without question imitated from Shakespeare's *Hamlet*.[28] An important innovation is made, to which the subtitle of the play—"The honest Man's Reuenge"—gives the clue. Chapman, in revolt against the bloodthirsty and hysterical Kydian hero, was shortly to create a Clermont D'Ambois who pursued his revenge by strictly honorable means. Tourneur goes farther than Chapman in his attack on the revenge tradition, and, adhering in every particular to the religious opinion of his day, produces a hero who is absolutely denied his revenge by the ghost of his murdered father and is strictly enjoined to

[26] "I will lay this maxime for my grounde, that pryde and vayne glory may produce Actions of bestially boldnes, but no man can haue true fortitude in ventering his life, who is not well resolued of the happy being of his soule after death," wrote Fynes Moryson in 1617. *Shakespeare's Europe,* ed. Hughes, p. 398.

[27] The increasing popularity of the villain in tragedy had already forecast some such reversal in the position of the two characters in the plot, even in so early a play as *Antonio's Revenge.*

[28] For an analysis of the plot, see A. H. Thorndike, "The Relations of *Hamlet* to the Contemporary Revenge Play," *PMLA,* Vol. XVII (1902), pp. 193-200; E. E. Stoll, *John Webster,* p. 112.

> Attend with patience the successe of things;
> But leaue reuenge vnto the King of kings.
>
> (II.vi)

The rôle of the revenging ghost is reversed, for when the apparition appears again it is not to urge on a sluggish revenger but to prevent Charlemont in the heat of his passion from executing a collective vengeance on the innocent Sebastian, younger son of D'Amville.

> Hold, *Charlemont!*
> Let him reuenge my murder, and thy wrongs,
> To whom the Iustice of Reuenge belongs.
>
> (III.ii)

The revenger, accordingly, has no choice but to suffer with what patience he can muster, under the double wrong of his own disinheritance and the murder of his father, until such time as Heaven wreaks its own vengeance. As Charlemont says (III.ii),

> You torture me betweene the passion of
> My bloud, and the religion of my soule,

and this conflict, following his one abortive outbreak, speedily reduces him to a suitable Kydian gloom without, however, its intermittent ecstasies. Barred from action, he loses interest in life and hopes only for death.

As a contrast to this quiescent figure, D'Amville plots with increasing success until finally the vengeance of Heaven falls: his two sons die, and he becomes distracted and kills himself by accident when about to administer the death blow to the unprotesting revenger. The relieved Charlemont quotes the moral of the tragedy:

> Onely to Heau'n I attribute the worke.
> Whose gracious motiues made me still forbeare
> To be mine owne Reuenger. Now I see
> That. *Patience is the honest mans reuenge.*
>
> (V.ii)

It was a platitude of theology for the opponents of revenge to repeat the biblical injunction to leave all vengeance to the Heavenly Revenger. The exact means by which God enacted His vengeance, however, were usually left to the imagination. Du Bartas contented himself with the affirmation of a providence which ruled men's lives:

> Gods sacred vengeance, serves not for defence
> Of his own *Essence* from our violence
> (For in the Heav'ns, above all reach of ours
> He dwels immur'd in diamantine Towrs);
> But, to direct our lives, and laws maintain,
> Guard Innocence, and Injury restrain.[29]

Thomas Wright (1601) shows that he believes in the direct intervention of God when he writes, "if his death were violent, or any way extraordinary, whereby it may bee gathered, that God extraordinarily rid the world of such a reprobate."[30]

Furthermore, offenders should not imagine themselves secure because they escaped for a time: "First, that in the preuention of worldly plots and stratagems he [God] commonly shews himselfe but at the last push, and seldome discouers our danger, till wee suppose our selues most secure" (1638).[31] Bishop Hall (1627) speaks of God as sometimes buffeting sinners "with their own hand . . . others with the fist of his dumb creatures,"[32] a circumstance closely parallel to the death of D'Amville. Several more contemporary comments on the direct vengeance of God will be reserved for the consideration of Massinger's *Unnatural Combat*, where they will prove more apposite.

Unquestionably Tourneur drew the leading theme for his play from the strong religious doctrines of the time. Yet Shakespeare's *Hamlet*, the influence of which is so dominant throughout the

[29] Joshua Sylvester, *Du Bartas His Diuine Weekes and Workes* (ed. 1641), p. 115.

[30] *Passions of the Minde* (ed. 1630), p. 270.

[31] Nathaniel Carpenter, *Achitophel, or the Picture of a wicked Politician* (1638), sig. D7.

[32] "Heaven Upon Earth," *Works,* ed. Wynter, Vol. VI, p. 20.

tragedy, may have given him the hint for the central situation. During his first appearance to Hamlet the ghost cautions him not to seek revenge on his mother but to leave her to Heaven and her own conscience. Later, in the cabinet scene when there is danger that Hamlet will forget this admonition, the ghost reappears to warn him. It seems very probable that Tourneur chose to elaborate into his main theme this hint given him in a minor situation by his master. The ghost's first admonition is taken over to cover Charlemont's religious course of action against his chief enemy, D'Amville. Shortly afterwards when Charlemont's fury is pressing him to forget the command, the ghost again appears, as in *Hamlet,* to enforce his behest.

What led Tourneur to this startling *volte-face?* We know that the traditional Kydian revenge play was so narrow in type that the form was not used by succeeding dramatists without considerable modifications in the treatment. It is possible that Tourneur was merely tinkering with the old machinery in order to produce a novel variation of an old theme which in essence was still popular. It is also probable that Tourneur, even more than Chapman, was in this play a reformer and moralist and that he was writing a propaganda tragedy with a religious hero and a higher moral to compete with the traditional amoral revenge play with its anomalous revenger. Where Chapman was to paint the revenge code of a well-bred gentleman, Tourneur produced the first tragedy to treat a revenge which in its action followed religious doctrine. *The Atheist's Tragedy,* with its insistence on the honesty of its revengeless hero, is one more indication that the convention of bloodthirsty revenge was no longer considered suitable as a motive for a hero.

Not only is the play one of the last of the Kydian tragedies until their partial revival toward the close of the Elizabethan period, but it also represents an intermediary stage in the final junction of the Marlowe and Kyd tradition. The two most conspicuous points of difference between the types lie in the choice of hero or of villain for protagonist and the cause—blood-revenge as a duty, or personal revenge for a real or fancied injury motivated by malice—which dictates that protagonist's distinct form of action.

Hoffman and *The Revenger's Tragedy* had endeavored to combine the most popular features of each form by fusing the two types of protagonists into one person who was revenger-hero, villain, and tool-villain rolled into one. The result, although the plays are interesting, was a moral chaos that could not long endure. Tourneur (following the line of development of *Titus Andronicus, Antonio's Revenge,* and to a slight extent *Claudius Tiberius Nero*) did not attempt a superimposition of such dissimilar material, but merely took over the most prominent features of each type and set them against each other, to form, theoretically, an ideal dramatic conflict. So the protagonist D'Amville is the popular villain motivated by malice and ambition; but forsaking the Marlovian formula in which this villain rises successfully and without appreciable opposition, Tourneur counterpoises the Kydian hero as an opposing force. The continual dramatic conflict of the Kydian tragedy, although the position of the two characters is reversed, replaces the single interest of the Marlovian form.

That *The Atheist's Tragedy* is imperfect results from the fact that theatrical morals had changed rapidly and that revenge, even in its purest form as an attempt at private justice for murder, was no longer a justifiable motive for a surviving hero. With Tourneur forced to substitute the vengeance of Heaven, his hero is made a motionless and undramatic figure and the greater part of the dramatic conflict is never realized. The possibilities of the general form, however, had been broached, and later dramatists were to develop and perfect Tourneur's uncertain experiment at counterpoising a revenging hero to a protagonist villain.

George Chapman's *Revenge of Bussy D'Ambois* was acted in 1610. By writing a sequel to his popular *Bussy D'Ambois* Chapman was forced to work in a form which was disagreeable to him. Superficially, therefore, the play agrees in purpose and structure with the older tragedies of revenge, but actually the spirit of Chapman, working in an uncongenial type, produced a work which turns upside down the most cherished conventions of the Kydian drama.

Traditionally, the revenger wanted revenge at any cost. Right and wrong, as with Hieronimo, were blurred by the lust for blood and the overwhelming passion for retaliation. As a consequence, such revenges as Hieronimo's, Titus's, and Antonio's were bloody in the extreme and were achieved by treachery and deceit. These hysterical men of blood and their melodramatic actions accorded ill with Chapman's correct idea of the dignity of the classical hero and the philosophical purpose of the dignified classical tragedy. The fevered action of the revenge play could have no place in his moral definition of tragedy prefixed to the drama: "Material instruction, elegant and sententious excitation to virtue, and deflection from the contrary, being the soul, limbs, and limits of an autentical tragedy." Even *Hamlet,* the greatest of the tragedies of revenge, would not answer to that description.[33]

Whereas *Hamlet* shows us the inner workings of a man's soul, Chapman's tragedy endeavors to teach virtue. Sufficient comment may be found about the Stoic doctrines of virtue on which Chapman founded the character of the revenger Clermont and which govern his actions. What has lacked general notice is that the conception of Clermont's revenge and his methods corresponds entirely to the ideals of the best English thought of the period, so that in the person of Clermont we have for the first time a stage-revenger who could be an English gentleman.

The law-abiding Englishman believed in allowing legal justice to right his wrongs. So Clermont at one point, weary with the importunities of his sister Charlotte, answers, "We must wreak our wrongs So as we take not more" (III.ii.103-4); in other words, a wrong cannot be righted by a murder which is outside the law. This question of taking the law into his own hands troubles him throughout. "I repent," he says, "(By any instigation

---

[33] T. M. Parrott, *The Tragedies of George Chapman* (New York: E. P. Dutton, 1910), p. 573.

in th'appearance My brothers spirit made, as I imagin'd) That e'er I yielded to revenge his murther . . . never private cause Should take on it the part of public laws" (III.ii.109-16).

The ethics of the revenge are finally resolved by the ghost of Bussy:

> To be His image is to do those things
> That make us deathless, which by death is only
> Doing those deeds that fit eternity;
> And those deeds are the perfecting that justice
> That makes the world last, which proportion is
> Of punishment and wreak for every wrong,
> As well as for right a reward as strong.
> Away, then! Use the means thou hast to right
> The wrong I suffer'd. What corrupted law
> Leaves unperform'd in kings, do thou supply,
> And be above them all in dignity.
>
> (V.i.89-99)

The sophistry of the first part of the ghost's address would not be accepted by any religious-minded Elizabethan, nor would the conclusion, since the prime tenet of his belief was that God would revenge all wrongs. Yet the courtier argued that private revenge was permissible in matters of honor where the court had no jurisdiction, and many more sober men were inclined to accept personal revenge as a regrettable necessity and a substitute for legal justice in times when the law was disrupted. Clermont, unable to secure justice from a corrupted court, would violate no point in the code of the Elizabethan gentleman by endeavoring to secure an honorable revenge in a private duel. Yet it must be remembered that Bussy was killed because of an adulterate union. Although this fact is conveniently ignored by Chapman, Clermont had no case in any court of justice, and, strictly viewed, his revenge was tainted from the start since it was conceived in an unjust cause.

But all this aside, Clermont somewhat reluctantly accepts the justice of his cause and endeavors to secure revenge like a gentleman. Montsurry's craven refusal of his challenge thereupon places him in a quandary. In the ordinary course of events the injured person's honor was held vindicated by the refusal of his adversary to fight, but this case was not one of simple personal injury to Clermont's own honor. Since Montsurry's action threatened to rob Clermont of revenge for murder, it could not be accepted. In such a case there is little doubt that the Elizabethan gentleman would have advocated open assassination by forcing his enemy to fight with equal weapons or else be slain outright. That indeed is the solution advocated by Clermont's friend Renel who is defending his scruples to Charlotte. Clermont's revenge, following this design, is entirely chivalrous. When Montsurry first lies on the floor and refuses to fight, Clermont spiritedly urges him to bravery and combat. On his continued refusal, Clermont, rather than soil his hands by stabbing a defenseless enemy, turns him over to a less finicky revenger, Montsurry's own wife, and when Montsurry is finally forced to action Clermont engages him as courteously and coolly as the purest of duelling etiquette prescribed. In contrast to Hamlet's action in forcing poison between the dying lips of the stabbed king, on Montsurry's death Clermont pronounces a benediction.

The last link that binds him to the England of the Stuarts is his refusal to attempt a revenge on the king for the murder of the Guise. This doctrine of the divine right of kings, so assiduously fostered by James, will be considered in its relation to the code of revenge in the account of *The Maid's Tragedy*.

Given Chapman's ideal of tragedy and of the tragic hero cast in the form of a Kydian revenge play, it was inevitable that various changes would be made. Superficially the play conforms to the standard pattern. A murder has been committed before the play opens. A ghost has called for vengeance, and the revenger has vowed requital. He is aided by a friend, finds obstacles in his path, hesitates, finally kills his enemy, and perishes. On closer examination, however, these conventional incidents are twisted to form a new pattern. First, the original murder was open and acknowledged; accordingly, there is never any doubt about the murderer. Then the audience misses the emotional shock of the appearance of the revelatory ghost since this episode and the revenger's vow are merely narrated. Next, the revenge is not the end-all and be-all of the revenger's existence. The traditional revenger had no other thoughts but of his vengeance; in fact, the continued brooding over his wrong and the problem of action was likely to turn him temporarily insane. Yet to Clermont his vow is not much more than a repugnant duty. He has many other concerns in life to attend to and many more pressing interests, as in his attachment to the Guise. The revenge is merely an episode and a rather disagreeable one at that. The obstacles in his path are not put there by the counter-intrigue of his intended victim but are chiefly caused by persons entirely unconnected with his revenge and relate to matters quite outside its province. His personal enemy is a shadow who is so wrapped up in his own self-preservation that he utterly neglects to set a counterplot on foot against the revenger. What interesting intrigue there is, therefore, has no connection with the revenge.

Thus while the revenge is the core of the play, most of the dramatic incidents that fill the time between the vow and the success of the revenge are unconcerned with its progress. Clermont and the Guise are of more moment than Clermont and Montsurry. The other revengers allied with Clermont are deliberately set aside at the start by his assumption of the duty, and, as far as direct action is concerned, are unimportant figures. Tamyra, who corresponds most closely in the plot to Bel-Imperia of *The Spanish Tragedy,* has little to do in the plan of the revenge and at its climax is, with Charlotte, simply a bystander. The hesitation of the revenger has no emotional dramatic value. Finally, the revenge is consummated according to the code of honor, and the audience is robbed of the thrill of an ingenious and exciting series of murders. The revenger is not killed in the dénouement of the revenge, and he commits suicide for reasons totally unconnected with his vengeance.

The philosophical and ethical content of this tragedy has often been emphasized.[34] It is entirely owing to this high ideal that Chapman wrote *The Revenge of Bussy D'Ambois* as it is. The inference follows that he did not approve of the ethics or manner of previous tragedies of revenge and that he was deliberately setting himself to raise the type by the infusion of a high dignity and a proper philosophy. The play is, in a sense, propaganda, and as such a dramatic failure. What is important, however, is not so much that Chapman the philosopher sought to elevate the tone of a revenge play by packing it with Stoic doctrines on the proper conduct of life in its various phases, as that he disapproved of the conventional bloody revenge acted on the stage and, as an ethical Englishman, wrote a tragedy which portrayed a revenge successfully carried through to its conclusion by a revenger acting according to the highest and most generous ideals of an English gentleman.

John Fletcher's *Valentinian,* dated 1610-1614, is almost completely a Kydian revenge tragedy, yet the changes Fletcher made in the form show once more that the pure Kydian type was not popular enough at this late date to warrant the portrayal of the protagonist as an entirely noble and justified revenger. *Valentinian* attests strongly to the fact that the Kydian motive as a mainspring for action was popular enough to be copied by such a fashionable dramatist as Fletcher, but that the old-fashioned Kydian characterization was not.

The central episode is entirely traditional in form, since it concerns the revenge taken by Maximus on his emperor Valentinian for the rape and suicide of his wife. The first two acts portray the injury, and the succeeding three the revenge. At the start, the development of this revenge is also Kydian. The shock turns Maximus slightly insane and delay is fostered by intense grief sapping his will to act. Further to accentuate the delay, Maximus is faced with the old problem of the Kydian revenger—the diffi-

---

[34] Parrott, *The Tragedies of George Chapman,* pp. 575-6.

culty encountered in securing vengeance on a more powerful person. Lastly, to clinch the matter, Fletcher adds the barrier of Divine Right, raising the problem of the justice of a revenge on one's king which he had already treated in *The Maid's Tragedy.* This situation is given a novel turn in *Valentinian,* for the delay is not occasioned by the revenger's own qualms of conscience (indeed, in the first scene he was shown as somewhat an iconoclast on the subject) but by the strong views of his best friend Aecius, who holds him back and at every opportunity puts obstacles in his path. To the standard list of physical and mental obstacles causing delay is added the new situation of mental conflict between loyalty to a friend and passion for revenge.

In the early action of the intrigue Maximus is as much a hero as Hamlet, but before long doubts arise about the perfect justice of his revenge. The Kydian revenger never thought of the injury to himself caused by the murder of his father or son but only of the outrageous injury to the slain victim. Maximus is revealed as a more self-centered individual who is about equally divided between grief for his wife and wrath that his own honor should be injured by a tyrant's lust and, if he hold back revenge, be subject to the idle gossip of the world. Hamlet was justified in seeking a means of revenge which would preserve himself, for his rights and his duty to his country demanded that he ascend the usurped throne. The purely private revenger, like Hieronimo, on the other hand, held his own safety precious only until it had secured him revenge, for the injury was such as to take away all desire for subsequent living. Maximus, suffering from just as severe a blow as Hieronimo, yet wishes to survive his vengeance by procuring "a safe revenge upon him" (III.iii).[35]

---

[35] The contrast with Hieronimo, however, is not so detrimental to Maximus as it might at first seem. Hieronimo was an old man who had little to live for after the death of his son. Maximus was a young and able soldier, at the height of his career, and could not have been expected to commit suicide simply because of the death of his wife. It is possible that Maximus's practical command to his wife to kill herself after her rape, while admirable according to Roman standards, was motivated to an extent by the lesson of the first scene in *Titus Andronicus* where Titus's stern Roman sense of duty forces him to an action which prevents the audience's whole-hearted sympathy for his later misfortunes.

The sturdy loyalty of Aecius to his emperor and his outspoken adherence to every tenet of the Divine Right of Kings, provides a contrast, as well, that makes just action by Maximus against Valentinian almost impossible. The parallel between Melantius of *The Maid's Tragedy* and Maximus will not hold. Melantius was a patriot and as such took every care to preserve his country from revolution and to deliver it safely into the hands of the next heir, despite his personal revenge on the king. Aecius, however, plainly warns Maximus that Rome, already shaking on its foundations, will suffer more than Valentinian if Maximus dares his revenge. No matter how secretly unimpressed the Elizabethan man in the street may have been by the doctrine of Divine Right, he would respond promptly to any suggestion of treason to his country, for he loved England itself more than he loved James. Aecius's appeal to patriotism over private wrong would strike to the audience's heart, and Maximus by his disregard of a loyalty higher than that accorded to a king would be considered extremely blameworthy in following his own private revenge at the expense of the ruin of his country.

Maximus, however, has the true blood-lust of the Kydian revenger. Just as Hieronimo by his excessive bloodiness became at the end a villain, so Maximus, led by his great love for his wife and an extreme regard for his own honor, exalts his vengeance not only over king and country but also over the sacred tie of friendship, and plans to wade to his revenge through the blood of his dearest friend Aecius who is the only insuperable obstacle.

Fletcher, who largely worked with the scene as a unit, was never over-careful of consistency in characterization if it interfered with a theatrical scene or emotion. Although the projected slaughter of his king and the ruin of his country give Maximus few qualms, the murder of his friend Aecius, once resolved, is attended with misgivings. Fletcher's inconsistency and straining of situation was never so absurd. Maximus, counting on Valentinian's bloodiness, incites his suspicions of Aecius by a forged letter in the knowledge that the tyrant will have Aecius killed and thus ironically remove the one remaining barrier to Maximus's re-

venge. Then when his plan succeeds, Maximus blames Valentinian for the result and promises Aecius revenge for the death to
which he himself has sent him.

> Goe worthy innocent, and make the number
> Of *Caesars* sins so great, Heaven may want mercy:
> I'le hover herabout to know what passes:
> And if he be so devilish to destroy thee,
> In thy bloud shall begin his Tragedy.—
>
> (IV.ii)

The absurdity is not altogether overshadowed by Maximus's sincere grief when he realizes too late just what he has done and
curses the motives which led him to plan revenge. But the die is
cast, his vengeance must be pursued, and in his stricken mood he
vows to follow his friend in death thereafter. His meditations on
the goodness of Aecius, designed to spur him to the deed, prove
so inflammatory to two of Aecius's young friends that without
his knowledge they take revenge from his hands, themselves kill
Valentinian, and commit suicide according to the stage tradition.

Maximus on his next appearance has not altered his mood. He
is horrified at the consequences of Valentinian's death, and, his
vengeance secured, sees nothing left for which to live. Once again
he realizes that his revenge will not stand the scrutiny of the
world because its means were definitely bad:

> Can any man discover this, and love me?
> For though my justice were as white as truth,
> My way was crooked to it, that condemns me.
>
> (V.iii)

He has encountered the problem which faced every bloody Kydian hero revenger and which none had solved without death or
retirement from the world as expiation. Maximus chooses death,
and is about to thrust his sword into his bosom when sudden
ambition assails him.

Now if that thrust had gone home, *Valentinian* would have
proved a complete Kydian tragedy with a hero who, beset by

overwhelming injuries, passionately—without thought of the consequences—carved out a correspondingly cruel and bloody revenge and was content to expiate by his own death the crimes which his headlong course had brought. Fletcher, writing in a more realistic age less liable to be swayed by the emotional storms of the Kydian tragedy of revenge, will not accept such a conclusion. The man had been so egoistic and callous that he had become a villain; therefore let him carry on his villainy and exhibit it for the benefit of the audience until he is shuffled off the stage by a good character so that there can be no mistake in the moral.

All consistency in characterization is accordingly sacrificed when, without any previous dramatic preparation, Maximus turns ambitious villain in truth and ascends the throne of the Caesars. Thereafter he becomes a stock villain with no relation to his former self. The worthy men of Rome dislike the choice, but with a complete turn about face Maximus cries, "If I rise, My wife was ravish'd well" (V.iii). Endeavoring to lure her with the pitiful lie that all was done for her sake, he forces Valentinian's widow, Eudoxia, to share the throne with him. He is fittingly poisoned at the coronation by his outraged victim who, after reciting the list of his crimes, is acclaimed with triumph for the deed. So ends the hero-revenger Maximus, and the failure of the attempt to carry the implications of the Kydian revenger to their last logical conclusion.

CHAPTER V

INTERLUDE: THE REIGN OF THE VILLAIN

I

*T*HE differences between *The Spanish Tragedy* and *Hamlet* on the one hand and *Hoffman* and *The Revenger's Tragedy* on the other, show that forces were at work which were to change the technique and spirit of tragedy. As the popularity of Kydian revenge tragedy ebbed, a new type of tragic drama developed in which vengeance for murder was no longer the emphasized theme. This new school of tragedy, which concerned itself chiefly with the depiction of villainy and horrors, had earlier been foreshadowed within the work of Kyd's imitators, but between 1607 and 1620 a series of plays which broke clean with the tradition established by Kyd held the stage.

The new trends which produced this change of type are clearly discernible even in the work of Marston, Chettle, and Tourneur. The coarse taste of the popular audience, already satiated with the rough and straightforward bloodshed of *The Spanish Tragedy,* demanded even more shocking scenes of blood and violence. The dramatists, therefore, exerted themselves to devise new and fiendishly horrible situations, fresh tortures, ingenious methods of poisoning, and gruesome scenes of depravity. With this portrayal of horror, strong enough to give a name to a new school of tragedy, went an increased emphasis on a complicated intrigue. Lastly, since he is the heart and soul of the intrigue, the opponent villain of Kyd is invariably raised to the position of protagonist. Strong sensation is substituted for strong emotion, and artificial points of honor for an inherent moral code.

The older Elizabethan drama of revenge was highly moral in that it raised (although infrequently attempted to solve) certain problems concerning man's life. The hero was set in a position which, as in *Hamlet,* wrenched his whole moral outlook. In *The Spanish Tragedy, Titus Andronicus,* and to an extent in *Antonio's Revenge,* tragedy came into the life of the hero with sufficient intensity to warp his character, drive him to insanity, and eventually to deal him ruin in victory. The type was, however, a narrow one, and the drift towards sensationalism and artificiality in the Jacobean age inevitably led audiences to demand more variety with less high seriousness. The people still wanted the highly colored and emotional declamation which had made the earlier plays so popular, but they preferred the more artificial, standardized, and hence less serious rhetoric of a villain to the essentially moral and real analysis of a tortured hero revenger. *Hoffman, The Revenger's Tragedy,* and to an extent *The Atheist's Tragedy* and *Valentinian,* had endeavored to cork the new wine in old bottles but without appreciable permanent success; indeed, nowhere is the fundamental disparity of the two philosophies more glaringly disparate than in Fletcher's tragedy. The trend was too strongly away from a worn-out convention.

For the subject matter of the new drama, themes were chosen in which the interest lay in violent, far-fetched, and surprising situations. Since these situations are what count, the typical play of this period is likely to be little more than a compilation of proved incidents without much heed paid to the methods of transition from one to another. The earlier tragedy had had its share of horrible incident but had used it as background material, as a testing ground for the human spirit. The violence of these new plays is portrayed for its own sake. Accordingly, since the horror itself is all-important, the reaction of the spirit is neglected and the characters on the stage are too frequently inadequate for the situation. The sound and fury is chiefly on the surface and characterization weakens and grows conventional, since it was sufficient for the dramatist—when the interest was held by the complicated intrigue—merely to portray types which would be recognizable.

Lacking the intellectual and emotional penetration in villainy of a Marlowe or a Shakespeare, the average author was content to outline characters who were merely the machinery for producing an arresting situation. This lack of sympathy from the author for his characters was transmitted to the audience, who viewed the play objectively and with only an intellectual interest in the types of persons presented to them. Emotions were not touched because the characters were not real.[1] An Elizabethan could identify himself with Hamlet or Hieronimo, in spite of the fact that he had never found himself in a similar situation, but he could view the actions of a Claudius Tiberius or a Mulleases only with objective indifference, appreciating the play merely in the successive thrills of horror at the violence of the action. His fancy could be caught by the melodrama; his emotions could not.

The growth of the interest in the portrayal of villainy, however, is the crux of the swing to action of horror, for to explain such creatures of evil it was necessary to exhibit horrors incredibly fantastic.[2] The blacker the villain, the more violent the horrors, and, usually, the more complex the intrigue. The difference between *The Spanish Tragedy* and *Titus Andronicus* is obvious. When this trend is carried to its logical conclusion we find either the compromise of *Hoffman* or else *The Atheist's Tragedy,* this last completing the reversal in importance of revenger and villain by presenting the revenger of blood as the opposing force to the protagonist villain. The interest in villains had succeeded in turning Kydian tragedy topsy-turvy.

One further element was to add to the importance placed on intrigue. Love in the Kydian tragedy had been confined either to the portrayal (though scarcely an extended one) of lust, as between the villain and the wife of his victim in *Hamlet,* or else to such idyllic interludes as in *The Spanish Tragedy.* The growing interest, as in *Antonio's Revenge,* in the love theme for itself as a motivating instead of a subsidiary element in the plot led naturally to a further complication and a greater fullness of plot interest as the driving force of tragic action.

[1] Several of these ideas are drawn from Agnes Mackenzie, *The Playgoer's Handbook* (London: Jonathan Cape, 1927), pp. 112-16.

[2] J. A. Symonds, *Shakespeare's Predecessors in the English Drama,* p. 45.

From the start the Elizabethan villain had been entirely self-conscious and entirely black, a complete embodiment of evil.[3] With the growing consciousness that revenge was evil, revengefulness—particularly for injuries less than blood—became almost exclusively a villainous characteristic. But villains were equipped with other motives than pure revengefulness. Envy, misanthropy, and especially ambition, often hold the stage almost unchallenged. The depiction of Italianate villainy undoubtedly received a strong impulse from the characters of the Italian stories to which the dramatists were turning ever more frequently for their plots.[4] It must be noticed that many of the proved theatrical incidents of Kyd are retained in the new tragedy. Accomplices are still tricked and murdered, a revenger of blood may appear (in the opponent's rôle), and the lust of the murderer for his victim's wife or daughter is frequently important as a mainspring of action. But if separate incidents and themes are reminiscent of the older drama, the form had changed decidedly, and a multiplicity of plot formulas have replaced the simple thread of the Kydian central situation.

The Machiavellian is, first of all, the protagonist. Revenge may be the driving force of his actions from the start, but more often it enters later and is allied with other motives such as ambition. Almost without exception the villain's revenge is for real or fancied injury rather than for murder, and frequently there is more than one revenger, for the accomplice may have his own private grudge to settle and may even turn against his master. The older serious meditation turns to invectives against the vices of the age. The ghost usually has no place, and hesitation is seldom presented. Insanity may play its part but is confined to a minor character. Since the revenge is conceived more from

---

[3] E. E. Stoll, *Shakespeare Studies* (New York: Macmillan Co., 1927), pp. 342-6, 349, 378 ff., 398 ff.

[4] See Vernon Lee's penetrating essay on "The Italy of the Elizabethan Dramatists" in her *Euphorion* (London: T. Fisher Unwin, 1884); and Creizenach, *The English Drama,* pp. 195, 219.

malice than duty and is combined with other motives, the interest of the audience is less concerned with the workings of the villain's revenge as a revenge than with the depiction of lust, villainy, and horror. As a consequence, revenge tends to be overshadowed by emphasis on situation and intrigue in spite of its real importance to the basic structure of the plot. The type of the revenge has some bearing on the construction of the play. There are revenges for simple insult or injury, the horrible revenges taken for adultery, the revenge of a cruel tyrant, and the revenge of an ambitious villain on those thwarting his rise. Often these various types are not separated and distinct but are united in one character or appear side by side in various characters.

Such plays as Marlowe's *Jew of Malta,* and *Alphonsus, Emperor of Germany* and *Lust's Dominion*, are early forerunners of the new school. Indeed, Marlowe has been called the sole progenitor of the type. The question will be considered later, but it may be said briefly that in general the Marlovian influence has been exaggerated and that the villain plays are a logical development of the old revenge play, with Shakespeare in *Titus Andronicus* and Marston in *The Malcontent* the important intermediaries.

2

The anonymous *Tragedy of Tiberius (c.* 1607) combines the theme dealing with the rise of an ambitious villain with that treating the atrocities of a tyrant and the final revenge taken on him. In this hybrid but popular type the customary pattern includes a villain who, as the accomplice of a villainous and insecure tyrant, urges him on to kill off all possible claimants to the throne. The accomplice, pretending to be the tyrant's tool, is actually the master, and as soon as the path is cleared for him plans to overthrow the tyrant and secure the throne for himself. Such a tyrant goes back on the Elizabethan stage at least as far as Preston's *Cambises*; he became a stock figure in such early plays as *Selimus,* and entered the Kydian form in *Alphonsus, Emperor of Germany* about 1597. This last play seems to have derived its chief inspiration from the early *Hamlet* with its usurper king and tool revenger Leonhardus.[5]

The accomplice Sejanus in *Tiberius* has little relation to Alexander of *Alphonsus,* but stems instead from the title character of Ben Jonson's *Sejanus* (1603) who was quickly Italianized as Mendoza in Marston's *Malcontent.* Such earlier villains as Aaron had taken pride in their artistry, but none had quite approached Sejanus in the scope of his evil plots.[6] Simple raw murder, as in the scheme of the insecure cave, is not enough; he must manipulate his victims by his intellectual ingenuity into destroying each other. Tiberius must kill his own son; the sons of Germanicus, Tiberius. For his own secret purposes he plays on the passions of Tiberius as on an instrument.

The ambitious intrigues of this accomplice villain bear the weight of the plot. Only one intrigue is motivated by private revenge: Sejanus bears a grudge for an unrequited injury against Drusus, the son of Tiberius. This grudge is not forgotten in the maze of intrigues against the other persons eligible for the throne. He secures a part of his vengeance by cuckolding Drusus, and then lays plans for his destruction. These compose the most elaborate scheme of the play and introduce a new situation to revenge tragedy: the murder of a victim by one dear to him who has been tricked into believing him an enemy. Thus Tiberius, infuriated by the false reports of Sejanus that Drusus was to poison him, forces the innocent Drusus to drink the poisoned wine which Sejanus says Drusus had prepared for Tiberius.

It is characteristic of the plays of the period that the author, having interested the audience with the various involved schemes successfully carried through by Sejanus, stumbles sadly in hastily

---

[5] For new facts about this play, see T. Starck, "The German Dialogue in *Alphonsus, Emperor of Germany*" and F. T. Bowers, "The Date and Composition of *Alphonsus, Emperor of Germany*" in *Harvard Studies and Notes,* Vol. XV (1933), pp. 147-90; F. T. Bowers, *"Alphonsus, Emperor of Germany* and the *Ur-Hamlet,"* MLN, Vol. XLVIII (1933), pp. 101-8.

[6] Tourneur's desperate attempt a few years later in *The Atheist's Tragedy* was more successful in the division of interest but failed because the device to soft pedal the revenger contrived to make him no revenger at all.

dramatizing his downfall. The bold and crafty Sejanus who tricks Tiberius into killing his son and who toys with the poisoned Julia is a vastly different person from the shabby rascal whose pitiful devices in the conclusion are so clearly discerned by the sons of Germanicus. This last episode, together with the hurried ending with its set horrors when each character takes his turn at dying, indicates all too clearly the loose hold on characterization when the insistence is on strong action.

The muddle in the author's mind is nowhere so apparent as in his treatment of the opposing force, here the blood-revenge of Caligula for the death of his father Germanicus. Feeling his way in an unfamiliar medium, the author has tried to retain the popular feature of the old tragedy, blood-revenge by a hero, which, however, is used as the counter instead of the main action. The result in unsteady hands is pure incoherence. If elaborated the revenge would secure so much of the audience's interest and sympathy that it would conflict with the avowed purpose of the play, the depiction of villainy. Consequently, the skeleton treatment awarded Caligula produces a caricature of the Kydian revenger with all that person's inherent dramatic weaknesses and none of his virtues. Caligula's unwarranted feigning of madness merits nothing but contempt, as does the excessive secrecy and regard for his own person forced upon him by the absolute necessity to delay for the external reasons of plot.

This weakness of touch is communicated directly to every other turn of the plot. The division of dramatic interest between the two major villains and a revenger of blood who was a minor character, was beyond the author's grasp. The numerous traditional incidents taken from earlier revenge tragedy are presented in such a conventionalized manner as to lose entirely their dynamic place in plot and characterization. The two villains are each so important that they confuse the plot-scheme, which consequently fails to afford a clear-cut issue and a continuous line of action and conflict. Part of this lack is undoubtedly owing to the apparent belief of the author that unconnected scenes of horror and blood were in themselves sufficient to produce a successful tragedy. *Tiberius* thus stands at the crossroads between the tragedy of Kyd and the new tragedy of the villain. It made a desperate attempt to combine the two forms, but the older elements in the plot are futile and the newer are still to be fused into a coherent whole.

3

Three characteristic plays of this period—John Mason's *Turk,* Middleton's *Women Beware Women,* and Thomas Drue's *Bloody Banquet*—may be selected as examples of the use of revenge-motives in the villain play.

The Turk (1607-1608) involves a maze of intrigues and revenges set in a new plot structure which was to prove extremely popular in later years. Two allied villains, using tools for their agents, each scheme secretly for the same object, come to cross-purposes, and destroy each other. Borgias schemes to gain the throne of Florence by destroying the Dukes of Venice and Ferrara and by marrying the Duchess Julia once his own wife Timoclea has been poisoned. Mulleases, the Turk, is apparently his accomplice in these schemes, but actually works against his master in order to secure the throne for himself. He secretly exposes her husband to Timoclea and uses her revenge as his means of destroying Borgias. Borgias, trapped, feigns death and starts his counter-revenge by killing Timoclea. Planning to accuse his former accomplice of this murder, he bursts in on Mulleases, already trapped by the Duke of Venice, and receives his death at the hands of the Turk but not before he has dealt him a mortal wound.

The major portion of the intrigue concerns the ambitious schemes of the villains which towards the end turn to mutual revenge. Revenge is freely used by these villains, however, to incite their accomplices to action. The good characters have little vital place in the action and prove only an indirect force in bringing about the catastrophe; for example, the efforts of the Duke of Venice, the hero, to revenge the supposed death of Julia are chiefly rhetorical. Ferrara, indeed, endeavors to perform some definite actions, but since he is burdened with the blood-guilt for the accidental death of Eunuchus, he falls a victim to Borgias.

Venice is made aware of the true nature of the plots with which he has been tricked by the merest accident of recognizing the supposedly dead Timoclea as the impersonator of Julia's ghost and by hearing Julia's shouts for help when Mulleases tries to rape her. Even then the situation is deadlocked until the appearance of Borgias draws Mulleases away from his human shield.

The revenge of Timoclea, the earliest and most important in the play, has no relation to the dénouement and is utilized merely to provide a series of incidents in the working-out of Mulleases' ambitious intrigue. The revenge of Ferrara for the supposed death of Julia ends in disaster. The parallel revenge of Venice is almost motionless and serves only to assure the audience that one of the good characters is working in the interests of justice. Finally, the villainous revenge of Borgias, conceived only in the last scene of the fourth act, provides the catastrophe, and is the only revenge in the play which is successful, even though the revenger strikes in self-defense and, as in *Hamlet,* after he has been mortally wounded. The sympathetic characters, since revenge has been actually removed from their hands, survive the play.

In the midst of the emphasis on pure intrigue it is interesting to note briefly the pervading influence, especially in the supernatural scenes, of conventions from the older revenge play. The appearances of the supposed ghosts are portrayed with the full panoply of *Hamlet,* to which there are verbal parallels; the choice of an infidel Turk as the protagonist would alone suggest *Titus Andronicus* and *Lust's Dominion,* even without the parallels of his lustful relations with the woman revenger.[7] Lastly, the great and frequent stress put on highly rhetorical speeches of blood and vengeance shows clearly that the convention of revenge, even in its new setting, was still a moving device to a theater audience.

The villain play *Claudius Tiberius Nero* was still so much under Kydian influence that it employed the revenge of a sym-

---

[7] For one incident especially reminiscent of *Titus Andronicus,* see Act III, sc. 4, where the lustful Timoclea importunes the impatient Mulleases.

pathetic character to dispose of the villain and end the play. *The Turk* followed the formula of *Alphonsus, Emperor of Germany*, but more especially of *The Malcontent*, in forming its catastrophe from the mutual revenges of two villains. This device was perfected in Thomas Middleton's first tragedy *Women Beware Women*, produced in 1613. The depiction of lust, one of the minor dramatic strands of Kydian tragedy which had become increasingly important in succeeding plays, here assumes a commanding position as the mainspring of the plot and the object of the drama's moral. Another of Kyd's conventions, the desperately revengeful woman, is taken over; and on these two minor elements of the old tragedy Middleton built his play.

In characterization he has followed the example of *The White Devil*, but with less artistry. His people are all either villains or fools; consequently, each revenge is bad in conception and execution. Since lust is the predominant motive there can be no delay by the revenger to fill up the action, nor can an elaborate and intriguing course of revenge complicate the play, for the motive of lust is not sufficiently dignified for such a full treatment. Therefore the chief interest of the tragedy lies in the new problem of construction forced upon the dramatist by the necessity for elaborating what had previously been material of subsidiary importance.

Middleton solved the problem by carefully interweaving three separate plots in such a skilful manner that the play is a coherent whole and never at a loss for appropriate action. Other tragedies—such as *The Second Maiden's Tragedy*—which were prevented by the simplicity of the central revenge from attaining sufficient complication of plot, had experimented with double plots very loosely linked, each containing its own revenge. Middleton, however, was the first dramatist to use as many as three different revenges, each one separate from the other and yet so interdependent that the chain of cause and effect is never broken.

Lust caused the Duke of Florence to seduce Bianca. Lust overcame the scruples of Isabella and Hippolito and flung them into incestuous union. Lust persuaded Livia to entertain Leantio as her lover. The threats of Livia's outraged husband caused the duke, through Bianca, to utilize Hippolito, wrathful at the affair between his sister and Leantio, as a tool to murder the inconvenient Leantio.[8] This initial murder, brought on by lust, begins the string of subsequent revenges. As a consequence of the murder of her lover, Livia reveals the awful secret of Hippolito's incest with Isabella. This news provokes the revenge of Guardiano for the injury done his Ward by the marriage with Isabella, to which Livia links her own revenge on Hippolito for the murder of Leantio. Livia's discovery of the incestuous pair causes the counter-revenge of Isabella. The cardinal's initial displeasure at his brother's adultery with Bianca hastens the death of Leantio so that the duke and Bianca may marry; but when the cardinal endeavors also to halt the marriage, Bianca determines to poison him to earn her future security.

These three murderous plots all result from Leantio's death caused by the lust of the duke and Bianca. To conclude this ingenious example of plot unity, all three revenge plots converge on an elaborated Kydian masque in honor of the duke's marriage to Bianca. Isabella's counter-revenge succeeds in killing Livia by the fumes from a poisoned torch although she herself perishes from the device. Guardiano is also slain ironically when, in a manner reminiscent of *The Jew of Malta,* he falls through the trapdoor onto the spikes he has prepared for Hippolito. But the two revengers' plan functions despite their deaths, and Hippolito, pierced by the poisoned arrows in the masque, runs on a sword to end his agony. Lastly, Middleton follows the popular account of Bianca Capello, Duchess of Florence, and depicts the back-firing of Bianca's schemes which results in the poisoning of the duke instead of the cardinal and in her subsequent suicide.

---

[8] The safer method of substituting a gulled but honest revenger for a paid tool villain to remove inconvenient opponents was a popular dramatic device with villains, as witness *Alphonsus, Emperor of Germany, Hoffman, The Malcontent, The Revenger's Tragedy, Claudius Tiberius Nero,* and *The Turk.* A variation on this, as when Vindici in *The Revenger's Tragedy* sends Lussurioso raging to destroy the supposed corrupter of the duchess, was produced by the hope that the tricked revenger would destroy himself in the process.

Middleton's contribution on his first appearance as a tragic writer, then, concerned itself chiefly with the ordering of the plot. Like the author of *The White Devil* he took over a sensational Italian story based on true life and elaborated it by the expansion of material which had always been a part of revenge tragedy. But sensationalism of incident and interweaving of plot failed to take the place of Webster's mastery of characterization. Middleton reaffirmed the importance of the masque play-within-a-play as a setting for a dramatic catastrophe, and popularized the device of the backfiring of revenge which had been associated with the revenge play since the *Ur-Hamlet*.

Although *Women Beware Women* is emphatically a villain play, and one that exploits the character of the revengeful villainess to the full, curiously enough it is so overrun with evil characters, each with his own particular grudge to revenge, that it lacks a real villain protagonist. The popular portrayal of lust, intrigue, and villainy, however, does not overshadow the importance of revenge to the plot. The first three acts present the necessary exposition and preparation. With the start of Act IV the train of revenge is laid and the revengeful plots absorb the whole interest of the audience until the dénouement. In its own form *Women Beware Women* has as much right to be called a revenge tragedy as *The Spanish Tragedy*.

Thomas Drue's *Bloody Banquet* (1620), as its title indicates, rested its hope for popularity on the horror of a human banquet, an incident from Seneca taken over by Kydian tragedy. There are verbal reminiscences of Shakespeare's *Hamlet,* the accomplice Roxano is disposed of with grim Kydian irony, and considerable interest is evinced in the damnation of the victims' souls. But these are merely the trappings of the older drama, for the play is simply a variation on the standard tyrant play of the type of *Claudius Tiberius Nero.* A villainous accomplice Mazeres schemes to overthrow his tyrant master. Revengeful plots are thus motivated by ambition and set in a framework of Fletcherian lustful intrigue. The usual counter-revenge swiftly destroys the villain but the revenger is himself killed by his sister in revenge for Mazeres. The human banquet concludes the play with the slaughter of the only remaining characters.

The atmosphere of easy licentiousness and the lack of moral reserves in the characters, together with the emphasis on a succession of strong theatrical scenes fundamentally unmotivated, exhibit clearly the influence of Fletcher. Such a villain play is completely released from the ethics of the Kydian form, even from the lip service paid by *Claudius Tiberius Nero*. Lust, ambition, revenge, all under the aegis of villainy, interlace in a hodgepodge of startling scenes. Without Middleton's firm grasp on character and situation there comes inevitably a disintegration. The audience cannot tell what to think about any character, since heroes are changed to villains in a flash and back again. Accordingly, the audience does not care. Theatrical fireworks engage the careless attention, galvanic shocks jerk the play forward to its culminating scene of vicious horror. This is the true amoral tragedy.

4

The Second Maiden's Tragedy and *Thierry and Theodoret* illustrate from their opposite poles the weakening of the Kydian formula during these years. The anonymous *Second Maiden's Tragedy* in 1611 attempts to dramatize two entirely unconnected plots of revenge. The first of these treats the story of Govianus, the Lady, and the Tyrant, and the revenge taken by Govianus on the Tyrant for the desecration of the dead body of the Lady. The second deals with the revenge of Bellarius on Votarius for an unnamed injury. It is in the story of Govianus that the closest resemblances to Kydian tragedy are found, since the underplot of Bellarius is no more than a comic *novella* story equipped with a tragic ending.

For the trappings of the main plot the author borrows, with no functional purpose in mind, from Shakespeare's *Hamlet, The Jew of Malta, Antonio's Revenge, The Malcontent,* but especially from *The Revenger's Tragedy* and *The Atheist's Tragedy.* Yet all these externals of blood and thunder tragedy are used simply as atmosphere for a sentimental romance. Govianus's Lady kills herself to escape the lustful advances of the Tyrant who has usurped Govianus's throne; Govianus entertains no thought of revenge until his Lady's ghost rises before him. She has come, however, with no demand for vengeance but simply to disclose the theft of her body. Govianus promises to restore her corpse to its tomb or else lose his life, and sensibly walks off to consult his brother about a plan of campaign.

The hysteria of the revenger at the appearance of the ghost is entirely missing; instead the lyrical atmosphere of the romantic love of Govianus and his Lady is emphasized, a romance so high-flown that Govianus delays vengeance at one point for the pure delight of seeing the ghost of his beloved again. It is only on her second appearance when, still unflurried, he has resolved to obey the spirit without more ado, that he definitely speaks of his course of action as a revenge. With a complete absence of dramatic internal conflict, he sets out and kills the Tyrant by a trick of cruel and ghastly irony; yet this revenge is motivated by no overwhelming passion for personal retribution, and in obedience to the ghost's command the revenger survives the catastrophe.[9]

The softening of the revenge motive is aided by the lyrical tone of the play's romantic story. Since the Lady is the first female ghost to appear to a revenger, the atmosphere of tender sentimentality would have been destroyed by having such a gentle spirit call for blood and vengeance. Her simple request, therefore, concerns only the proper burial of her body. Masque-like spectacle displaces the rough and gloomy horrors of the Marstonian form of tragedy up to the catastrophe where a ghastly scene of horror marks the fall of the Tyrant.

[9] The lack of turmoil in the whole idyllic atmosphere of the play makes this ending suitable, in spite of the fact that Govianus is twice stained with blood. The sudden stabbing of Sophonirus is prepared for by the earlier incident in which Govianus pretends to pistol Helvetius sent on the same errand. Presumably, since Govianus was king in theory he would be considered justified in killing any of the adherents of the usurper, or even the usurper himself. Since a king, according to the doctrine of Divine Right, was above all earthly laws, so, perhaps, Govianus escapes from the consequences.

If the author of *The Second Maiden's Tragedy* persistently refused to allow Kydian revenge to disrupt the idyllic atmosphere of his sentimental romance contrasted with the villainous plots of the Tyrant, the collaborators in *Thierry and Theodoret* (of uncertain date) were equally firm in excluding it from their fast-moving and complicated tale of villainy. Fletcher and Massinger construct a pure villain tragedy concerned with the ambitious machinations of Brunhalt whose lust for power is so great that she cheerfully murders both her sons who stand in her path. The main interest lies in the intrigues of Brunhalt and in the tragic accidents which result. Actual revenge plays such an extremely unimportant part as a motivation for action that it is limited to Brunhalt's murder of Theodoret, who had first infuriated her by his strictures on her vicious life and who was an ever-present danger to the continuance of her sway over her other son Thierry. This revenge is achieved at the start of the third act, yet the murder has no repercussions and but the slightest effect on the future ordering of the plot.

Indeed, the plotting of the whole play is thrown together in a curious fashion. Traditional characters of revenge tragedy appear, situations are begun which would normally lead to revenge as the motivation for the future course of action, and then nothing happens. The play is cluttered with type characters and stock situations which have no apparent reason for their being, since they are never utilized, except that they are dramatic conventions. Every revenge situation for which the author seems to prepare the audience is without its conclusion. Ordella does not revenge herself—even so mildly as Massinger's later duchess of Milan—on her betrothed husband Thierry when he attempts to murder her. Further, since she is unconscious of Brunhalt's plot against her, she is completely neglected as a revenger. Thierry, by refusing to believe Brunhalt's final avowal of Theodoret's legitimacy, cannot be the revenger for the murder of his brother which he has been led to condone. Martel, the close friend of the murdered Theodoret and an intimate of his daughter Memberge, makes no move to revenge, and cheerfully takes service under the master who has refused to prosecute Theodoret's death.

Lastly, considerable pains have been taken to prepare the audience for Memberge in the rôle of revenger for her slain father. But after her first furious demand to Thierry for vengeance, a scene in which she seems willing to contemplate incest with him if it will procure revenge, she does not appear again until it is time to stand mute beside the bed of the dying Thierry and receive Martel as a husband.

Middleton had been vitally dependent upon revenge for the motivation of a plot of villainous intrigue, and even such a writer as Thomas Drue recognized its value. The author of *The Second Maiden's Tragedy* had softened the theme so that revenge was not so much personal retaliation as a simple recovery of one's right, but Fletcher and Massinger here entirely disown its necessity. With all the smoke in their plot, there has been no fire; the dramatists really fail by promising in the exposition what is not delivered in the catastrophe. This unfulfilled promise makes for a lack of satisfaction with the play, and certainly for an unintegrated and confused plot. Whatever the reason—whether the collaboration was not smooth, or the dramatists erroneously believed that revenge was no longer effective as dramatic motivation, or whether the play was too hastily written to bother with a linked plot of cause and effect—*Thierry and Theodoret* presents an interesting example of pure villainy entirely usurping the normal interest in revenge as a motivation for tragic action.

5

The Maid's Tragedy, written by Beaumont and Fletcher and dated prior to 1611, is not properly a villain tragedy, although it does contain several strong portraits. Its chief interest here lies in the introduction of a strain of romance in tragedy, a feature quickly caught up by other dramatists as in *The Second Maiden's Tragedy*; the emphasis on theatrical situations without much regard for consistent characterization, a facile trick which thereafter was the curse of minor playwrights; and, more specifically, the popularization of the problem arising from the clash of blood-revenge with the doctrine of the Divine Right of Kings.[10]

This last topic was a timely one, for the matter of the assassination of kings was giving England many uneasy moments. Various attempts had been made on Queen Elizabeth's life; the celebrated Gunpowder plot of 1605, suspected as coming from the Jesuits, was still vividly fresh; and the murder of Henry IV by Ravaillac in 1610 caused a new wave of fear. King-killing and popery were closely allied in English minds,[11] and they recognized that dangerous ideas could be gained from classical accounts of tyrannicides[12] and from Italian doctrines.[13]

The popular trust in absolute monarchy in England reached its peak near the close of Elizabeth's reign;[14] and in consideration of the power conceded the queen, it is at first surprising to find very little expression in her reign of the *Jus Divinum*. She herself firmly believed in the theory, but with the realization of the instability of her claim to the throne her Tudor sagacity prompted her not to press views which might prove a double-edged weapon. Not so James. In the year 1598, five years before he inherited the throne of England, James wrote his *Trew Law of Free Monarchies,* the first and most comprehensive of his political writings and the first complete pronouncement of the supreme monarchical theory which had arisen out of Tudor absolutism. Throughout his reign in England he boldly maintained the strict doctrine

[10] For a summary of the doctrine, see J. N. Figgis, *The Theory of the Divine Right of Kings* (Cambridge at the University Press, 1922), p. 5.

[11] J. B., *The Coppie of a Late Decree of the Sorbone . . . touching the murthering of Princes* (1610), sigs. B₁ᵛ-B₂.

[12] Hobbes, *Leviathan,* ed. Waller, Chap. XXIX, p. 237; Sir Thomas Elyot, *The Book called the Governour,* ed. Eliot, Book III, Chap. VI, pp. 193-4; T. B. Howell, *State Trials,* Vol. III, p. 579; Francis Osborne, "A Discourse upon Piso," *Works* (ed. 1673), p. 373.

[13] Joseph Hall, "Quo Vadis? A Just Censure of Travel," *Works,* ed. Wynter, Vol. IX, pp. 556-7.

[14] As an instance of the extreme lengths to which the theory was pushed, the lawyer Richard Crompton declared in 1587 that since kings were ordained to govern, subjects must submit to all their ordinances although these should be against the very word of God. *A Declaration of the End of Traitors* (1587), sig. B₄.

of Divine Right. In his *Defence of the Right of Kings* he declared that kings were "the breathing images of God upon earth." They were not only "God's lieutenants upon earth" and "sat upon his throne" but even by God Himself they were "called Gods." Kings may "make and unmake their subjects: they have power of raising, and casting down; of life, and of death. . . . To Emperors or Kings that are Monarches, their subjects bodies and goods are due for their defence and maintenance."[15]

No matter what sins the king committed, he was subject only to divine, not to human justice,[16] and no subject should so shake off his obedience as to contemplate a private revenge.[17] This doctrine of absolute and passive submission was re-enforced by the idea that a tyrant was sometimes chosen by God in order to punish the sins of the people. Tyrants, accordingly, must be suffered with patience. George Whetstone (1586) says roundly, "He that resisteth because the king is a tyrant encreaseth his sinnes, and doubleth Gods wrath, who sendeth Tyrants to punish the sinnes of the wicked."[18] Any other view led to punishment, since no loophole was left to evade the doctrine of passive obedience and non-resistance. In 1615 one Owen was condemned to death in England merely for maintaining that it was as lawful for any man to kill an excommunicated king as for a hangman to execute a condemned person.[19] In 1622 "Mr. Knight, a public lecturer at Carfois in Oxford, taught that people might withstand their prince, in case he should compel them to idolatry, or offer violence against them in that case, as Rochell doth. And being called in question thereof, he vouched Paraeus upon Romans xiii; whereupon he was committed, and M. Paraeus's

---

[15] *The Political Works of James I,* ed. McIlwain (Harvard University Press, 1918), pp. 248, 307, 308.

[16] John Dunster, *Caesars Penny, or a Sermon of Obedience* (1610), p. 15.

[17] "Crumms fal'n from King James's Table," *Miscellaneous Works of Sir Thomas Overbury,* ed. Rimbault (London, 1856), p. 268.

[18] *The English Myrror* (1586), p. 202. See also, Dunster, *Caesars Penny* (1610), p. 3; Thomas Becon, *The Catechism,* ed. Ayre, p. 302; Richard Clerke, *Sermons* (1637), p. 224; John Norris, *Christian Blessedness* (ed. 1692), pp. 74-5.

[19] Thomas Birch, *The Court and Times of James the First,* Vol. I, pp. 362-3.

book upon the Romans burned by spiritual command at Oxford, and others in London.[20]

In view of the strong feeling of the times, *The Maid's Tragedy* dealt with an extremely ticklish subject when it portrayed the personal revenge of a subject on a king. The opinion still existed, moreover, that it was dangerous to allow the stage to suggest such deeds to an audience.[21] The manner in which the authors constructed their play so as to avoid giving offense[22] is an interesting example of their fluid morality. There are two logical revengers: Amintor and Melantius. Amintor, the man most deliberately and personally injured by the king, refuses with theatrical loyalty to lift a hand in vengeance against his traitorous sovereign. An unquestioning adherent of the *Jus Divinum*, he shrinks from obtaining justice at the expense of God's anointed. The character is saved from ludicrousness only by the occasional futile outbursts which show Amintor's underlying manhood. In one instance he actually draws his sword against the king, only to be charmed

> there is
> Divinity about you, that strikes dead
> My rising passions.

Again he bursts out:

> A Baud! hold my breast, a bitter curse
> Seize me, if I forget not all respects
> That are Religious, on another word
> Sounded like that, and through a Sea of sins
> Will wade to my revenge, though I should call
> Pains here, and after life upon my soul.

Finally, a fresh insult shatters the last remnants of his control and he is rushing sword in hand to secure vengeance when dissuaded

---

[20] Walter Yonge, *Diary,* ed. G. Roberts (Camden Society, 1848), pp. 61-2.

[21] J. Greene, *A Refutation of the Apology for Actors* (1615), p. 25.

[22] For proof that this point was not theoretical, see James's perturbation when a play touching the murder of a ruler was acted before him in 1620. *Calendar of State Papers Venetian (1619-1620)*, Vol. XVI, p. 111.

by Melantius, who fears the sudden overthrow of his own carefully laid plans.

Here is manifestly a new, fashionable, and decidedly original motivation for delay in vengeance, and Beaumont and Fletcher with their delight in artificial and strained situations play it to the hilt. Certainly in its own artificial way this motivation produced scenes fully as effective theatrically as did the motives for delay treated in earlier plays. The revenger does not hesitate because of lack of knowledge or opportunity, or of partial insanity caused by a too full realization of the enormity of his task; but instead from the very fact that he knows his enemy and that it would be both high treason and a religious crime to act other than "passive obedience" with "sighs and tears." The conflict in his mind is, theoretically, put on the high plane of struggle between every natural impulse of earthly man and the strict code of human and divine law, intensified by the special circumstances of the doctrine of Divine Right.

Amintor, as the hero of the play, cannot relinquish his revenge too easily without losing his manliness and yet cannot take revenge without becoming an arrant villain. A character of Elizabethan tragedy in the clutch of two such strong and opposite forces is naturally marked for death because there is no solution to either. The specific reason for his death is found in his broken betrothal to Aspatia: even at the orders of his sovereign, this was a crime which in tragedy could not go unrequited. Further to justify his death he is saddled, although unknowingly, with the blood-guilt for slaying the disguised Aspatia, and his subsequent suicide is his only possible course. If this had been a Kydian tragedy Amintor would have slain the king before his own death, but he is too romantic a figure finally to turn bloody revenger and villain, and the revenge is left to other hands.

In searching for a revenger the dramatists resorted to the Italianate convention of relationship by which the family of the guilty woman took an equal concern in her honor with the husband. Thus Melantius, Evadne's brother and close friend of Amintor, becomes the logical revenger. In the early scenes his character is skilfully prepared for the part he is to play. An exceedingly proud and choleric man, who is used to command and cannot brook opposition, he is a soldier with the military's touchy honor and therefore a man accustomed to direct and forceful methods of maintaining that honor. In contrast to Amintor who is a courtier of the king, Melantius by his prowess in the field is the chief defender and preserver of his country. In a sense, then, he is endowed with royal attributes which the unworthy king has relinquished in favor of a voluptuous life.

This last point is of some importance, since Melantius, who plans the revenge and is an accessory before the fact to the murder of his sovereign, survives at the close of the play and is not held blameworthy by the new ruler. Three matters made it possible for Beaumont and Fletcher to draw Melantius as a hero. His whole attitude, without hesitation from start to finish, shows that his deserts, while incapable of changing his rank as a subject loyal to the dynasty, have placed him on a higher level of equality with this one king than Amintor, so that he occupies a position important enough to justify the direction of a private revenge on his monarch. Theoretically, of course, no such position was tenable under Divine Right unless the avenger felt himself to be an agent of God sent by divine mission to remove a wicked king, an errand to which Melantius never pretends. Secondly, he is no traitor to his country. He has no thought of usurping the rule, and, in a sense, by his armed revolt holds the country in trust for the next lawful heir. That the new ruler offers him amnesty without serious misgivings is proof that he holds Melantius free from villainous motives.

Of paramount importance, however, is the fact that Melantius does not execute the revenge himself but delegates it to his sister Evadne. Such a scene involving the sudden reversal of character and situation was a favorite with Beaumont and Fletcher and the admiration of their audience. Evadne had been drawn as the villainess of the play, the scornful adulteress without an atom of consciousness of her moral guilt. The theatrically effective struggle between brother and sister, the abrupt *peripetasis* when by physical force she is frightened into a realization of her crime, and her eager acceptance of the duty of revenge for a mortal injury, undoubtedly formed the high point of the play, as it still is its climax. Legally, of course, Melantius is equally guilty as accessory, but sentimentally he escaped the stain of blood in awakening his sister to vengeance for her moral ruin. He must not stain his hands, because he must survive to justify the vengeance, but Evadne—a woman already smirched with adultery and therefore by dramatic ethics doomed—makes the ideal revenger. The same opaque sense of moral values which led to her adultery, sends her flying to Amintor in the firm belief that her bloody expiation has washed her white as snow. When Amintor turns from her in loathing, normality is restored and her suicide follows as a matter of course.

It is not difficult to see how Beaumont and Fletcher avoided giving offence to the precise James. The declamatory lines sedulously upholding in every article the doctrine of Divine Right which were sprinkled in full measure throughout Amintor's speeches and confirmed by his actions, were flattering in the extreme since they carefully copied James's own utterances. The dangerous Catholic question was totally ignored. Also, the doctrine of loyalty was strongly emphasized. Melantius was no revolutionist, usurper, or Jesuit, but a man driven to action by deeds of his sovereign which could never be laid at James's door. All personal application was removed, and the theme carried up to the stratosphere of improbable romance, since James by no stretch of the imagination could ever have feared an English Evadne. A vast gulf stretches between *The Maid's Tragedy* and *Gorboduc*.

Finally, for those squeamish stomachs which revolted at even the most romantic suggestion of regicide, the concluding lines of the tragedy contain the moral hinting directly at the instigation of Heaven.

> May this a fair example be to me,
> To rule with temper: for on lustful Kings
> Unlookt for sudden deaths from heaven are sent!
> But curst is he that is their instrument.

Just as God, according to belief, sent evil kings as a punishment to the people, so He could dispose of them. But as a warning to fanatics who might believe in their Heaven-sent mission, "curst is he that is their instrument." Evadne, cursed already by a mortal sin, was the only fit instrument for the vengeance on her sovereign.

The Maid's Tragedy is exceptionally interesting in the history of the revenge play chiefly because of its theme, which was the first tragic development of a question suggested but not elaborated in such chronicle histories as *Richard II* and *Edward II* and in Chapman's *Revenge of Bussy D'Ambois*. The ending with its hint of vengeance from Heaven is a statement of what was always implicit in Kydian tragedy, a theme which was to assume a greater importance in the work of later dramatists.

Fletcher's *Bloody Brother* (1616-1624) treats the same problem but with the more dangerous Kydian revenger of blood. Here the peril is escaped not by the nature of the revenge, as in *The Maid's Tragedy,* but by the nature of the ruler who is a villainous usurper. The play is of the type first codified in *Claudius Tiberius Nero* which deals with the rise of a tyrant. The structure of the plot follows a well defined path. The first two acts are devoted to the rise of the villain to the throne, the third and fourth to the consolidation of his position by fresh atrocities, and the fifth to the blood-revenge of the relatives of his victims. The villain is spurred on and aided by a villainous accomplice who meets his death in the downfall of his master. The greater part of the play is devoted to the intrigues and bloody deeds of the protagonist, since the intrigue of the revengers is neither lengthy nor complicated.

In spite of a wide variety of Kydian conventions in situation, there is an explicit disavowal of the purity and justice of Kydian revenge. Sophia, the mother of Rollo and the murdered Otto, curses her parricide son but refuses even to be present at a discussion of revenge. On the other hand, Matilda, their sister, has no such qualms; and it is she who aids, and in the end applauds, the action of Edith in seeking revenge on Rollo for the murder of her father. The character Aubrey, Rollo's adviser, is the one from whom the audience is expected to take its lead. Patriotism, loyalty to his country, is his abiding principle. Fully realizing Rollo's crimes, he yet endeavors so to advise his master that he may preserve the country and rule in peace. Aubrey refuses to take part in any conspiracy against Rollo, and even accepts from him his own death warrant without thoughts of revenge.

In contrast, Edith glorying in her deed appears contaminated by the essentially dishonorable means she has employed to trick Rollo to his death. It is worthy of note that Aubrey considers she has sinned, and, although he promises to lift the rigor of the law from her, he orders her to a convent to expiate her deed for the remainder of her life. Like a true revenger content with any fate once her vengeance is secured, Edith departs cheerfully to her life-long sequestration. Her noble accomplice Hamond was already removed by death from what would have proved Aubrey's reluctant justice.

The resolution of *The Bloody Brother* presents the strongest possible evidence for the taint which by this time explicitly clung to the Kydian revenger of blood, no matter how strong and relatively pure his motives. In three different ways Fletcher's *Valentinian, The Maid's Tragedy,* and *The Bloody Brother* had reached this conclusion. It was unfortunate that his later imitators found the surface glitter of his theatrical incidents irresistible, and were led astray by the undoubted inconsistencies of morality within his dramatic action and characterization. For Fletcher, the greatest force within these years, was fundamentally sound; it was the imitation of his superficial weaknesses that caused the eventual destruction of Elizabethan tragedy.

6

If Fletcher was the most influential playwright within this period, John Webster was the greatest and his treatment of the villain play the most thoroughly artistic. *The Duchess of Malfi* did not, as sometimes asserted, bring to a close the tradition of revenge tragedy. It did, however, provide in its plot structure the artistic climax to the particular type of drama which had been in the direct line of descent from Kyd and Marlowe, Marston and Tourneur, and marked the temporary discard of the much modified Kydian plot formula. Webster, together with Fletcher, is the bridge between the older Elizabethans and the so-called decadent drama of Massinger and Ford.

Webster's debt to Kydian tragedy in *The Duchess of Malfi* has been noted in detail—the wanton bloodshed, torture, use of the tool villain, omens, and the like.[23] Only the structure of the plot and the position of the tool villain will occupy us here. The play is peculiar in that the protagonist (the duchess herself) is the victim of the villains' revenge. This much and no more Webster found in his source. The problem, how to bring the guilty persons to justice, remained. If the death of the duchess were delayed until the dénouement, the villains in some inexplicable manner must become so involved as to bring disaster on their own heads or else be disposed of hugger-mugger by Antonio. The Kydian formula would suggest the murder of the duchess to be followed by the revenge of the distraught Antonio, but this would involve not only a decided wandering from the source but also a certain loss in the more pitiful and ironic aspects of the story. Webster clung to his source and accordingly was forced to create original machinery for his catastrophe, a task complicated by the loss of his major hero and the necessity for the early loss of his minor.

The solution came through the extension of the action of the tool villain. Bosola is no mechanical villain of the Lorrique type. He is, instead, a misfit, a man of worthier talents forced into a degrading position and, with a brutal philosophy, making the most of it by the thoroughgoing manner in which he plays his part. If he must be a villain, one senses, he has decided to be an efficient one. Enough flashes of his independent better self are shown to stir the interest of the audience and the more to horrify them by the cynical brutality that follows. Indeed, Bosola has an almost surgical interest in torturing the human spirit to see how

23 E. E. Stoll, *John Webster*, pp. 93, 118-45.

much it can endure before the veniality he seeks as the excuse for his existence is forced to the surface.

The unworldly bravery of the duchess proves to Bosola that his theories are false; but his character is so well conceived that his sympathies are not fully enrolled until he is made aware of the fate that awaits him at the hands of an ungrateful master. Already shaken by his experience with the duchess, he is cast completely adrift from his convictions by this second shock, and takes to himself the office of revenger for the duchess upon the men who have ruined him. With dramatic irony the first step in his new rôle is the unwitting murder of Antonio, the man whose life he had resolved to save. Bosola knows then that his life, tainted by years of evil, is doomed, and with that knowledge he becomes the impersonal agent of Death. In the mortal scuffle with his enemies that follows he meets his end, but not before he has seen one of his foes ironically slain and has with his own hand stabbed the second. The fatal retribution begun with the murder of the duchess has at last descended on the guilty parties.

This retribution is the keynote of the play, but it does not come from a Kydian revenger, for in a sense the villains bring it directly upon themselves. Ferdinand goes mad, the cardinal is no longer able to control his accomplice Bosola, and the resultant internecine strife works the havoc. The accomplice had always been the weak link in the Kydian villain's schemes. Webster followed the tradition of the weak link, but exalted the irony of the catastrophe and provided a more fitting doom for his villains by removing the element of accident from the accomplice's betrayal and founding such betrayal on a psychological change in character.

The White Devil (1609-1612), which immediately preceded *The Duchess of Malfi,* is, however, Webster's real masterpiece in the villain play. In a sense it may be said to complete the merging of the Kyd and Marlowe revenge play last considered in *The Atheist's Tragedy.* Just as Shakespeare by his emphasis on character had in *Hamlet* created the apotheosis of pure Kydian tragedy, so Webster, to a lesser degree and in a lesser medium, by the same artistic means rather than by any important tinkering with the construction of plot, achieved in *The White Devil* a welding of the most popular features of Kyd and Marlowe. The result is a complete synthesis and the finest villain play of the period.

Superficially the plot seems somewhat old-fashioned.[24] A villain, in order to marry a villainess, has her husband and his own wife secretly murdered. The fact is suspected, and the wife's brother and lover join forces as revengers. They set a trap by which they kill the villains and their accomplices although one of the revengers also falls. The vital change from Kyd, unrevealed by such a bald outline, comes in the position of importance these two sets of opponents occupy in the plot, but more especially in their characterization. The title indicates whose play it is. The victim of the revenger is the protagonist, as in the usual villain play, yet, as with Kyd, the balance of conflict is maintained since the revenge is conceived early and the revengers' intrigue occupies an important part of the play. Definitely it is not the Marlovian *deus ex machina* suddenly raised to bring about a quick catastrophe.

It is chiefly in the characterization, however, that Webster differs. Here is a villain play in which, contrary to Swinburne's opinion, the characters are not all black or all white but all—even to the possible "good" characters—are gray. The provincialism combined with the intense moral loathing which led Elizabethan tragic writers to portray their Italian villains as impossible pieces of living evil has been replaced by a calmer and more realistic point of view. Webster's villains are not the grinning, self-conscious puppets of the Machiavellian tradition, glorying in evil and at war with religion and good. The Elizabethan Machiavellian villain provoked interest only by the fascinated horror of the audience, but it is evident that Webster's Vittoria, by every means possible to his hand, is intended to appeal to a fascinated sympathy. Therein lay the great change Webster introduced to revenge tragedy; but as with Shakespeare the example was too high

[24] Stoll, *John Webster,* pp. 93, 117-18.

for the melodramatic tastes of the other dramatists and was little emulated except by Ford and by Middleton in *The Changeling*.

Webster took advantage of the fact that a villain as protagonist will receive sympathy if the audience is not morally disgusted by his unalloyed and unromantic depravity, and if the other prominent persons are not sufficiently virtuous or interesting to ally the audience on their side against the protagonist. The overriding passion for Vittoria which possesses Brachiano is so genuinely felt that the affair is removed from the level of low intrigue and to some extent is raised to the company of the great though illicit loves which have always gained the sympathy of the world. There is no doubt that the means by which he achieves possession of Vittoria are evil, but, except for a few casual moments, Brachiano is not shown as a wicked man who falls in love but as a proud, imperious man whose passion drives him to wicked ways. His very pride and cool insolence compel from the first an unwilling admiration, and the very force of his passion which leads him in death to turn away from his own son and to ask for "this good woman," if it does not legitimize his moral guilt at least provokes the most intense sympathy. The contrast with Barabas and Aaron self-consciously reciting their crude crimes is marked.

A greater glamour enfolds Vittoria. Her wit, her courage, her beauty make her a fit mate for Brachiano. It is her play, and she invests it with a quality of magnificence to which no audience can be cold. Webster's leavening has extended even to the highly conventional character of the tool villain. Flamineo is no gulled Pedringano or comic relief Lorrique. In a halting and imperfect way Webster has tried to dignify his essentially undignified rôle by raising the quality of the man within it. Malcontent, pander, murderer, the force of his vitality and depraved cynicism yet makes him a far more important figure in the play than his actual position warrants.

Webster has humanized his villains by substituting for the religious tradition of "the devil incarnate" real persons with more than their share of vice yet treated so poetically as to arouse the sympathetic as opposed to the antagonistic interest of the audience; moreover, he has strengthened that sympathy by his treatment of the revengers. Like his villains, they are gray. Their revenge is actuated neither by the pure religious frenzy of the Kydian hero revenger nor by the malicious self-interest of the Marlovian villain. They occupy a halfway ground between the two extremes, and Webster, in order not to overthrow the balance of sympathy, is at some pains to taint slightly the purity of their motives and consequently the justice of their action.

Francisco de Medicis, the chief revenger, is already at odds with Brachiano and is endeavoring the downfall of Vittoria before the murder is committed. To his revenge for the murder of his sister is added, accordingly, more than a share of private grudge which has been adequately revealed in the biased trial of Vittoria. Furthermore, he shows a consciousness that some discredit attaches to the revenge by the pains he takes to keep his plans from the Cardinal Monticelso, who, as uncle to Vittoria's murdered husband, might reasonably be expected to sympathize with and even to join the revenge if it were just or allowable.

The second revenger Lodovico is drawn from the start as a desperate, bloody man. He has no just grounds whatever for a revenge except that he was illicitly in love with Brachiano's murdered wife, a motive which largely removes him from the rôle of hired *bravo* but does not warrant blood-revenge. Even this violent man has qualms about the justice of the sworn vengeance and at one time would have withdrawn had he not been tricked by Francisco into believing the deed countenanced by Monticelso. His cry—"Why now our action's justified"—when following the slaying of Brachiano the conspirators learn from Zanche the actual facts of the murders, is as enlightening as to his dubious state of mind as is Francisco's cynical reply:

> Tush for Justice!
> What harmes is Justice? we now, like the partridge,
> Purge the disease with lawrell: for the fame
> Shall crown the enterprise and quit the shame.
>   (V.iii.277-80)

Such sentiments on either side are not those of Kydian revengers. Neither were the means by which the revengers secured the death of Brachiano likely to be considered the acts of good men to an Elizabethan audience.

The close of *The White Devil* when Lodovico is led forth to be tortured and executed and the young Giovanni uncompromisingly declares Francisco a villainous murderer, represents an hostility to the revenge which is more in keeping with the end of *The Revenger's Tragedy* than with *Hamlet*. There is no doubt that Vittoria and Brachiano are guilty and have pulled their doom on their own heads. Yet Webster balances the scales so nicely that the means of their doom—the revenge of Lodovico and Francisco —has no religious sanction and is conducted in as blameworthy a manner as the deeds which raised it. This realistic rather than melodramatic treatment of a revenge story marks Webster's *White Devil* as almost unique. Not only has he successfully amalgamated the interest of an audience in a Kydian revenge and a Marlovian villain protagonist, but he has also added a new type of treatment which is realistic without becoming bourgeois and thrilling without the introduction of caricature.

CHAPTER VI

THE DISAPPROVAL OF REVENGE

I

FROM the very first, revenge in Elizabethan tragedy had been associated in some form or other with the tacit disapproval of the audience. This statement at once needs qualifying, but in essence it remains accurate. Despite the occasional difference in the ethical judgments made by an audience in a theater as compared with those of real life, Hieronimo's course of revenge with its bloody conclusion must have alienated the audience to the point where it looked upon him as a villain. The upshot was that the audience accepted his cause as necessary and just, but was temperamentally incapable of wholehearted sympathy with the un-English Machiavellian maniac who closed the play. If this view seems too strong, or Hieronimo not a fair example, it may be stated with justice that the audience sentimentally sympathized with the Kydian hero revenger and hoped for his success, but only on condition that he did not survive. Thus his death was accepted as expiation for the violent motives which had forced him to override the rules of God and, without awaiting the slow justice of divine retribution, to carve out a bloody revenge for himself. The heroes were unbalanced by the force of the shock and the burden of their difficult duty. Whatever the outcome of the revenge, even the most sympathetic characters like Hamlet were so twisted and warped by their overwhelming experiences that they could never return again to a normal life on earth. Who but an incurable sentimentalist could conceive of Hamlet's receiving the crown after the death of Claudius, marrying, and living happily ever after? The grand sacrifice—death in victory—was the revenger's only possible lot.

The implications of this Pyrrhic victory finally led to the transformation of the hero to the villain protagonist who yet retained exactly the same revenge motives as the Kydian hero. Three separate explanations may be advanced for this sea-change. The dramatists realized that by this road lay the easiest way to vary the monotonous Kydian formula which had been overworked. They perceived the growing popularity of the villain and were anxious to please the audience's taste although unwilling to abandon a tried plot structure. They recognized the fact that the compromise between stage and public morality in the treatment of a bloody revenge could no longer be effected and that the audience could not accept a murderer as a hero no matter how just his motive.

Whether any one of these explanations points to the positive force, or whether it was a union of all three which dictated the change, would be too vexed a question to decide precisely. It is most probable that each exerted an influence but that the third was the real mover. The prime importance of the audience's ethical reaction may be buttressed by two pertinent facts. When the later dramatists on occasion revived the strict Kydian formula, they were forced to adopt some such painful compromise as in *The Atheist's Tragedy*. Furthermore, the bourgeois drama —most representative of the people—shows unmistakable aversion to the ideals and spirit of the revenge play.

In the second period of the revenge play, when the villain reigns supreme, revenge still plays an important part in the structure of the plot, but the interest is frequently shifted from the workings of this revenge to the general villainy of action and the evil intrigues of the protagonist. When revenge is undertaken by the good characters against the villain, it is usually hurried over and excused. The revenges of the villains, however, are portrayed with gusto, particularly when they lead to mutual destruction.

In this period revenge has no advocates. *The Turk* and *Women Beware Women* illustrate the doom of all persons who for their own evil ends harbor vengeance. *The Maid's Tragedy* ostentatiously inveighs against revenge on kings. *The White Devil* shows an evil revenge taken for a theoretically just cause, and *The Duchess of Malfi* the retribution which befalls a villainous revenge. During these years, also, in such plays as *The Revenge of Bussy D'Ambois*, *The Atheist's Tragedy,* and to some extent *The*

Maid's Tragedy, The Second Maiden's Tragedy, and *The Duch-ess of Malfi,* we hear the first didactic murmurings of the re-ligious doctrine which bade the relinquishment of all vengeance to Heaven.

The plays of the second period showed a disapproval of revenge by their putting it in the hands of the villains, but this disapproval was more implied than expressed. It was left largely for the next development of the revenge play, a period covering roughly the years 1620 to 1630, to express openly and forthrightly—sometimes even in the form of a problem play—the absolute disapproval of revenge under any circumstances. Individual earlier plays had touched on this disapproval and indirectly forecast the develop-ment, but in these years a succession of tragedies was produced which leaves no doubt that a well defined movement was on.

The first propaganda play, immediately preceding this distinct third period, is *A Fair Quarrel* written in 1616 by Thomas Mid-dleton and William Rowley on the problem of the ethics of duel-ling. This work was followed in 1619 by Massinger's *Fatal Dowry,* which for an objective, strictly logical, and non-romantic criticism of revenge was not surpassed in the period. The major dramatists, Massinger, Rowley, Middleton, Ford, and D'Avenant, in almost every one of their plays during this period treat of revenge as a cruel, mistaken, or useless motive. Each playwright used different methods. Massinger in *The Fatal Dowry* expressed the views of the man in the street and in *The Unnatural Combat* the religious disapproval. Ford shows the cruelty of the duty to revenge in *The Broken Heart,* the uselessness in *'Tis Pity She's a Whore,* and the evil results of rash vengeance in *Love's Sacrifice.* Middleton's greatest expression of the working of revenge on character and after-circumstance occurs in *The Changeling.*

This period, however, was not exclusively under such softer in-fluences. The plays of Massinger, Rowley, and Ford are fre-quently replete with blood, horrors, and many of the conventional situations of the old revenge tragedy. It is the conclusions of their tragedies, the larger interest apportioned to the problems of ethics in vengeance, and the decreased interest in the depiction of villainy, which mark the difference. Thus even though imbued with the new spirit, the major playwrights carried on some of the old traditions. Minor playwrights also harked back to the old school in such plays as Goffe's *Orestes* and D'Avenant's *Albovine,* without the leavening found in the work of their betters. Moreover, Shirley, although he once showed the influence of the period in *Love's Cruelty,* was gradually reviving and perfecting the traditional use of revenge as the dominant note of an entire play. There is, then, this undercurrent of the bloody revenge tragedy carried over from the first and second periods which runs through the years when the best dramatists seem to be deliberately striving towards a more religious and humane treatment of the theme.

2

Middleton and Rowley's *Fair Quarrel* (1616) and Goffe's *Orestes* (1623) represent the opposite poles of dramatic effort in these years. *A Fair Quarrel* is not a propaganda play against all duelling, as is sometimes believed, but only against the hasty and ill-grounded quarrels which were the curse of the time and so frequently led to "honorable" murder. The central theme is not Captain Ager's refusal to fight any duel, but his refusal to the point of absolute disgrace to fight a duel in a cause he believes unjust. The significance of the play in the development of the sentiment concerning revenge lies in the fact that the hero refuses revenge when his honor is injured but his ultimate ground uncertain, and that he prosecutes his vengeance like a gentleman when presented with a just cause under the duelling code. The conception of personal honor held by the gentleman of the time is carefully analyzed, and a higher code of conduct, still based on the same premises, is offered. By this new code and by Ager's actions in accord with it, not only are all revenges of villains for unjust causes entirely thrown out of court, but, more important, the methods by which a gentleman could take revenge are firmly limited. This sentiment indicates a verdict that the treacherous means of even the best of tragic revenges, were "unfair" and not to be countenanced by valiant gentlemen who esteemed their honor.[1]

In contrast to this reasoned analysis of a contemporary problem, Goffe's academic tragedy *Orestes* (1623) presents perhaps the most consciously contrived succession of horrors and bloody incidents of the whole Elizabethan period. But it is significant that in a play which attempts to outrival Seneca on his own ground, Goffe turns to the Kydian tragedy of the past and thereby Anglicizes a play which by rights should have been a servile imitation of Latin models. Hints from Seneca's *Agamemnon* are quite apparent, but Goffe's real models have been *The Spanish Tragedy, Antonio's Revenge, Hamlet,* and *The Revenger's Tragedy,* with overtones of *Macbeth* and perhaps Massinger's *Duke of Milan*. Of greater importance is the fact that the blood and thunder do not hide the inescapable moral and psychological view of revenge and its consequences.

Justice is forgotten in Orestes's passion for horrible and purely personal retaliation. He vows:

> Hell and the furies shall stand all amaz'd,
> *Alecto* shall come there for to behold
> New kindes of murthers which she knew not yet:
> And nature learn to violate her selfe.

The inhumanly horrible torment and final slaughter of Aegystheus and of Clytemnestra placed his vengeance beyond all earthly bounds as the work of an insane evildoer. Goffe has not retreated from this conception in the crucial fifth act. The revenger's words justifying his revenge and seeking to claim the throne are those of an impudent and callous villain. It seems clear that Goffe at least partially understood the psychology by which the sudden shock of the murder of a father, the consequent turning-inward of the grief and the forced repression of the normal

---

[1] For an analysis of the play in the light of the duelling code of the time, see F. T. Bowers, "Middleton's *Fair Quarrel* and the Duelling Code," *Journal of English and Germanic Philology,* Vol. XXVI (1937), pp. 40-65.

outlet of instant vengeance, would so work on the character of an erstwhile good man that, when the path was made clear, his pent-up emotions would burst out in terrible retribution. Goffe comprehended that such an action was made possible by the buckling of the revenger's moral nature under the burden of an unbearable wrong which he had been too long helpless to right.

The tragedy was not, then, merely the external action of death and destruction, but also the more inward tragedy which turned good men like Hieronimo and Orestes into villains by the warping of their characters under the strain. Although the play exhibits, as had no previous tragedy, the unadulterated ferocity and the raw emotions of revenge, the conclusion is definitely turned against applause for vengeance. The self-destruction of Orestes and Pylades, with Goffe's view of the causes of the madness which had assailed Orestes after his vengeance, are closely linked to the conception of Middleton's *Changeling*—the most artistic play of this decade—that murder is its own reward and that the murderer carries the seeds of his destruction within his own breast.

3

Interesting as are *A Fair Quarrel* and *Orestes* as representative of the two extremes within this period, they can scarcely be called typical. If the spirit of this era was comprehended within the work of any one man, that man was Phillip Massinger. The story of his *Fatal Dowry* (1619) is shortly told. Charalois discovers his wife in adultery with Novall, Jr., and, killing the man, hales his wife before her father who is forced to admit that she is deserving of death. On this pronouncement Charalois stabs her in cold blood. The case for the murder of Novall, Jr., is prosecuted at law by Novall, Sr. Charalois is acquitted but is immediately stabbed by Pontalier, a friend of the slain man. Romont, friend of Charalois, kills Pontalier in return, and is banished by the judge, who delivers the moral of the play.

Although the scene is laid in France, the characters are not noble or royal as was customary in tragedy, but good, honest, upper middle-class citizens who might just as well be Englishmen. Nor are the situations strained or inflated. The actions of the characters, and indeed the whole background, would carry no foreign implications to the English audience. The spectators were viewing their own kind set on the stage in a tragedy. Understandably, along with this bourgeois atmosphere goes an entirely hard-headed bourgeois disapproval of revenge.

No other course was possible. The London citizen could be thrilled by a Kydian revenger and horrified by the magnificent villains of conventional tragedy, but this interest was largely based on their distance from the citizen. Such characters had no place in realistic English plays like *The Yorkshire Tragedy* or *Arden of Feversham*. This fact had already been recognized by bourgeois dramatists, who had perforce thrown out entirely the inflated conventions of revenge tragedy in their realistic portrayal of contemporary murders. One anonymous dramatist had even gone so far as to poke ostentatious fun at the Kydian plays in the Induction to *A Warning for Fair Women* (*c.* 1598) when the popularity of the school of Kyd was at its height. Except for this Induction and the play's epilogue, however, the criticism had been only by implication, and it was not until *The Fatal Dowry* that the solid London citizen heard from the stage a "common sense" exposition of the harms that resulted when people took their revenges into their own hands instead of resorting to the law, as any honest man would do.

In *The Fatal Dowry* there are no hysterical revengers of blood or deep-dyed Machiavellian villains. The complicated intrigue of revenge is therefore missing, and we have instead a well ordered drama of the interplay of character and circumstance. No man is entirely a villain. Novall, Jr., is a weak fop and Pontalier, the murderer, a loyal but hotheaded soldier with the military man's love of direct action and distrust of civilian justice in matters which concern his honor. Novall, Sr., is a flint-hearted usurer, but he, as the chief person injured by his son's death, contents himself with endeavoring to secure legal justice.

The question raised by the play really hinges on the characters of Charalois and, to a lesser extent, Pontalier. Charalois in all things endeavors to act the part of a gentleman. It is true he takes justice to himself when he kills Novall, Jr., but the immediate slaying of an adulterer caught in the act was held manslaughter by the law of England and therefore practically certain of pardon. Furthermore, he refuses to assassinate the cowardly Novall, and insists on the honorable revenge of a gentleman by personal combat. While Charalois's action is called a "brave revenge" and "noble justice" (V.ii), that of Pontalier is conceived in desperation and—because of its purely personal grounds as contrasted to Charalois's insistence on justice—in contempt of law.

The catastrophe shows the unromantic view which Massinger held of these two revenges. Charalois is acquitted of murder by the court on the judgment that though he had overstepped the strict letter of the law in killing Novall, Jr., his injuries were sufficient to merit mercy. Pontalier thereupon takes justice into his own hands and stabs him, only to fall himself under the dagger of Romont. Then comes the lessons Massinger has to teach. Charalois dies because

> what's fall'n upon me
> Is by heaven's will, because I made myself
> A judge in my own cause, without their warrant.

Pontalier dies with this repentance:

> I receive
> The vengeance which my love, not built on virtue,
> Has made me worthy, worthy of.

To conclude the matter Romont is banished:

> For you, Romont, although, in your excuse,
> You may plead what you did was in revenge
> Of the dishonour done unto the court,
> Yet since from us you had not warrant for it,
> We banish you the state.

The judge speaks the moral of the tragedy:

> We are taught
> By this sad precedent, how just soever

Our reasons are to remedy our wrongs,
We are yet to leave them to their will and power
That, to that purpose, have authority.

No more trenchant criticism of the revenge play was ever spoken
in the theater; and it expresses the realistic view of a law-abiding
middle class. For the first time in a play the romantic stage conventions of personal justice were outspokenly contrasted to the
legal and moral code by which the vast majority of Elizabethans
lived.

Massinger has refused to allow sentiment to stand in the way
of his strict application of the common sense doctrine of lawful-
ness. Charalois by killing Novall, Jr., had temporarily usurped
the law and made himself the judge of equity. More important
still, the widely accepted motives which led him to such an action
are condemned. To the world as to himself, Charalois was seeking only justice. But his almost fanatical insistence on rigid justice took no account of the tempering of mercy. Ironbound
justice turned the stabbing of his wife into murder. Pontalier's
revenge, according to his own confession, was not built on virtue;
the vengeance of Charalois was built on too much. Massinger,
accordingly, goes far beyond what even James I in his treatises
on duelling was striving for. With Massinger, slaughter even in
hot blood takes away the prerogative of Heaven and of the earthly
courts of justice, and so is not to be pardoned. Personal justice,
even for the strongest cause, is entirely ruled out. The place to
seek justice is in the courts, which alone have the power of dis-
pensing it.

"The measure of the satisfaction wch is required at the hand of
ordinarie Iudges at more leashure and in a lawfull manner vn-
doubtedly will both carrie a greater credit in the worldes conceate,
and likewise be more large and full then a priuat passion is able
to extort, wch in a presse of men distempered and disordered doth
rather preuaile by chance then attempte vppon certaintie
(c. 1614)."[2]

2 Cotton MS. Titus C IV, fol. 467.

The Duke of Milan (1620) is a more Italianate production, drawing its inspiration directly from the first period of Kydian revenge tragedy as modified by Chettle and Tourneur. The number of Kydian conventions used to work out the variation on the Herod-Mariamne story of the central situation provide an assurance that the revenge of Francisco, the brother of the seduced Eugenia, is the moving cause of the action and the part of the plot most interesting to the audience. The emphasis put on the relations of the duke and his wife Marcelia usurp the early action, but once the foundation is laid the play concerns itself chiefly with Francisco's vengeance, the importance of which is attested by the anticlimactic fifth act.

Massinger contrives a curious variation, however, when he insistently withholds, except for the slightest of hints at the start, the underlying motives for Francisco's thirst for vengeance. He leaves no doubt in the minds of the audience that Francisco is seeking a serious revenge, but the real reasons—which lie beneath the conventional villainous revenge on Marcelia for rejecting his advances—are left in the dark. For the first two acts Francisco has been portrayed as the traditional ambitious villain who hopes to make Marcelia's love the stepping-stone to the throne, but from the point of Marcelia's repulse it is clear that he has some deep-seated and unrevealed cause for his revenge. It is not until the fifth act with the appearance of Eugenia and the revelation of the wrong done her by the duke that the whole story is put before the spectators.

What led Massinger to this peculiar holding back of vital information is a matter for conjecture. He may have felt that the mystery of Francisco's true motives would lend an air of interest to his proceedings which would be missing were his reasons known. Moreover, the withholding of the information which reflected severely on the duke gave the audience a fairer picture of the duke and a greater sympathetic interest in his relations with Marcelia than would have been felt had the duke been known from the beginning as the debaucher of Francisco's sister and the marked victim of his revenge. This last point is of some importance by virtue of its effect on the audience's judgment of Francisco's character. Massinger did not intend the spectators to sympathize with Francisco's vengeance; yet that was precisely what would have happened to a certain extent had the duke been painted in blacker colors and the audience been apprised from the start of Francisco's secret. Francisco owned a good cause but Massinger, both by holding back the reasons for his cause and by portraying merely the evil side of his revenge for Marcelia's rebuff, left no doubt in the minds of the audience that he was a villain. When the revelation of his revenge is finally made, the contrast between Francisco and Eugenia clinches the view of his character. For all Eugenia's bloodthirsty avowals, it is Francisco who plots and carries out the last desperate revenge and Eugenia who blenches at the terrible means in which her brother exults. She stands as a seriously wronged woman who without due thought has loosed the destructive force of her villainous brother.

The Duke of Milan is linked in spirit to *The White Devil* by its just apportionment of guilt and its refusal to give a sympathetic gloss to a villainous revenge made for a good cause.[3] No effort is spared to prevent the audience from romanticizing the revenge and from feeling that the cruel means of revenge were justified by the seriousness of the original injury. For this reason it seems likely that Francisco is made a villain in his own right and allowed to embark upon a tainted revenge before the purer original grounds are revealed on which he has superimposed his base motives. By this modification of earlier tragedy the dramatist gives the first four acts a superficial resemblance to the standard villain play. But Massinger is close to Webster, for technically the comparative justice at the hidden base of the revenger's motives differentiates this work sharply from such absolute villain plays as *Claudius Tiberius Nero, The Turk,* or *The Bloody Banquet.*

---

[3] Compare the moral of the play as given by Pescara: "And learn, from his example, there's no trust In a foundation that is built on lust." The duke was guilty in his seduction of Eugenia and in his animal uxoriousness which incapacitated him for reasoned action and so caused him to murder his wife. Francisco's revenge was occasioned as much by his lust for Marcelia as by his sister's injury. Both revenger and victim, then, were stained.

The White Devil and, in some respects, *Valentinian,* both of which looked forward to the spirit of the third period, are the best parallels.

Yet Massinger's play in this new period exhibits a curious difference. Webster and Fletcher had been content to use revenge as a dramatic motive for what it was worth, and had left chiefly to the audience the task of evaluating the final justice and the morality of the vengeance. In *The Duke of Milan* it seems probable that Massinger did not trust to this more or less impartial procedure, and that he felt impelled to banish the real reasons for revenge as a dramatic motive for as long as he could without disrupting entirely his plot. The curious withholding of the comparatively just motives for Francisco's vengeance, therefore—a procedure which undoubtedly injures the chain of cause and effect so necessary for a satisfactory tragedy—may perhaps be laid to the influence of the growing disapproval of revenge.

Massinger's *Unnatural Combat* in 1621 represents his final word of disapproval upon earthly private revenge, but much of the play is shrouded in darkness. The tendency, which could be adequately explained in *The Duke of Milan,* towards the withholding of vital information about antecedent action as a spring for present motivation, is here elaborated to such an extent that it degenerates into a decadent device for securing mystery by illegitimate means. The dark doubts engendered by the hidden motives in the revenge of Malefort, Jr., on his father would be dramatically legitimate were the play concerned solely with this situation. But since the unnatural combat of son and father which gives the play its name[4] is totally unconcerned with the main action of Malefort, Sr.'s incestuous affection for his daughter Theocrine, and serves merely to emphasize at a later date the tragic tangle Malefort has made of his life, Massinger's deliberate mystification falsely leads the audience to connect the enigma of

[4] It is possible, however, that Massinger intended a double meaning, and that the title, "The Unnatural Combat," may also refer to Malefort's struggles against his incestuous lust.

the son with a story behind the mystery of Malefort's feelings for his daughter. And, of course, no such story exists. Theocrine actually is his daughter, and his incestuous passion is real.

The most indefensible holding back of information concerns the status and motives of Montreville. Here the influence of *The Duke of Milan* is most marked. Both plays introduce their villain as a friend of the protagonist, and in both, minor characters comment on the strangeness of the friendship. But whereas some real information, even though fragmentary, is given in *The Duke of Milan,* here no hint is forthcoming of the important story of Montreville's relations with Malefort, Sr., which antedate the action of the play. In *The Duke of Milan* there is very shortly no doubt that Francisco is a villain with a grudge, but Montreville, while not portrayed as an especially admirable character, does not reveal the depths of his villainy until the final scene of the last act when the debauched Theocrine is thrust out of the fort to lie sobbing at her father's feet. As in *The Duke of Milan* the tragic story results from the act of the protagonist in giving a woman—here a daughter instead of a wife—into the care of the villain. Finally, in both plays the real cause of the villain's long-delayed revenge is not revealed until the fifth act.

To all intents, revenge is of quite subordinate interest in the play, since there is no indication until the last act that any revengeful action has been on foot. The action is portrayed at its face value, and the audience is left to guess at the mystery behind it until the revenge motivation which explains the action is finally disclosed by laying bare the motives of Malefort, Jr., and Montreville. Indeed, the main revenges of the play do not untie the knots at the end. It requires a thunderbolt from Heaven to kill Malefort, Sr.; and Montreville at the conclusion is captured by Beaufort, Jr., and his father who happened on the scene only because of a minor revenge on Malefort, Sr., for wrecking the marriage of the son and Theocrine.

As various early eighteenth-century comic dramatists revelled in drawing a realistic picture of fashionable vice so long as they reformed the hero at the end, so some dramatists of this third period of Elizabethan tragedy, no matter how much they show an ethical disapproval of revenge in the moral of their plays, seize eagerly on the more flamboyant and horrible incidents of the older revenge tragedy to give excitement to their plots. The treatment of incest first begun in the old *Hamlet* had furnished a minor situation in various early tragedies, as had the unnatural love of a murderer for the wife or daughter of his victim. This theme of incest is expanded almost to the point of nausea as the central situation of *The Unnatural Combat.* The choice of subject may be excused as necessary for the special catastrophe of the play, but not the detailed treatment which indicates clearly a decadent pandering to the tastes of Massinger's audience.

The unique catastrophe, when God Himself directly intervenes and kills Malefort, Sr., by a bolt of lightning, is a logical progression to the last step in the dramatic portrayal of the religious contention that all revenge should be left to God. Various plays, such as *The Maid's Tragedy, The Atheist's Tragedy,* and *The Fatal Dowry,* had stated without equivocation that their tragic endings had been brought about by Heaven. Such statements corresponded not only to the religious views of the time in which God slowly but surely punished all sins, but also to the contemporary ideal of moral tragedy.

The idea that tragedy never encouraged vice but instead discouraged its audience from emulating vicious practices by showing the inevitable retribution which overcame villains, was used by Thomas Heywood in 1612 as the bulwark of his argument in favor of plays: "If we present a tragedy, we include the fatall and abortive ends of such as commit notorious murders, which is aggravated and acted with all the art that may be to terrifie men from the like abhorred practises."[5] This he reenforces by the

---

[5] *An Apology for Actors,* p. 53. This defense, and the particular moral of the ending of some tragedies, was forced upon the playwrights by the arguments of the Puritans that the representations of crimes on the stage encouraged criminal tendencies in the members of the audience. See Stubbes, *Anatomie of Abuses* [1583], p. 143; I. G[reene], *A Refutation of the Apology for Actors* (1615), pp. 55-6. A hundred years later the same argument was going on: see Arthur Bedford, *Serious Reflections on the Scandalous Abuse and Effects of the Stage* (1705),

well known story of the hearer who was so moved by the representation of a murder on the stage that she confessed to her own black deed.

The opinion that tragedy taught a moral by representing the vengeance of Heaven on guilty persons was firmly infixed.[6] Every tragedy, accordingly, had to bring ruin to its evil characters, and their destruction was conceived in the minds of thoughtful spectators (if not always indicated in the play itself) as the result of the indirect workings of Heavenly Justice. Massinger, however, has constructed such an arch-villain in Malefort, Sr., that the standard moral would not have been strong enough to express the unutterable loathing for his unnatural crimes. His deeds were too evil to be punished merely by his destruction at the hands of a Montreville seeking revenge for the loss of Theocrine, for the moral would then be too obscure. A concrete and active example of Heaven's direct vengeance was necessary; ergo, the thunderbolt which swept him cursing to his damnation.

While the indirect workings of supernatural vengeance through a human medium (as in *The Maid's Tragedy*) were universally believed in, the conception of the direct and active intervention of God in His own Person in human affairs was not so common.[7] Various references, however, may be found as parallels to the slaying of Malefort, Sr. The contrast between direct and indirect intervention was described in 1627 by Bishop Hall: "God strikes some immediately from Heaven with his own arm, or with the arm of angels; others he buffets with their own hands; some by the revenging sword of an enemy; others with the fist of his dumb creatures: God strikes in all: his hand moves in theirs."[8] Nathaniel Carpenter (1638) warned sinners that "God sits not as an idle

pp. 25-6, repeated verbatim in Bedford's *Sermon Preached in . . . St. Butolph's Aldgate . . . occasioned by the Erection of a Playhouse* (1730), p. 13.

[6] See John Reynolds, *The Triumph of Gods Revenge Against Murther* (ed. 1670), sig. A₂.

[7] In Elizabethan tragedy the closest approach had been in the conclusion of *The Atheist's Tragedy* when Mountfort brains himself with the axe he is raising to execute the innocent Charlemont.

[8] "Heaven Upon Earth," *Works,* ed. Wynter, Vol. VI, p. 20. Cf. also Burton, *Anatomy of Melancholy* (Bohn Library, 1923), Vol. I, pp. 203-5.

Spectator, but interposeth himselfe as a chiefe Actor on the theater of worldly actions."[9] Deaths occurring by accidents in theaters or illegal assemblies were attributed by interested opponents to divine retribution.[10]

The Unnatural Combat carried forward the plot-disintegrating formula of *The Duke of Milan* by which necessary information is withheld concerning the reasons behind the action. In the fate of Malefort, Jr., it followed the theme of *The Fatal Dowry* with its moral refusal to admit the rights of private justice. But chief of all it worked out to the logical conclusion of stage representation the religious ideas of the day about the intervention in human affairs of the personal retribution of Heaven. As *The Duke of Milan* purported to teach that "there's no trust In a foundation that is built on lust," so *The Unnatural Combat* points the moral of its spectacular catastrophe:

> May we make use of
> This great example, and learn from it, that
> There cannot be a want of power above,
> To punish murder and unlawful love!
>
> (V.ii)

The moral is even sharper than in *The Fatal Dowry,* for in *The Unnatural Combat* God Himself is shown as the revenger and not merely the punisher of those who usurp His privilege. No more concrete and terrifying lesson could be presented as proof that revenge should be left to a God Who was altogether capable of its administration.

4

James's contemporary propaganda on Divine Right was neatly put to dramatic use by various playwrights. The ethics of a private revenge on kings had concerned Fletcher in *Valentinian, The Maid's Tragedy,* and *The Bloody Brother.* This test case for revenge was seized on in this period by William Rowley and by D'Avenant.

---

[9] *Achitophel, or the Picture of a wicked Politician* (1638), sig. D$_7$^{v}.

[10] See *The Autobiography of Sir Simonds D'Ewes,* ed. Halliwell-Phillipps (London, 1845), Vol. I, p. 238.

Rowley's *All's Lost by Lust* is usually dated 1619, although there is a possibility that the play was not composed until 1623.[11] The catastrophes of both the main plot and the underplot are motivated by revenge: the first for the rape of a daughter, and the second for the infidelity of a husband. In conformity with the views of this period both revenges are futile. Margaretta, in the subplot, realizes she is forestalling Heaven in seeking a personal revenge on her faithless husband Antonio, and asks pardon for her sin (III.ii.25-28); yet she is still so much the dupe of the revenge code as to call revenge a manifestation of a high spirit (III.ii.88-89), and to label her private revenge an act of justice (IV.ii.19-20). Her retaliation, however, spends itself on Antonio's accomplice Lazarello, and when Julianus causes Antonio's death she commits suicide, followed by Dionysia, Antonio's paramour.

The main plot treats the ethics of a private man's revenge on his sovereign. Julianus, the revenger, is first portrayed as a simple, loyal subject who fully acknowledges his master's kingly prerogative. Yet with the revelation that the king has raped his daughter Jacynta, his mind becomes affected and he instantly resolves on the fatal means of vengeance by deposing the guilty king Roderigo in favor of his erstwhile prisoner Muley Mumen. Retribution for this disloyal revenge follows swiftly when the Moor, in revenge for Jacynta's refusal of his love, has father and daughter killed. The moral appears in a speech by Julianus to Muley Mumen when he has been blinded and is about to die:

> This worke
> Is none of thine, tis heauens mercifull iustice,
> For thou art but the executioner,
> The master hangman. . . .
> I was a traytor to my lawfull King,
> And tho my wrongs encited on my rage,
> I had no warrant signde for my reuenge,
> Tis the peoples sinnes that makes tyrants kings,

[11] *All's Lost by Lust,* ed. C. W. Stork (University of Pennsylvania Series in Philology and Literature, XIII, 1910), p. 30.

And such was mine for thee, now I obey,
But my affliction teaches me too late:
On bloody reuenger, finish up my fate.

Two important ideas are here expressed. Julianus sees the Moor as the instrument of Heaven for revenging the wrong he, Julianus, has done Roderigo by his traitorous revenge, and so is able to accept his fate placidly.[12] A comparison may be made with the moral of *The Maid's Tragedy*. Jacynta had called the vengeance of Heaven upon Roderigo's head for her rape (II.i.141-2), and this divine retribution was presumably executed in the uprising led by Julianus. But since Heaven's instrument who brings about the death of kings is accursed, Heaven in turn raises the Moor to revenge the crime on Julianus.

The second point lies in the ethics of Julianus's revenge on his king. It must first be considered that he did not kill his sovereign privately and by deceit as did Evadne in *The Maid's Tragedy* or as Maximus purposed in *Valentinian*. Such a vengeance was held ignoble by all men. Instead, Julianus chose a public revenge, which of all revenges was accounted by the Elizabethans to have the best tinge of honor. But though his cause was good and his injury grievous, the motives with which he executed his public revenge were bad, for they did not purpose true justice "for any publike good, nor for the amendment of the delinquent, nor for the immunity of the part offended,"[13] but instead were born of personal retaliation pure and simple. With such motives, "Publike Revenge, whether it be executed by a Magistrate, or sought by a private man, if it proceed out of Envy, Hatred, Thirst of blood, or Cruelty, or if by any other meanes it be tainted in the impulsiue, formall, or finall cause, doth in that respect become pri-

[12] Some such idea was commented on by Richard Clerke: "All euills of punishment whether lighting on the wicked for reuenge, or on the godly for their tryall, vpon whomsoeuer, for what cause, or to what end soeuer, are from God, all. Shall I instance here in some particulars? It skils for the checke of most mens readinesse, to runne vpon the meanes, to curse, and seeke reuenge on them, not considering that God sends them." *Sermons* (1637), pp. 180-1.

[13] William Ames, *Conscience With the Power and Cases Thereof* (ed. 1643), Book V, Chap. III, p. 115.

vate and unlawfull."[14] Julianus was equally guilty with Margaretta in forestalling Heaven, and more guilty by breaking the
doctrine of Divine Right which asserted that tyrannous kings
were sent by God as a punishment and must therefore be patiently endured. Finally, in contrast to Melantius of *The Maid's
Tragedy,* Julianus had put private revenge over patriotic duty and
had knowingly ruined his country in order to secure retaliation
on its ruler.

D'Avenant's *Albovine* (1626) is such a mixture of inextricably
confused Kydian and Fletcherian traditions that any clear-cut
point of view is undiscernible. The play begins as a standard
tyrant play, with Rhodolinda and Hermegild as patriotic revengers. But the purity of this and of the Kydian blood-revenge
for her father murdered by Albovine is soon obscured by a
reversal of character in which Rhodolinda becomes a lustful adulteress and Hermegild an ambitious Machiavellian super-villain.
When the audience must cope with an incredible tangle of Fletcherian villainous intrigue combined with fashionable heroic love
direct out of tragi-comedy but adorning a tragic hero, the result
can be only utter confusion.

In this his first tragedy, a work which perhaps was never acted,
D'Avenant's loose conception of characterization leads to a play
entirely lacking in tragic ethics. He never quite makes up his
mind whether Albovine is a villain or a hero; Rhodolinda, a patriot or an immoral revenger on her sovereign. And when the
ultimate revenger Paradine, whose courses have been bloody
enough to warrant death twenty times over, survives the murder
of Albovine to be healed of his wounds, all ethical content is lost.

In *The Cruel Brother* (1627) the moral confusion and blurred
motive have largely been corrected. The credit for this forward
step must go to D'Avenant's acceptance of the changed view of
revenge which marked the period in his treatment of Foreste's
revenge for the rape of his sister by his duke. The duke repents
his deed and tries to halt the plot he has formed to murder For-

14 William Ames, *op. cit.,* p. 116.

este. The Fletcherian lustful ruler has thus been considerably softened, and there are other sides to his character than his lust. He is in many ways an admirable man, but his original crime has made forfeit his life, and he is ironically killed in the place of the man he was hastening to save. The incident of an intending murderer being hoist by his own petard was scarcely new, but D'Avenant has contrived an ingenious ironical twist to the commonplace situation.

D'Avenant's disapproval of private revenge affects Foreste's character. Foreste is distinctly modelled on Charalois of *The Fatal Dowry,* and the frequent references to his honesty and loyalty leave no doubt that he is to be regarded as a good man. But as with Charalois, a too great rigor and a callous cruelty arising directly from his impetuous forthrightness turn justice into ethical wrong. In addition, he is tainted with the bloodthirsty vindictiveness which followed on the injury to Italian honor. His brutality when he suspects his wife of infidelity is shocking, and the extreme course he takes with his sister is entirely in accord with the Italian tradition so incomprehensible to the average Elizabethan. Hence Foreste is faulty in his goodness, and through the cruelty which gives the play its title forfeits his life.

Of interest is the recurrence of the debate on the sanctity of a ruler in his relations with an injured subject. The eventual relinquishment of their revenge on the duke by Foreste and Lucio, his sister's husband, is all the more effective in its lesson by its lack of Fletcherian theatricality. Of moment, too, is the mutual forgiveness of the duke, Lucio, and Foreste as they lie dying, caught up in the duke's plot which he had countermanded too late.

Lucio is the only truly innocent character who suffers death in the catastrophe. His slaying is undoubtedly a remnant of the tragedy of blood, but there is an indication that the lack of ethical justice in his end disturbed D'Avenant sufficiently to bring forth a futile apology. The moral of the play, which again echoes the theme of the vengeance of Heaven, indicates that D'Avenant had not wholly conquered his dramatic medium, for the closing lines are an admission of structural weakness:

> So intricate is Heaven's revenge 'gainst lust
> The righteous suffer here with the unjust.

5

In *The Changeling* (1622) by Thomas Middleton and William Rowley we reach the artistic culmination to the ideas of the third period. In its own way the play is to their period what Shakespeare's *Hamlet* was to Kydian revenge tragedy.

As is usual, various stock situations of revenge tragedy are present. The main plot emphasizes a lustful intrigue which results in a murder. A revenger of blood appears who delays from insufficient information and in consequence becomes slightly distracted under the strain. The ghost of the murdered man rises before his murderer. The villains slay their accomplice in true Kydian fashion. Yet to these standard situations a new expression is given, for the revenger is thwarted by the suicide of the guilty persons themselves who have found that the results of their crime were more than they had reckoned. Revenge, then, is not a simple requital of blood for blood exacted by a duty-bound revenger despite the counterplots of his opponents, as in the early plays; neither does vengeance fall from Heaven or result from the hidden workings of divine retribution. Middleton and Rowley rise in psychological perception far above any other Elizabethan dramatist except Shakespeare and Webster in their treatment of the problem so as to show that life carries its own vengeance for crime.

We need no bloody Tomaso to stab Beatrice or fiery thunderbolt to strike her to the earth: her punishment in the form of the inevitable consequences attendant on such a deed begins immediately after she has instigated the murder of Alonzo. By staining her hands with blood she has put herself into the power of her hated accomplice De Flores and is forced to undergo the hell of prostitution to him on the night of her marriage to a noble man whom she loves. In the torture resulting from her position lies the revenge for her crime. This concept is clearly understood by Middleton and is emphasized several times by Beatrice herself. The demands of De Flores immediately after the murder of Alonzo bring home to her at once the forfeit she must pay:

> O misery of sin! would I'd been bound
> Perpetually unto my living hate
> In that Piracquo, than to hear these words!

Her deed has instantly lowered her to the level of the man she has most despised, as he points out with justice:

> Look but into your conscience, read me there;
> 'Tis a true book, you'll find me there your equal:
> Pish! fly not to your birth, but settle you
> In what the act has made you; you're no more now.
> You must forget your parentage to me;
> You are the deed's creature; by that name
> You lost your first condition, and I challenge you,
> As peace and innocency has turned you out,
> And made you one with me.

Broken-hearted, she cries, "Vengeance begins; Murder, I see, is followed by more sins." Just before her death she sums up the retribution that has overtaken her.

> Beneath the stars, upon yon meteor
> > [*Pointing to* De Flores.]
> Ever hung my fate, 'mongst things corruptible;
> I ne'er could pluck it from him; my loathing
> Was prophet to the rest, but ne'er believed:
> Mine honour fell with him, and now my life.—

In a sense, De Flores may almost be regarded as the personification of Beatrice's evil angel. Certainly his character and the use to which he puts his particular position in the plot as accomplice constitute the best and most original treatment of that dramatic type.

It is thus entirely in keeping with Middleton's conception that revenge should not come from an outside force, the revenger of blood, but should result from the mutual destruction of the criminals. Beatrice has been sadly disillusioned by her excursion into murder. Her pride has been humbled and her fastidious honor soiled, so that she eagerly embraces suicide, for " 'Tis time to die when 'tis a shame to live." She is no natural murderer, since she is not black enough to deal callously with the consequences: when these overtake her, she is ruined. The grimly ironic manner in which the dramatists work out their theme, and the theme itself—that murder is its own reward and that revenge is obtained by the effect of the murder upon the people concerned—lie amazingly near to the modern heart with its liking for the psychological probing of action, and are the personal triumph of Rowley and Middleton.

6

Critics of John Ford's *'Tis Pity She's a Whore* (1627) have usually concentrated on Ford's decadent treatment of passion and on the incestuous love story of Giovanni and Annabella. But when esthetics are put aside and the play studied from such a comparatively narrow point of enquiry as the treatment of revenge, it is seen that Ford has merely completed the trend towards hinging revenge on sexual passion seen already in Fletcher and Massinger. One of the important results in Ford is to narrow appreciably the causes from which his revengeful action springs and thus to limit the range of his characters. The conventional Machiavellian villain, for example, is found in only one of his plays.

In the construction of *'Tis Pity* Ford followed the example of Massinger in *The Roman Actor* in creating for emphasis a story which is not in itself a revenge plot but is set against a background of revenges to which it is eventually linked. In the conduct of these revenges Ford is absolutely in accord with the ethics of his period. If any one theme besides the incestuous passion of Giovanni and Annabella runs through the play, it is the sense of impending doom to the guilty lovers from the forthcoming revenge of Heaven. The Friar warns him, "Repentance (sonne) and sorrow for this sinne: For thou hast mou'd a Maiesty aboue With thy vnraunged (almost) Blasphemy." On Giovanni's refusal, he warns him again: "in thy wilfull flames Already [I] see thy ruine; Heauen is iust." Giovanni is finally won over to attempt a course of repentance in order to avert the vengeance of Heaven, but if it fails to subdue his passion he resolves to trust his fate, no matter what the end.

> All this I'le doe, to free mee from the rod
> Of vengeance, else I'le sweare, my Fate's my God.

On his failure the Friar prophesies:

> But Heauen is angry, and be thou resolu'd,
> Thou art a man remark't to tast a mischiefe,
> Look for't; though it come late, it will come sure.

Lastly, Richardetto feels confident, in relinquishing his revenge on Soranzo, that Heaven's vengeance is working through the discord in Soranzo's marriage to Annabella.

Hence whatever may be said of Ford's too great sympathy for his guilty couple and of his dangerously inflammatory arguments in exaltation of passion over worldly laws, there is no more doubt in his mind than in Giovanni's that the laws of God have been violated and that God will eventually punish the criminals. It is, indeed, this final realization which at the last throws Giovanni on his fate and sends him a raging berserk to the banqueting hall, resolved to sell his life only at the cost of his enemies' destruction. In the ethics of revenge and the strong emphasis on the vengeance of Heaven working itself out in human affairs, Ford is entirely in sympathy with the spirit of Tourneur's *Atheist's Tragedy* and the great dramas of Massinger, Rowley, and Middleton.

To return to the construction of the play: against this story of the love of brother and sister and the workings of Heaven's vengeance on them is set a series of revenges. Three of these are aimed at Soranzo, Annabella's husband, and thus serve to keep him in the audience's view until it is time for him to clash with Giovanni. The first is that of Grimaldi, a rival for Annabella's hand, conceived for the injury Soranzo has done in setting his servant Vasques to chastise Grimaldi. This minor revenge is utilized by the more important revenger Richardetto, who is attempting to destroy Soranzo for committing adultery with his wife Hippolita. Lastly, there is the revenge of Hippolita on Soranzo for discarding her in favor of Annabella. These revenges are skilfully woven into the play to provide a continuous opposition to Soranzo up to the fifth act, which is occupied with the conflict of the revenges of Soranzo and Giovanni.

When these different revenges are examined, it is seen that not one is entirely free from taint. Grimaldi's is too serious for the original injury and is made villainous by its treacherous plan. Only a flagrant act of injustice by a powerful patron saves him from a deserved fate when he slays an innocent man in error. This tragic occurrence has a sobering effect on Richardetto who, like Vindici and Hoffman, has been a revenger in disguise. His intrigue ends abruptly, he sends his niece to a convent, and soon after gives up all thoughts of personal retaliation in favor of Heaven's justice. It is worthy of note that not only was his injury the most serious of all, but that he is spoken of as a good man (II.709-12), and since he relinquishes his vengeance he is the only revenger to survive with honor at the close of the play. Hippolita's previous incontinence invalidates the justice of her revenge and makes it wholly malicious. Her purposed treachery makes her ironic fate pure poetic justice.

The vengeance of Heaven works itself out in the mutual destruction of the two revengers Soranzo and Giovanni, the action for which starts almost immediately after the unsuccessful conclusion of the minor revenges. Up to the point of his discovery of Annabella, Soranzo has not been portrayed as the traditional Machiavellian villain, nor yet entirely as a good man. Like Sforza in *The Duke of Milan* he has been guilty of criminal incontinence in the past and, by the manner in which he casts off Hippolita, of callous heartlessness in the present. His action in setting Vasques to quarrel with Grimaldi, moreover, has not been wholly admirable. The villainy appearing after his discovery of Annabella's guilty secret is caused rather by the too passionate and bloodthirsty nature of the Italian revenger of infidelity than by any formal Machiavellism. Soranzo's character, therefore, is closely modelled on the vindictive husbands of the Italian *novelle* and on the Elizabethans' conventional opinion of the treacherous and bloody Italian revenger. As such he plays his part to perfection. Unable to force the name of her lover from his wife by brutality, he dissembles, and his faithful Vasques is soon in possession of the secret. The outrage of the injury is soon matched by the outrageousness of the revenge. Spurred on by the Spaniard Vasques to a state of revengeful frenzy in which he begins "to turne Italian," crying "Reuenge is all the Ambition I aspire, To that I'le clime or fall; my blood's on fire," he orders the treacherous banquet and Giovanni's assassination. He falls by Giovanni's hand but is content to die "in death well pleased, that I haue liu'd To see my wrongs reueng'd on that *Blacke Deuill*" by the dagger of Vasques. Vasques, since his deed was not done for himself and since he was a foreigner, is merely banished, and departs rejoicing "that a *Spaniard* out-went *an Italian in reuenge*." The atmosphere of the *novelle* is clear.

It is difficult at first to understand why Giovanni should call his deed a revenge. The first mention comes when, immediately after he has stabbed Annabella to forestall Soranzo's plot, he cries: "Reuenge is Mine: Honour doth loue Command." Holding her bloody heart aloft before the company, he answers his father's horrified query of his sanity:

> Yes Father, and that times to come may know,
> How as my Fate I honoured my reuenge:
> List Father.

Lastly, as he stabs Soranzo,

> *Soranzo,* see this heart which was thy wiues,
> Thus I exchange it royally for thine,
> And thus and thus, now braue reuenge is mine.

The explanation must go back to the very beginning of the play when, promising the Friar to attempt penance, he vows, "All this I'le doe, to free mee from the rod Of vengeance, else I'le sweare, my Fate's my God." The inference is that on his failure God removes His protection and Giovanni accordingly with desperate courage throws himself for better or worse upon his fate. Buoyed up in this conviction with paranoiac hardihood, the normal functions of his mind are gradually destroyed and he begins to feel that he can outface God Himself.

The audience, therefore, must either accept this outside force of fate which has seized on him from the beginning and remorselessly propelled him towards a bloody end; or else it must see that the wine of his incestuous union has gone so strongly to his head that he has become afflicted with illusions of extra-human grandeur which have so affected his sanity (perhaps, as hinted, already unbalanced by excessive study) that he becomes a bloody and maniacal villain.

By calling his deeds a "revenge" and glorifying his "justice" which has no need for God's mercy (V.2541), his warped mind has lost so much touch with normality that he boasts:

> why I hold Fate
> Clasp't in my fist, and could Command the Course
> Of times eternall motion; hadst thou beene
> One thought more steddy then an ebbing Sea.

It is this madman with his "revenge" who shortly makes a panegyric to his incestuous sister's purity, stabs her, and, bearing her bloody heart impaled on his dagger point, goes foreknowing to meet his doom, more than half-believing that he can overcome it. Not only the Friar, who fulfils the functions of chorus, but also his own repentant sister, is set for contrast against this fantastic figure.

It appears, therefore, that *'Tis Pity She's a Whore* can scarcely be called an immoral play. Annabella's confession,

> Beauty that cloathes the out-side of the face,
> Is cursed if it be not cloath'd with grace,

puts a quietus to the glamour of their love, and although the insane Giovanni carries on the intoxicated illusion, an end respectively in repentance and madness cannot be called a special pleading. If nothing further were needed, there was no Elizabethan who would not turn in horror from Giovanni's baseless and bloody vengeance on the man who, he believes, must be killed in revenge because he had dared to destroy the enjoyment of incestuous passion. Every revenge in the play is tainted, and with the exception of Richardetto's every one ends in death or disgrace to its conceiver. Ford is entirely in accord with the ethical spirit of the tragedy of his time.

As with *'Tis Pity* there is a tendency for critics of Ford's *Broken Heart* (1629) to mistake for the dramatist's own statement of the moral, the arguments of a character in a fevered state of emotion. It is not at all certain that the play "powerfully suggests that obedience to the promptings of the heart would conform to a higher morality, than passive acceptance of the [conventional] fetters."[15] The moral seems rather a double one: first, the cruelty of enforcing love; and, second, the fact that a man must always pay for his past misdeeds. To these may possibly be added a third, the cruelty of the duty to revenge.

The first moral needs no explanation. The attempt to part the lovers Orgilus and Penthea provides a lesson in unhappiness to everyone in the play and eventually drives Penthea to madness and death. Linked directly with this theme is the second moral, that Ithocles must suffer for the sufferings he has caused the lovers. It does not matter that Ithocles is no villain but an honest, upright, admirable man who admits the injury, wishes it undone, and excuses it with a perfectly legitimate defense that his youth and inexperience made him ignorant of love's commanding power. His act permanently stains him (V.ii.2392-5).

But the key to Ford's conception lies in the character of Orgilus. This "angry man" is not a perfect hero; instead, like

<hr />

[15] S. P. Sherman in *John Fordes Dramatische Werke,* ed. W. Bang (Materialen zur Kunde des älteren Englischen Dramas, XXIII, 1908), p. xi.

Charalois, Orestes, and Foreste, he is a just but too cruel revenger, and there is even a hint of a predestined fortune which he blindly follows (I.iii.375-81; III.i.1092-5). From the start of the play he is a hidden volcano which may erupt at any moment. He does not, apparently, conceive his revenge on Ithocles until moved beyond endurance by Penthea's madness, but the grudge which he nourishes is continually aggravated by the happiness of Euphrania and Prophilus and then by the sudden fortune in love of Ithocles. The coals of his antipathy are glowing, and need only an occasion to flame. Tecnicus the Philosopher (like the Friar in 'Tis Pity) recognizes the danger in his brooding and twice warns him against revenge, the first time by a disquisition on true honor and the second by the ambiguous couplet,

> Let craft with curtesie a while conferre,
> Reuenge proues its owne Executioner.

How little his precepts of true honor founded on legal justice (III.i.1075-82) affected Orgilus may be shown by Orgilus's triumphant acknowledgment of his crime as "Honourable infamy" (V.ii.2472). Even the overwhelming passion of Orgilus for Penthea is tainted by his demands on her. It should be noted that she indignantly refuses his rash pleas for possession, and remains a chaste wife. It does not seem that Ford conceived their love as one which should overleap the bounds of convention but rather as one which must perforce bow to the stronger convention and so destroy its lovers.

Orgilus as a revenger is no Kydian hero nursing his vengeance until a fit opportunity appears. Although the possibility of his revenge is always present, it is not until the middle of the fourth act with the madness of Penthea and his own partial distraction that he resolves to revenge her. Therefore his previous reconciliation with Ithocles, prompted by the powerful urgings of his father, has not been a Kydian trick to lure the victim into a false sense of security. The emphasis has all been on the repression of emotions from which his revenge finally springs; once the vengeance is determined there is no portrayal of intrigue until he comes on the stage to trap his victim and kill him.

The revenge is consummated almost sorrowfully, and gently—as becomes an act of justice—rather than with the usual triumphant brutality. Of Ithocles and this present deed he says,

> the reasons
> Are iust and knowne: quit him of these, and then
> Neuer liu'd Gentleman of greater merit,
> Hope, or abiliment to steere a kingdome.

So just does he feel his cause that, as he later confesses, he was forced to use trickery only to leave no loophole for escape. He has no sense of outraged retaliation but only of justice. Hence the lack of interest in the workings of the revenge plot and in Orgilus as a haunted revenger,[16] the portrayal of Orgilus as a wronged man suddenly driven beyond the bounds of reason by Penthea's madness and death before he thinks of revenge, the restraint in the act of vengeance, and finally the construction whereby the revenge concludes the fourth act, leaving the entire fifth act for the working-out of the fates of the various characters—all indicate a softening of the convention of revenge on the stage.

A further indication is the prominence attached to the stories of Euphrania and Prophilus, and of Calantha and Ithocles. Although the first is a parallelism used to enforce by contrast the misery of Penthea and Orgilus, and the second partakes somewhat of this purpose, the spectacular story of Calantha, as indicated by the title, is more than a subsidiary plot to a revenge theme. *The Broken Heart* is actually concerned more with the problem of frustrated love and the reactions of various people to the emotion of love than with the progress of a revenge. In this conception of dramatic material it follows *The Changeling, The Roman Actor,* and to some extent *'Tis Pity,* in the relegation of revenge to a secondary importance in the plot, while the interplay of

---

[16] The disguise of Orgilus and his reconciliation with Ithocles, two important devices used by the conventional revenger, are here removed from connection with the revenge.

character and circumstance (not pure intrigue as in the tragedies of the second period) steps forward as the foundation of drama.

Love's Sacrifice in 1630 carries on this softening of revenge by showing the evil results which befall when the revenge is not conceived on just grounds. Superficially, the play bears a decided resemblance to the villain-tragedies of the second period in that the tragic action is started and kept moving by the revengeful plots of villains who are using the revenge of a good character to destroy their enemies. Although the first hint had come as early as *Alphonsus, Emperor of Germany* in 1597, the specific grounds of this secondary revenge—adultery—and the spurring on of the injured husband or close relative to vengeance, had first been utilized as a part of his villainous schemes by Mendoza in *The Malcontent,* and was copied in *The Revenger's Tragedy, The Second Maiden's Tragedy, The Duke of Milan, The Bloody Banquet,* and *Albovine.*

Ford, however, makes a new use of old materials. The villainous Fiormonda conceives a malicious revenge on the Duchess Biancha from jealousy at an absurdly small fancied slight. This revenge is heightened and made serious by the discovery that Fernando, whom she vainly loves, spurns her suit because he is in love with Biancha. She vows revenge and, with the aid of her accomplice D'Avolos, plots the ruin of the lovers by the duke's revenge. The revenge of a subplot, performed upon the faithless Ferentes in a Kydian masque by the women he has debauched, joins the main plot by its use as a capping argument against Fernando. In a manner reminiscent of Vasques and Soranzo, the villains raise the duke to a fever heat of revenge, bring him to the lovers, and, when he hesitates and is about to relinquish his vengeance, force him to stab Biancha.

So far the pattern is conventional enough, but Ford's treatment of the love of Fernando and Biancha has overshadowed the interest in the revenge plot; as a consequence the main interest is in the lovers and in the effect of the revenge on them. Although considerable time is spent on the machinations of D'Avolos, the direct intrigue of Fiormonda is scantily portrayed, and the revenge plot assumes an importance chiefly when it is concerned with the passion of love in such incidents as the rousing of the duke's jealousy. Moreover, the main theme of the play—the love of Fernando and Biancha—is not the conventional lustful intrigue but a typical Ford conception where the lovers by remaining chaste are elevated in nobility above the bounds of loyalty or the marriage vow, and their fundamentally illicit relationship is viewed through such a rosy glow that the injured husband is morally on the defensive instead of justified in resenting his wife's essential infidelity. Thus in spite of the Kydian seriousness of the duke's revenge with its solemn kneeling vows and care for the purity of his motive,[17] the technical chastity of the lovers, which in Ford's peculiar view completely vindicates them, upsets the justice of the duke's revenge.

This unusual portrayal of love leads Ford away from the pattern of the revenge play. The duke relinquishes his revenge on Fernando when he is convinced of his wife's physical chastity, and, after he is once prevented from committing suicide, both he and Fernando kill themselves for love of the dead Biancha in what amounts to a contest to join her in heaven. Curiously enough, even though D'Avolos is led away to execution, Fiormonda, the outright villainess of the play, survives and is merely enjoined to a life of penance.

Love's Sacrifice, coming in 1630 at the end of the period, is a transition play. On the one hand it shows a softening of the revenge motive by the greater importance placed on another theme, by the view that the revenge was cruel and unjustified since it was not substantiated according to Ford's ethics, and by the sparing of Fiormonda, the remorse of the revenger, and the catastrophe unconnected in its purpose to a revenge intrigue. Yet in spite of the shift in emphasis in the play, there is no gainsaying that considerable interest is developed in the progress of the revenge of Fiormonda through the actions of her accomplice

[17] See the duke's warning to Fiormonda to take care that no private grudge or maliciousness has moved her to arouse his jealousy (Act. IV, sc. i, ll. 1967-80).

CHAPTER VII

THE DECADENCE OF REVENGE TRAGEDY

I

*T*HE dramatists of the fourth period of revenge tragedy in the last decade of theatrical activity before the Commonwealth were perforce imitators. Almost every source for dramatic invention had been exploited; almost every situation had yielded its last combination and every type of character its ultimate modification. There were seemingly no more worlds to conquer, and the huge weight of accumulated dramatic tradition lay heavily on any aspirant to originality. Moreover, the high imagination of the Renaissance which had animated Kyd, Marlowe, and Shakespeare had given way to second thoughts which were invariably cynical. The age, in its literature as well as its mood, had lost its freshness and inspiration. The drama was becoming worn out.

No new ideal was found to revivify the old tragic situations. The inspiration which had produced the great tragedies of Massinger, Middleton, and Ford had faded. The new playwright Shirley, the only dramatist of consequence in this period, was more concerned with brisk, sharply outlined plots than with ethical conceptions of character and justice. Shirley turned to the past and contented himself with re-arranging in an energetic and efficient fashion the best of the older drama's incidents and characters. He found revenge as a leading motive in the older drama, and so utilized it as an important keystone in his own. Therefore, revenge in Shirley is usually free from the implications of the third period and is more nearly related to its functional use for plot complication and handy motivation in the second period, or to the interest in revenge for its own sake in the Kydian drama.

The stage was losing touch with the common audience for whom the older dramatists had written, and in its appeal to a more courtly group it found a fashionable artificiality more popular than its former direct approach to the deeper emotions. Dilettantism in playwright and audience ended sincerity. The influence of Fletcher was the most powerful, and pure plot with its accompaniments of strained situation and incoherently characterized action became the hallmark of tragedy among the minor writers. They had neither the ability, nor the taste, nor the impulse for searching the inner tragic depths of human character. In default, through sheer lack of inventiveness they fell back on traditional material for motivating death, and more and more came to use private blood-revenge as the chief means for setting their characters in opposition and creating suspense of plot. No sense of the ethical problems which had motivated the great revenge tragedy of the past obtains. The glittering tricks of Tourneur, Fletcher, and Massinger were slavishly copied. And because complication and ingenuity of action must replace legitimate tragic purpose, the artificial Machiavellian villain was revived, fresh scenes of vicious atrocity imagined. Not decadence but disintegration appeared. Against the relatively clear brilliance of Shirley's *Cardinal* must be set the maniacal happenings in *The Fatal Contract* and the impossibly confused motives and incidents of *The Marriage Night*.

2

One of the strong currents in this decade was the trend towards the dramatization of Greek or French romance. Such plays are usually tragi-comedies and often anticipate in their heroic ·spirit the tragedy of the Restoration. In general these dramas cut themselves off from the type of revenge tragedy, but in a few the influence of the older form is curiously visible.

Henry Killigrew's *Pallantus and Eudora* (1634) is of interest in showing what happens to the traditional motive of a son's revenge for his murdered father, when it is placed in a tragicomedy. When Pallantus discovers that Timeus, son to the usurping King of Crete, is plotting his death, he cries:

> Some God give me temper,
> Or too much Rage, instead of a Revenger,
> Will turn me a Stock, a Fool. Hear me yee

Banisht Gods (for I may justly fear
If that your powers are absent any where,
'Tis from this place where Tyranny doth raign)
On this Altar I doe vow, to be your
Martyr, If not your surviving Instrument,
Nere to let fall your Vengeance, till it light
On those which slew the King, your King, the
Image of your Goodnesse. . . . Which slew
My Father, and last resolv'd on me.
Had I a thousand lives, I'd 'gage them here,
And think your judgement yet not bought too dear.

To this religious invocation for justice and the vow of revenge may be added other traditional incidents such as the conspirators' solemn oath to unseat the usurper, and the revenger's own disguise. This revenge of Pallantus extends through the play, but the treatment is not that of Kyd. The personal revenge for blood is largely swallowed in the public revenge of the conspirators, and the influence of Fletcher runs in a debased form throughout. Pallantus, indeed, manages to slay the usurper, but his love for the daughter of his victim is heroic rather than lustful, and the devices employed to secure the marriage of these two veil the essential situation in artificial generosity and changeableness of character which look forward to the later heroic tragedy and rob the play of any further blood and vengeance.

Heroic love has also taken its toll in Lodowick Carlell's *Osmund the Great Turk*, perhaps revised about 1637 although its original composition definitely goes back to 1622. The underplot exhibits a revenge in the straight *novella* tradition, and is finally wound up in an imitation of the revengeful murder of Zenarchus by Amphridote in Thomas Drue's *Bloody Banquet*. The main revenge plot is under the heroic influence.

Because his soldiers threaten revolt on account of his unmanly love-sickness, the Emperor Melcoshus has slain Despina, the object of his love and of that of his loyal favorite Osmund. When Osmund learns of the murder, he casts off all ties of loyalty and swears a bloody revenge on his sovereign master: "it may be her faire Soule hovers about to see how they will use her deere Companion: if so, oh let it heare my vow: by Mahomet and all the powers of heaven I swear with speed to be reveng'd upon thy cruel murderer, all his brave former acts are by thy innocent blood washt from my remembrance, I was not more his slave then he was thine: confirm'd with many thousand oathes, and most unjustly he hath not onely broke those bands, but with thy deere blood died his villainie in grain, so that they cannot change their horrid colour in my memorie, till I take equall vengeance, but I must needes come short both that I am by his example taught, and that I shall but kill a murderer when thou diedst innocent."

Fortified with this resolution he hides in the garden to await his victim, and while there overhears a group of conspirators plotting the assassination of Melcoshus. With heroic scrupulosity he says, "What's this I hear, how ere in me it is but justice to take *Melcoshus* life, in them 'tis damn'd treason, which I'le prevent; nor shall they frustrate me of my revenge, their hands are far too base." He thereupon joins Melcoshus, and in the fight the conspirators are slain but Melcoshus receives a mortal wound. Osmund turns on him to consummate his revenge. He and Melcoshus then proceed to indulge in a long argument over the merits of their respective cases until Osmund finally relinquishes his revenge and reconciles himself to the emperor. Melcoshus dies and Osmund, with nothing left for which to live, stabs himself.

The blurring of the characters in the Fletcherian manner is pronounced. Despina is never certain which one she loves, and Osmund performs miracles of self-sacrifice in refusing her love in favor of his sovereign. A scene of horror is presented when Orcanes, the principal figure of the underplot, has an eye gouged out on the stage. Finally there is the artificial contest of generosity at the end between revenger and victim, mingling with the vexed question of the revenge of a subject on his king, by which heroic virtue triumphs over revenge.

D'Avenant's *Unfortunate Lovers* (1638) is a Fletcherian tragedy which, like *Albovine,* is chiefly concerned with love and
politics, but unlike *Albovine* has little emphasis on revenge. The
love stories and the obstacles met by the lovers furnish the bulk
of the action, although eventually the characters are maneuvered
into such serious situations that revenge is the only solution.
The revenge of the villain Galeotto causes the tragic outcome
of the love stories and creates the counter-revenge of Altophil
for the rape of his beloved Arthiopa. This revenge, sympathetically, takes the form of a fair fight with Galeotto in which the
villain is slain. Altophil, once embarked on his course, must
continue.

> I have begun
> In blood, and must go on. Inhuman guilt
> Is so dispers'd and grown so strong, that now
> Revenge from every valiant hand will be
> Acknowledged lawful and divine.

With the aid of his friends he entraps the second villain, the
lustful tyrant Heildebrand, and kills him in combat, ignoring
the pleas of his beloved to leave his revenge to God. As a consequence, he himself is mortally wounded, and Arthiopa dies of a
broken heart.

Small use is made of traditional incidents of revenge, although
Altophil stabs Galeotto repeatedly in the names of the injured
persons, and exhibits to Heildebrand the dead bodies of Galeotto
and his daughter. No space is devoted to the intrigue of the
revenge plot, and, displaced by the treatment of the love story,
it is introduced merely to bring about the deaths in the catastrophe. It is interesting to see, however, that the hero who refuses
to trust to a Heavenly vengeance pays the penalty for his pre-
sumption even though he revenges as an honorable man in fair
combat.

Although there is considerable laxness in this period in demanding the penalty for bloodshed, *The Rebellion* (1640) by

Thomas Rawlins is remorseless in its application. The play is really a tragi-comedy perverted into a tragedy by unnecessary bloodshed at the end. Superficially the work exhibits strong revenge motivation, but actually the revenge is no more than a conventional means of setting hero and villain in conflict. Machiavel, an ambitious villain, is jealous of the popular Antonio and for that reason vows revenge on him. His plots for ruining Antonio force him to flee to save his life, but unfortunately he kills the governor of the city by accident in making his escape. In the confusion Machiavel has been wounded by Antonio, and this gives him a concrete reason to pursue his revenge further. Vengeance, however, is limited to ordering a spectacular death for Antonio if he is captured.

A detailed intrigue for Machiavel's advancement now usurps the stage. He and his wife join with another ambitious pair, each secretly purposing to dispose of the other once the throne is secured. Much space is devoted to the idyllic love stories of Antonio and Aurelia, and of Evadne (his sister) and Sebastiano. The two pairs of lovers meet the exiled king in disguise and, more from loyalty than from any desire for revenge on Machiavel, decide to aid him. By acting in disguise as tools to the villains they second them in their internecine strife and consequent destruction, but Antonio is arbitrarily killed in the catastrophe. Actually, revenge has caused the banishment of Antonio and once puts him in later danger; otherwise its sole purpose is to motivate Machiavel's last stab which kills the hero.

Of chief interest is this recurrence of the remorseless doctrine of blood for blood found in most revenge plays. The killing of the governor in self-defense, otherwise unnecessary, was inserted only to justify the tragic death of Antonio at the close. On his escape Antonio cries,

> Now I repent too late my rash contempt:
> The horror of the murtherer will still
> Follow my guilty thoughts, fly where I will,

and as he lies dying at the end, he says to his love Aurelia,

it was thy love
For to deceive the law, and give me life:
But death, you see, has reach'd me: O, I die;
Blood must have blood, so speaks the law of heaven:
I slew the governor; for which rash deed
Heaven, fate, and man thus make Antonio bleed.

In many other dramatists the doctrine of blood for blood had covered a stern ethical purpose, but Rawlins by his superficial and arbitrary use of the theme illustrates the sterile conventionalism which in the minor plays of the fourth period had attached itself to the great incidents of revenge tragedy.

3

In these years the one playwright who at all approaches the spirit as well as the methods of the great dramatists is James Shirley, who was able to become the master of dramatic tradition rather than its slave. He was no old-fashioned anachronism, but the one dramatist who was not thrown off balance by the demands of his age. He wrote for his time, indeed, but through his sureness of touch was alone able to bring forth something of the old tragic spirit, albeit imperfectly, in new garments.

His earliest tragedy, *The Maid's Revenge* (1626), is a straightforward single-plot play of a villainous revenge which calls down upon itself a bloody retribution. The drama approaches ethical awareness only when Vilarezo, the father whose sternness has caused the whole tragic action, realizes that his too just harshness has made him the real villain. One might also include the conception of the accomplice Velasco, who is no Machiavellian but rather a hot-headed man whose revengeful passion, like that of Laertes and Foreste, leaps over normal bounds. He is a villain only inasmuch as he has not been sufficiently injured to justify the lust for Antonio's blood which unbalances him.[1]

Catalina, the chief villain, is in the direct line of descent from such wholeheartedly unscrupulous women as Tamora, Timoclea,

[1] Shirley is at some pains to make clear that Velasco has never been betrothed to Berinthia. See Act II, sc. iii.

Brunhalt, and Livia and Bianca. Her serious revenge has no basis in real injury but is purely malicious. The mere fact that her sister Berinthia has been chosen instead of herself by an eligible lover leads to a whole labyrinth of crime in which she poisons her sister, instigates her father to destroy the lover Antonio, and by this act brings about the death of her brother Sebastiano. In her intrigues she makes use of an accomplice, Velasco, whom she tricks and endeavors to saddle with the blame for her misdeeds.

Very noticeable is a return to the Kydian device of parallel incident and characters. Thus Velasco, the accomplice, is also a revenger and for the same reasons as Catalina. There is the contrast between the bold and cowardly suitors Velasco and Montegro, the poisoning of both Berinthia and Catalina by the maid Ansilva, the courting of the servants to parallel that of their masters, and the parallelism at the duel between the emotions of Berinthia in love with Antonio and Castabella with Sebastiano. A further Kydian influence shows in the portrait of Berinthia who, driven to desperation by her injuries, resorts to a bloody and criminal revenge. Bel-Imperia is, of course, the progenitress of this type of woman-revenger, but it was also popular with Fletcher, as witness Gabriella in *The Triumph of Death* and Edith in *The Bloody Brother*. Fletcher's penchant for strained emotions gained by artificially posed conflict is copied in the duel between the friends Sebastiano and Antonio, each in love with the other's sister, with the sweetheart of each man viewing the action with emotions appropriately torn between brother and lover.

Two incidents, however, illustrate how Shirley voluntarily relinquished dramatically effective but standardized situations. In his source Catalina rid herself of her accomplice Ansilva by poison, but Shirley has preferred to make the death of Ansilva an act of poetic justice. Secondly, there is a decided softening of revenge in the fact that Castabella enters Sebastiano's service disguised as a page, not to take revenge on him for the death of her brother but merely for the romantic reason of the tragi-comedy heroine—to be near her lover. In fact this tragi-comedy atmosphere almost succeeds in destroying the play as a tragedy. The ending is far from inevitable, and if the duel had not developed fatally the play could well have turned to comedy. The one really clear-cut element in the play is the emphasis on revenge for its own sake, purely and simply as a dramatic motive and not as a means of bringing forward the moral.

Love's Cruelty in 1631 again mixes other elements with revenge. Briefly the play describes how Bellamente discovers his wife Clariana and his friend Hippolito unlawfully together, but, contrary to custom, abandons his revenge. Later when he discovers their second meeting he refuses to be convinced of their innocence and rushes off to secure aid for his revenge. The couple, although they are technically innocent this time, kill each other in desperation, and the husband, realizing the truth, dies of a broken heart.

The play seems to be composed partly under the influence of Heywood's early sentimental tragedy *A Woman Killed With Kindness.* Heywood had first put into dramatic form, though with a less noble conception than Middleton's *Changeling,* the punishment which arises from the erring characters' consciousness of their guilt in the place of the punishment of an exterior physical revenge. This conception is present in *Love's Cruelty*, although largely overlaid by Bellamente's materialistic refusal to take revenge in order that the outside world may not know of his disgrace, a motive found in Shirley's *novella* source. The lack of substantiation for the final revenge, which is forestalled by the suicide of the lovers, is somewhat reminiscent of Ford's *Love's Sacrifice.* And the ruthless creed that erring though repentant characters must eventually suffer for their misdeeds is similar to Ford's *Broken Heart.* In general, the weakening of the revenge theme, first by Bellamente's initial refusal to revenge, and second by the ordering of the catastrophe only indirectly from revenge, definitely links the play to the widespread softening of revenge in the period just closed.

In *The Traitor* (1631) Shirley revives the traditional plot dealing with the rise of an ambitious villainous accomplice. In accordance with his usual technique the plot is simplified. The tyrant is a tyrant in only one thing—his lust for Amidea—and the plans of the villain Lorenzo for the downfall of his master revolve about only one situation and the characters incidental to it. This villain is moved purely by ambition until his plans are thwarted by Sciarrha, whose revenge he has endeavored to use as a means of killing the duke. Counterpoised to Lorenzo's subsequent revenge on Sciarrha is Sciarrha's on Lorenzo when he discovers he has been made a tool. Linked closely to the main plot is also the revenge of Sciarrha on Pisano for deserting his sister Amidea in order to marry another woman, and his abortive revenge on the duke for endeavoring to debauch Amidea.

Lorenzo is the typical Machiavellian villain whose mind is fertile in villainous projects and quick in extricating himself from danger. He relies both on paid accomplices and on tricked tools. He flatters, lies, turns face with equal readiness. Playing upon the duke's lust, he neatly separates Amidea from her lover Pisano in order to bring her to his master, fires her brother Sciarrha to deadly revenge against the duke, and when the duke's repentance fosters a reconciliation he sets Sciarrha off on a fresh revenge against Pisano which will either destroy him or make him powerless. Finally, when he has himself murdered the duke, he almost succeeds in pinning the infamy on Sciarrha before he is finally slain by Sciarrha's counter-revenge.

The revenger Sciarrha owes a considerable debt to Foreste in D'Avenant's *Cruel Brother*. Like Foreste he is described as "all touchwood" and as "rough-hewn." Both are blunt, straightforward, and both become tainted with blood-guilt by the murder of their sisters to cheat the lustful designs of their rulers. Sciarrha realizes that he has waded so deep in blood by the murder of Pisano and the subsequent slaying of Amidea that he has "wounded [his] own soul Almost to death" and is "more spotted than the marble." Clearly he is no guiltless hero-revenger; yet he is not all villain. Shirley has carefully worked out the successive changes in character in an upright young man who is suddenly confronted with a series of terrible situations with which he copes in the only way known to him—by direct and bloody action. His growing callousness and recklessness as he lets his hot-headed temper run away with him are carefully delineated, as are his increasing despair and the care with which he keeps his younger brother Florio from taking an active part in the revenge. Finally, after the murder of his sister completes the doom begun by the slaying of Pisano, he becomes a vessel dedicated only to the destruction of Lorenzo and the duke before he himself meets oblivion. The death which accompanies the satisfaction of his completed revenge is actually a relief from an over-complicated and ruthless life.

With *The Traitor* Shirley's bent for simple, clear-cut plots emphasizing revenge is brought into contrast with the plays of the third period just concluded. In this bloody story with its strong situations presented so as to excite unusual emotions in the characters, Shirley in his own way is doing what the earlier, more strict revenge tragedies had done. The Kydian drama by means of the overpowering duty to revenge had aroused abnormal emotional excitement in its revengers, with each successive stride in the revenge throwing the overstrained emotions of the revengers into high relief. Shirley portrays these emotions as arising from various strong situations which are not always originally connected with revenge but from which revenge is the only possible escape. The title of the play truly indicates that the villain Lorenzo is the protagonist, but in few villain-plays is the part of the opposing revenger, originally the accomplice, given more prominence or more superbly woven into the rising action. With such earlier plays as *The Maid's Revenge* (1626), *The Cruel Brother* (1627), and *Love's Sacrifice* (1630), *The Traitor* in 1631 typifies the revival of interest in the earlier revenge play, with its treatment of the motives for revenge as a legitimate source of action and character, instead of a mere means of pointing a practical moral.

The Cardinal (1641), Shirley's greatest tragedy, completes the trend by presenting in a brilliant fashion a clear-cut, coherent Kydian revenge tragedy, polished and simplified in his best manner. The play has been most often compared to *The Duchess of Malfi* because of consequences resulting when an interested person tries to enforce affection. This theme, however implicit in Webster's tragedy, was not put forward with the vigor found in *The Cardinal,*[2] and Ford's *Broken Heart* with its powerful lesson on freedom of choice seems more probable as the source for Shirley's special and conspicuous pleading.

The Cardinal is not an especially derivative play, however. Shirley went chiefly to *The Spanish Tragedy* for the larger construction of his plot, and though various other dramas contributed characters and incidents, these were chiefly used to bring the old Kydian tragedy up to date. An outline of *The Cardinal* fits almost point for point into the outline of Kyd's play. In both there is much preliminary action leading up to the murder which is to be revenged. In both this murder is committed by a jealous lover to rid himself of his rival who has won the heroine's heart. Both murderers are backed by intriguing villains who are anxious for the marriage to raise the fortunes of their houses. The murder calls forth the counter-revenge, which is ordered with extreme deceit and dissimulation including a feigned reconciliation. While Rosaura, like Hieronimo, goes mad from excessive grief, the portrayal of her madness is more closely allied to *Hamlet,* since she resolves to pretend insanity in order to deceive her enemies but from time to time lapses into actual distraction. Like *Hamlet* is the emphasis put upon her melancholy. A masque is used to commit a murder, a body is exhibited, ingenious deaths are contrived with great irony. An effect somewhat similar to Bel-Imperia's self-immolation after her revenge is secured in Hernando's suicide.

Various other details are taken from the dramas which developed the Kydian form. The lust of the villain for the victim

---

[2] See especially the king's speech after the murder of Alvarez (Act III, sc. ii) and Rosaura's dying forgiveness (Act V, sc. iii).

of his schemes is prominent in such plays as *Antonio's Revenge* and *The Atheist's Tragedy,* although the closest resemblance comes in *Alphonsus, Emperor of Germany, The Bloody Brother,* and *Sicily and Naples,* from which last, perhaps, the particular form of the cardinal's revenge may have been borrowed. Hernando, the accomplice, has been compared to Bosola. It is true that in the disinterested quality of their revenges they bear a certain resemblance, but Bosola's previous position as accomplice to the villains is a wide variant, and a closer approach to type may be found in Hamond in *The Bloody Brother* who has been himself directly injured. Stephanos in *The Roman Actor* has the same disinterested motives, but other suggested parallels to Baltazar in *The Noble Spanish Soldier* and Ziriff in *Aglaura* are wide of the mark, as are comparisons of Hernando as revenger to Sciarrha and to Vindici.[3] Indeed, Hernando corresponds most closely in his position in the plot to Hermegild in the Albovine story.

These matters of influence aside, *The Cardinal* is an expert work of the theater. The situations are clear-cut, the action rapid, and the characters strongly drawn. Action, however, has taken the place of the Kydian emotion with its accompaniments of a hesitating, overwrought revenger, blood and thunder, and ghosts. Rosaura's madness does not come until late and is sparingly exhibited. One moment she is seen planning to pretend madness, and the next as insane in fact. Since this change from sanity to actual distraction is accomplished off-stage, the audience is not permitted to see the slow disintegration of a mind as in *The Spanish Tragedy, Hamlet,* or *Antonio's Revenge.* Similarly, there is no hesitation, and much of the important planning of the intrigue is done off-stage. Pursuing an entirely different course from that of Kyd, Shirley has his characters do their thinking behind the scenes. All the audience sees is the thinking which has turned into action. Such a method makes invariably for a brisker play

---

[3] R. S. Forsythe, *The Relations of Shirley's Plays to the Elizabethan Drama* (Columbia University Press, 1914), p. 186.

but a more shallow one; the polish has rubbed up the surface at the expense of the inner glow.

Yet the brilliance of Shirley's achievement, particularly when viewed in the light of the sterile treatment of revenge in the dilettante plays of his contemporaries, must not be minimized. If in bringing the old revenge tragedy up to date he has lost much of the emotion and the high tragedy of a soul on the rack, if his characters are slightly too facile in conceiving and acting revenge, he has at the same time sloughed off the bathos and hysteria, the rant and bombast, which at times had made the Kydian form a butt for laughter. His characters are ordinary persons in an ordinary world, who set about righting their wrongs as best they can. Some remnants of the older tradition persist, as in Rosaura's real madness under the weight of her burden and in the constant references to the religious and expiatory nature of the revenge for her dead lover Alvarez. Yet even if Rosaura's distraction does not fit too smoothly in the plot, the revengers' talk of sacrificing to the ghost of Alvarez is necessary to show the nobility of Hernando's character and the essential justice of the vengeance. Without it, Hernando would have been a malicious man exploiting Rosaura's grievance for his own small ends.

The plays of the fourth period, especially that group yet to be considered, show in general an extreme degeneration in the convention of revenge. Only perfunctory motivation and action are given to a serious Kydian blood-revenge; consequently, all the true Kydian ethical spirit, the moral approach to a vital problem of character, is entirely missing. Although his *Cardinal* is not entirely divorced from this fault, Shirley has created a true revenge tragedy in which the entire play centers upon blood-revenge for murder. Vengeance is not perfunctorily relegated to the background until it is time for the catastrophe, nor is it hidden in artificial obscurity of motive. He has achieved a nice balance of characters and situation; in pure construction and actability *The Cardinal* is one of the best of the Elizabethan revenge plays. Furthermore, there are evidences in his careful delineation of character that Shirley up to a certain point in the play intended a conception of life which would closely approach the ethical content of the best revenge tragedy.

The early, or Kydian, tragedy of revenge had presented a hero-revenger who, forced by his overwhelming duty and outraged passion into too bloody courses, had lost all ethical adjustment to normal life and was eventually forced to pay the penalty in death. The necessarily treacherous and evil course of his revenge soon produced the feeling that he could not have been a good man even at the start, and we have such bad revengers in a good cause as Hoffman, Vindici, Maximus, and Francisco. The natural transition was thereupon made to the convention that revenge was the prerogative of villains alone, as exemplified in the villain plays *The Turk* and *Women Beware Women*. The realization grew, however, that good men did revenge, and that there still remained dramatic material in showing the results of their departure from heavenly and earthly laws on a practical plane of morality. A form of problem play, such as *The Fatal Dowry*, was produced. This form in the best plays yielded to the broader artistic conception of life as a balanced whole in which people are neither all good nor all bad. The justice of revenge was occasionally recognized but also its harms and cruelties in a social as well as a personal sense. *The White Devil, The Changeling, The Roman Actor, The Cruel Brother, The Broken Heart*, and *Love's Sacrifice* all in one way or another portray this feeling. Shirley himself in *The Maid's Revenge, Love's Cruelty*, and to some extent in the portrait of Sciarrha in *The Traitor* had written in this mood.

The Cardinal may roughly be placed in this genre although the conception is not so clear or consistent. The cardinal with his ambitious schemes is the real villain, and his murder is truly the catastrophe of the play. Columbo is not wholly an evil but more an overrough and cruel man who lacks entirely the finer sensibilities which would have released Rosaura from her painful contract. Shirley is forced to produce the conflict between Hernando and Columbo to provide sufficient motivation for Hernando's revenge, but even greater emphasis is laid on Hernando's generous espousal of Rosaura's wrongs so that he is in effect her champion. Hernando himself partakes a trifle too much of the overbloody nature of the misled revenger. His anger is rather too personal and pronounced, and he betrays himself when he fiercely desires the damnation of the cardinal's soul as well as the destruction of his body. Hernando, however, is definitely no hypocrite; and his expiatory death, while it does no more than forestall the certain justice of the king, places him in the ranks of those revengers who were willing to suffer death for a good cause. At any rate, the noble method of revenge by formal duel in which he engages Columbo should remove him from the category of a villain.

Rosaura, the duchess, is a more complex person. It is her misjudgment of Columbo's character which really produces the tragedy. Not strong enough to resist with frank integrity the combined pressure of king and cardinal, she has weakly allowed herself to give the impression of acquiescence to Columbo's courtship, and so has involuntarily deceived him in a serious matter which he cannot forgive. The feeble exercise of her wiles in the writing of the letter, the fatal misinterpretation which, owing to her past deceit, Columbo gives it, and finally the reckless and injudicious haste with which she accepts his playful release and rushes into marriage, form a pyramid of feminine error which, when dealing with a man of Columbo's nature, can lead only to tragic consequences. Moreover, feminine jealousy plays its part in her revenge. The last push is given to her resolution by Columbo's vengeful and ostentatious courting of one of her ladies-in-waiting. She plans to seek a bloody revenge on Columbo and the cardinal, who she firmly believes instigated the murder of her Alvarez, and then to die.

So far her portrait has been that of a humanly faulty but not a vicious woman, and her resolution not to outlive her revenge has greatly purified her motives. Almost immediately, however, and with no perceptible motivation, she forgets her resolution and promises to marry Hernando if he is successful in her revenge.

In consequence Rosaura allies herself to the hated class of Elizabethan husband-poisoners who had made the same promise to their accomplices, and, on the stage, to such villainesses as Rhodolinda in *Albovine* who had offered the same conditions to Paradine. This incident causes the most grievously blurred morality in Shirley's play, and is the one loose thread in his plot. Rosaura never refers to it again except in a distorted form in her ravings, which Hernando misapplies. Furthermore, the plan is never put into execution. Hernando kills himself immediately after he has stabbed the cardinal, in spite of his expressed eagerness of a few moments before to live to enjoy Rosaura. The insertion of the incident is puzzling, because immediately afterwards Shirley reverts to his former conception of Rosaura and never pursues farther the red herring of her villainy.

In her vengeance Rosaura is single-minded to a fault. She persistently believes that the cardinal instigated the murder of her husband and, in fact, accuses him to his face. Yet Shirley has given no indication of such a fact, and the cardinal's comments during the masque which precedes the murder show distinctly that he has no connection with it. He answers Rosaura with an eloquent denial and a spirited defense of his championing the cause of his nephew Columbo which should convince any audience that he was innocent of any connection with the murder. Rosaura pretends to believe him, but her acceptance is pure dissimulation, for on his departure she disclaims her feigned reconciliation and starts her plans for his murder. The cardinal has admittedly been guilty of corrupting his sovereign, of forcing Rosaura's match with Columbo, and of securing the reinstatement of Columbo after the murder of Alvarez. His brilliant and sound defense to Rosaura, however, places him in the minds of the audience as an erring ambitious man but not a murderer, and so not deserving of a revenge for that murder. Some sympathy must inevitably have been taken away from Rosaura on her refusal to believe him and on her immediate plans to secure his death for an act of which he was innocent.

So far the interpretation has been only what is latent in Shirley's text, and has avoided as much as possible that facile error of reading into Elizabethan plays the nuances and conceptions which may be present only in the critic's own mind. Such a warning is necessary when we find that the ordering of the catastrophe destroys the whole of the more subtle distinctions in character which seem to have been built up in the evolution of the plot. According to what has gone before we should expect to find a clearly expressed or implied moral, not only on the faultiness of the characters but also on the inevitability of the result; or at least we should expect a suggestion that Rosaura, while grievously wronged, had in her turn mistaken justice and committed wrong.

On the contrary, the characters who have been gray throughout the drama suddenly part into black and white. The cardinal, from whom all Machiavellism had been missing, appears with an absurd villainous scheme of rape and poison to revenge Columbo. When Hernando's stab foils his plans, the person whose eloquent and sincere defense has shown him to be merely a man and so deserving of some meed of sympathy, suddenly turns black villain and, with atheistical deceit, tricks Rosaura to her death. Rosaura, certainly a femininely faulty woman, by the metamorphosis of the cardinal is transformed into a guiltless heroine, whose cruel fate is universally mourned with not the slightest hint of censure. The change is too sudden and too sweeping to be caused by anything other than a weakening of conception, the result of Shirley's occasional theatricality. The collapse in characterization of the cardinal, the key figure in the drama, into a mere stage villain is peculiarly similar to the metamorphosis of Barabas, caused by whatever means, from a creation of humanly villainous grandeur to a bogey man to frighten children. With the collapse of the cardinal all ethical spirit in the characterization vanishes. The play fails to fulfil its brilliant promise. Fletcherian theatricality has destroyed the real potentialities of the last great tragedy of revenge.

4

The trend in Shirley's plays was towards the use for tragic motivation of a serious revenge, which may even be the blood-revenge of the first period. The same general formula is found in the dilettante drama of the time composed by young men of the court and universities. In these plays the final degeneration of revenge tragedy occurs, for consistent characterization and ethical purpose is entirely ignored in the striving for ingenious and surprising situations of horror and shock. These playwrights fell heir to all the vices of dramatic tradition and flaunted them as virtues. The earliest imitated the worst of Fletcher, and when the later imitated these imitations the result is indescribable.

William Heminge's *Jewes Tragedy* and *Fatal Contract* are typical. The years 1637-1638 have usually been assigned for these plays, but they may have been written as early as 1628 and 1630 respectively.[4] *The Jewes Tragedy* presents a confused account of the capture of Jerusalem. Much of the play is taken up with a complicated intrigue among three ambitious Jewish captains. Several conventional incidents of revenge tragedy are used. Eleazar, the chief villain, goes mad after he has killed his father; and insanity overtakes Titus, the victorious Roman general, in this instance with a total lack of motivation. A ghost appears and the supernatural is freely employed for portents. Various horrors include the torturing of Gorion before the eyes of his son Joseph, and Miriam's Thyestean banquet on the limbs of her son.

Although the action of the play is chiefly devoted to the internecine strife of the three captains and their eventual overthrow by the Romans, a revenger appears in the person of Zareck, the accomplice of Eleazar. Zareck has solemnly sworn revenge for his father's wrongs and, like Vindici, has become the tool of the three villains in order to accomplish their destruction. Never has an active revenger had a less causal part in the plot. Zareck is a debased Castrato of *The Fatal Contract*, this latter a character who, as a tool-accomplice, at least sets his own plots working in con-

---

[4] A. Harbage, *Cavalier Drama* (New York: Modern Language Association of America, 1936), pp. 128-9, 261-2.

junction with the schemes of his masters. But Zareck contents himself with carrying out orders, a device which happens to be sufficient to bring about his enemies' downfall. The subtlety of this conception of revenge is quite unperceived. After each deed which Zareck performs according to his master's instructions, he gloats "It works," as though he himself had contrived it to cause their destruction.

Heminge evidently—as shown by Joseph's accusation against Zareck at the conclusion—conceived him as an active force, but the conception fails lamentably since Zareck originates nothing; indeed, it is not until the end of the play is near that the audience realizes Zareck is supposed to be a revenger. His place, with absolutely no change in the plot or characterization, could as well be taken by an ordinary villain-accomplice who has no thoughts of private vengeance. Revenge in *The Jewes Tragedy,* therefore, is a purely artificial and perfunctory gesture in accordance with the traditional motivation of villainy. It is entirely subordinate to the plot and interferes with none of its workings.

Not so with *The Fatal Contract,* which makes a disastrous attempt to combine the Kydian and Fletcherian forms of revenge tragedy. Rather more space than it deserves will be devoted to this play because it is entirely typical of its school in its borrowings from the past and in the use it makes of these materials.

A rough outline of the various intrigues will show the tortuous maze of revengeful plots and counterplots which so excited the admiration of Heminge's friends in the dedicatory epistle.

(1) The revenge of Fredigond, an ambitious and villainous queen, starts the play. This revenge is for blood and is centered on Dumaine and Lamot, whose fathers had killed her brother for the rape of Crotilda when Fredigond's son Clotaire was in reality the guilty person. To this revenge is allied her ambitious intrigue to kill her husband Childerich and place her favorite Landrey, with whom she is an adulteress, on the throne. This plan also requires the deaths of her sons Clovis and Clotaire since they have opposed her affair with Landrey and stand in the way of his suc-

cession. She is aided in her plots by an accomplice Castrato, who is a Moorish eunuch. Fredigond poisons the king and places the blame on Dumaine and Lamot, whom she has inveigled to court on promises of reconciliation, but they escape. After further intrigue directed against her sons and Aphelia, which is unsuccessful, she abandons her revenge.

(2) Clovis, robbed of Aphelia, his betrothed, by Clotaire and rejected by her, revenges himself by inciting Clotaire's jealousy of Aphelia with forged evidence. He joins the rebel troops and, capturing the city, ascends the throne after Clotaire's death.

(3) Clotaire, his jealousy aroused, takes revenge on the innocent Aphelia by imprisoning her and allowing her to be tortured.

(4) Dumaine and Lamot revenge themselves with patriotic intent by raising a rebel army to overthrow Clotaire and Fredigond and free their country from such atrocious rulers.

(5) With them is joined young Brissac who revenges himself on Clotaire for the death of his father from a broken heart and for the ill treatment of his sister Aphelia.

(6) Running through the whole play is the revenge of Castrato on the entire royal family. Castrato is really the raped Crotilda in disguise, although this fact is not revealed until she lies dying in the catastrophe. As a disguised accomplice she endeavors to forward those plots of the queen against Clotaire and Clovis which will result in their deaths, and at the same time instigates the two brothers against the queen. When the queen's plots fail and she retires, Castrato, who has previously failed in an attempt to have Clotaire kill the queen and Landrey, allies herself with Clovis. Castrato brings about Clovis's discovery of the adulterous pair and takes into her own hands their murder. As the accomplice of Clovis she arouses Clotaire's jealousy and carries through the whole intrigue. When Clotaire wavers she spurs him on and herself tortures Aphelia with Clotaire's consent. Crotilda's revenge in the guise of Castrato is principally for her rape by Clotaire, but at the end there is confusedly brought in the idea that she is also a blood-revenger for her father, who had presumably suffered death by the queen's revenge for her brother.

(7) The catastrophe links all revenges except that of the queen, which had earlier been abandoned. Clotaire has Aphelia tortured. Clovis captures the city. When news is brought of his brother's success, Clotaire gives Castrato a pistol with which to kill him, Clotaire. Castrato for the first time reveals herself as the revenger of Crotilda. She opens the curtains concealing the dying queen and Landrey, and triumphs over Clotaire by recounting the whole course of her intrigue. Clotaire now realizes the innocence of Aphelia and begs for life. Castrato weakens, hesitates, and finally returns Clotaire's sword on condition that Clotaire kill her. Clotaire stabs her as Clovis and young Brissac break into the room. The dying Castrato reveals her identity as Crotilda, Aphelia dies of "inward and Externall injuries," and Clotaire succumbs from a broken heart.

The confusion and blurred motivation of the play result from several causes. The construction is loosely that of Kydian revenge tragedy where, as in *Hamlet,* the injury has been committed before the beginning of the play and the action from the very start is chiefly concerned with the revenge for that injury. In such tragedies the problem of the dramatist is to find sufficient complication and intrigue to fill the five acts. Kyd's own devices were too narrow for imitation on a large scale. Marston expanded the counterplot and gave more action to his villain in matters not wholly connected with the revenge, in this way reversing the construction of *The Spanish Tragedy.* Chettle created a number of victims for his revenger and so pieced out the action with a multiplicity of revenges. In this construction he was followed by Tourneur in *The Revenger's Tragedy,* which exercised a considerable influence on *The Fatal Contract.*

Crotilda, by adopting the disguise of Castrato, follows the procedure of the disguised revengers in Chettle and Tourneur. Like Vindici she becomes an accomplice of her enemies in order to secure her revenge, and takes every opportunity to set them at odds. Similarly, she has a number of victims marked for revenge. She has been injured by only one person, Clotaire, but, as with Hoffman and Vindici, she extends her revenge to include the whole family. Thus she intrigues at one time or another for the deaths of Clotaire, Clovis, Childerich, Aphelia, Fredigond, and Landrey. As in *The Revenger's Tragedy* an internal strife in the family of her enemies is substituted for the lack of counterplot caused by the revenger's disguise. This extraneous action is borrowed chiefly from *Hamlet*[5] and from *Thierry and Theodoret*.[6] The influence of *Hamlet* is strongest in the language, but there are several parallels in characters and minor situations. Lamot and Dumaine had been students at Wittenberg when, before the opening of the play, the queen's brother was murdered. As suggested by her name, Aphelia is somewhat similar to Ophelia. Her father Brissac is obviously modeled on Polonius, and her brother, in that he strives to preserve his sister's honor and later to revenge her, is suggested by Laertes.

Thierry and Theodoret was the most important source for the conception of the characters and for the relationships of Fredigond, Clovis, Clotaire, and Landrey. The lustful Fredigond and her paramour Landrey are copied from Brunnhalt and Protaldy. Each queen becomes enraged with her sons for opposing her adultery and seeks to enthrone her favorite. Each endeavors by inflammatory speeches to set her two sons in conflict so that one may kill the other. To some extent Childerich resembles Thierry in that the queen poisons him in order to continue her adulterous intrigue. Landrey and Protaldy are sharply differentiated from such ambitious accomplices as Mendoza and Sejanus, since they are figureheads who do nothing themselves and leave to their queens the planning and execution of the intrigues in their favor.

Various incidents were borrowed from other plays. The use of pretended ghosts is taken from *The Turk,* the patriotic motives of the minor revengers from *Albovine* and *The Roman Actor,* the incident of the forged letter possibly from *Valentinian,* and the lust of the king for Aphelia from any number of plays such as *The Second Maiden's Tragedy, Women Beware Women, Valen-*

5 J. Q. Adams, "William Heminge and Shakespeare," *Modern Philology*, Vol. XII (1914), pp. 51-64; D. J. McGinn, *Shakespeare's Influence on the Drama of his Age Studied in Hamlet*, pp. 40-8.

6 *The Fatal Contract*, ed. O. Junge, pp. 33-41.

tinian, All's Lost by Lust, and *The Traitor.* Revenge gained by inciting a husband's jealousy bears many resemblances, some verbal, to *Othello,* but may well have been partially suggested by *The Duke of Milan* or *Love's Sacrifice.* Aphelia's materialistic brazenness in arguing for the dissolution of her betrothal to Clovis resembles closely Biancha's speech defying the duke in *Love's Sacrifice.* Both are out of character and would seem at first sight to mark a change to villainy in the women, yet in neither case does the dramatist feel that anything out of the way has been spoken. The unexpected resurrection of a character supposedly dead is paralleled in Fletcher's *Cupid's Revenge.*

To return to the main revenge of Castrato, there is an obvious parallel to *The Revenger's Tragedy* when the revenger's chief enemy uses him as a pander to one closely connected with him. Similar also is the device of the revenger in each play to destroy his enemies by exposing the lust of their mother and sending them to interrupt her in the adulterous act. Castrato's setting the brothers at odds over the woman they desire is also found in Tourneur. Massinger in *The Unnatural Combat* but more especially in *The Duke of Milan* had withheld for some time the vital fact that his supposed accomplice was actually a serious revenger for a wrong deep in the past. Heminge borrows this trick, as well as the reason for the revenge, from *The Duke of Milan* but reduces it to absurdity. Castrato for a time seems motivated by nothing but sheer pleasure in evil-doing. Gradually the audience learns that he hates the whole family and is determined to destroy them, but no reason is given for this determination. At the very last moment Heminge further endeavors to trick the audience. Castrato, with the queen and Landrey already disposed of and his enemy Clotaire in his power, seemingly throws off all restraint and announces he is the revenger of the rape of Crotilda. It is not until he inexplicably weakens, and, in a scene reminiscent of *Albovine* and *The Traitor,* taunts Clotaire into slaying him that, for the first time, the audience discovers his real identity as Crotilda herself.

The Fatal Contract is motivated exclusively by revenge. Into the modified Kydian construction of *The Revenger's Tragedy* is set a Fletcherian plot of Fredigond and her intrigues to put her paramour on the throne. Even this is partially motivated by blood-revenge, and from the interplay of various minor revenges guided always by the main revenge of Castrato-Crotilda, Heminge has woven his complicated plot. The familiar characters, the surprises and endless turnings of the various intrigues, apparently delighted an audience whose interest was no longer in the exploration of character but simply in the ingenious resolution of shocking situations. The decadence of the drama is clearly shown in the reasons which led Heminge to hold back the identity and the motives of his chief revenger until the last possible moment purely for the artificial surprise involved.

The decadence of the minor revenge tragedy of the fourth period is even more clearly apparent in the blurring of the dramatist's ethical treatment of his characters. Clovis, who has treacherously incited his brother to kill his wife, emerges as the surviving hero. Aphelia, who breaks her sacred betrothal vow in order to be a queen and brazenly defends her lack of faith, is delineated as the purest type of mistreated womanhood. Clotaire, who has raped Crotilda, and has been a villain to his brother and a cruel and jealous husband consenting to a horrible torture for his wife, is allowed to die in a noble manner of a broken heart, and is treated as a good man who errs only by being too foolishly jealous. Finally, Crotilda, as evil and villainous a revenger as ever trod the stage, is considered a noble heroine. By her very disguise as a Moor she would alienate the audience from Castrato at the start, and this detestation would be increased at every fresh villainy. As Castrato she boasts:

> Thus on all sides the Eunuch will play foul,
> And as his face is black he'l have his soul.

Not content with planning the death of Fredigond, she insists as well on the final villainous act of damning her soul in death. The cruel murders of Landrey and the queen, the exultation in their suffering, and at the last her hideous torture of Aphelia, put upon her the stamp of blackest villainy.

Yet with the revelation of her sex and true identity, and with her refusal to kill Clotaire, the audience is expected to turn about face and, forgetting her whole past, to accept her as a heroine worthy only of pity. Dumaine, her brother, speaks of her atrocious deeds as a "brave revenge," and even the injured Aphelia, whose breasts she has just seared with hot irons, sympathizes with her sad case. Such a total confounding of all ethical judgment had never before been found in the Elizabethan tragedy of revenge, and the very fact that sympathy instead of moral disgust could be asked for such a character indicates the approaching dissolution of the tragic drama.

Sir John Suckling's *Aglaura* (1637), one of the most fashionable of the dramas during these years, betrays the dilettante workman in its equipment with two fifth acts, one comic and the other tragic. The motivation of the play is as perfunctory as the tragic spirit.

On the surface the play is a revenge tragedy, since from the very start its most prominent character is seeking a blood-revenge. Ziriff, however, is a cardboard revenger. For three years he has lived at court in disguise, seeking power and an opportunity to revenge his father's death. Yet so fundamentally unimportant is this motive that only late in the fifth act is the audience told of the identity of the slayers or the circumstances of the killing. Then we vaguely learn that the king had destroyed Ziriff's father in a general revenge for Ziriff's adulterous love for Orbella, the queen. Poorly worked out as this motive is, it is considered sufficient for Ziriff's main revenge. To make matters worse he adds a curious revenge on the queen for having been unfaithful to him with Ariaspes, and a third revenge on Ariaspes and Iolas for having striven to interfere with the love of his friend Thersames for his sister Aglaura.

Ziriff's revenges are the movers of the plot and so the most important factors in the play's action, but the main interest of the dramatist is concentrated rather on the love story of Thersames and Aglaura. Ziriff dwindles from a protagonist revenger to a friend and helper of Thersames. All his actions now center on protecting the lovers; indeed, it is likely the cold and perfunctory theme of blood-revenge for a father was added merely to give him sufficient motivation to take an interest in opposing the king. The various subplots are all concerned with love and various pairs of lovers, and have nothing to do with working out the revenge. Since the revenger's disguise prevents his enemies from knowing him, the opposing force is not concerned with the revenger. Instead the king plots against Thersames, and the ambitious villains Ariaspes and Iolas intrigue against the king. The shortness of the play and the great prominence given to the love story prevent any adequate characterization and any substantial treatment of the ambitious villains.

Aglaura is replete with petrified conventional characters and situations which have not been expanded. There is the lustful king, the ambitious accomplice, the revenger of blood, the lustful love story set against an idyllic one, a revengeful woman, ingenious poisoning, ironic deaths, and the exhibition of bodies. The tragic fifth act welters in blood for its own sake. The catastrophe of D'Avenant's *Cruel Brother* is elaborated and made more purposeful, for the king dies at the hands of his own men set to kill Thersames. Ziriff stabs Iolas in revenge for the villain's plot against Thersames, and, since

> love should have
> A nobler way of justice than revenge
> Or treason,

he fights a formal duel with Ariaspes, his successor in the love of the queen, and kills him. By a fatal error Aglaura kills Thersames and dies of a broken heart. To complete the slaughter, the queen slays Ziriff with the poison Ariaspes had given her to murder the king, and is herself killed by one of Ziriff's friends who is held for torture at the conclusion. In all, fifteen people are killed on the stage.

Not only does the grafting of a revenge on a love story produce a dramatically unsound plot, but the blending of blood-revenge and revenge for an unfaithful adulterous love lends a certain incoherence to the character of Ziriff. This confusion is not abated by such cheaply artificial tricks to secure suspense as occur when for the space of an act the audience is led to believe that Ziriff is betraying Thersames and Aglaura although in reality he is working for their preservation. The motive of blood-revenge in *Aglaura* is merely a conventional device to fill the stage with death at the close. No play of the fourth period better illustrates the perfunctory nature and sterility of the Kydian revenge tragedy in the closing years of the Elizabethan drama.

Samuel Harding's *Sicily and Naples* (1638), never acted, is an example of a University exercise in blood, lust, and intrigue. With justice the complimentary poem by S. Hall comments,

> The *Fatall* sisters sure are muses growne,
> Else whence proceeds this *Fatall Vnion?*

In general the play conforms to the type of the rise of an ambitious villainous favorite. The villain Ursini has a notable ancestry in Elizabethan tragedy, but his model may be discovered in Nicholas Downey's prefatory poem:

> *Sejanus, Catiline's* damn'd treachery
> Liues in *Vrsini's* treasons, there is not
> BEN'S *Fox* can scape the policy o'th plot.

Ursini, like Mazeres of *The Bloody Banquet,* and to some extent Francisco of *The Duke of Milan* and Abrahen of *Revenge for Honour,* conceives a passion for Calantha, Ferrando's niece, and hopes to win her as a first step to Ferrando's throne, to be followed by the assassination of his ruler. The construction of his intrigues is strongly influenced by Suckling's *Aglaura,* the admired tragedy of its day and one set against *Sicily and Naples* in Hall's prefatory verses.

Ursini's tool is Zisco who, like Suckling's Ziriff, is a revenger on his sovereign for the ruin and death of his father. With both characters the wrongs of the father are left in obscurity; further-more, the sister of each disguised revenger is concerned in the plot and each brother revenges her dishonor. It is true that there is no definite indication in *Aglaura* that Ziriff was a Moor, but his name and the impenetrable disguise which is easily doffed (like Zisco's in Harding's dénouement) seem to point to that fact. Castrato in *The Fatal Contract,* however, is probably also an influence since he and Zisco exult in their deeds which they vow will be as black as their skins. The catastrophe is partly based on *Aglaura* when a character is killed in bed through mis-taken identity. Here also death coming to a substitute in the nuptial bed is closely paralleled in the underplot of *All's Lost by Lust,* but Harding attains a certain originality by doubling the situation. Felicia, intending to convert Ferrando, has substituted for Calantha, and so falls the victim of the revenge her own brother Zisco has set for Calantha.

To show the extremely derivative nature of these dilettante plays, more parallels may be mentioned. Certain specific incidents are curiously similar to some of the business in the old *Alphon-sus, Emperor of Germany.* The relation of Zisco to Ursini as tool-revenger whom the villain uses for his own ends is like that between Alphonsus and Alexander. Both revengers are bloody and headstrong, and both, at the suggestion of their masters, rape the bride of their enemy as a means of revenge. Both have the hallucination that the shades of the dead are urging them to re-venge. A resemblance to *Albovine* appears when in each play the conquering king marries the daughter of the man he has slain and falls the victim of her blood-revenge which has been set in motion by another injury he has done her. A slight parallel to D'Avenant's *Unfortunate Lovers* occurs when Charintha, un-justly accused of unchasteness, refuses to marry her lover lest it injure his honor. The disguise of Felicia as a boy page to be near her lover may have been suggested by *Philaster* or *The Maid's Revenge.* Various injured women joining in revenge on one man are met with in *The Roman Actor* and *Love's Sacrifice.* Very similar to scenes in *The Maid's Tragedy* and *The Traitor* is Ursini's defense of himself when accused before his master. Undoubtedly *The Duke of Milan* exercised a general influence. In Harding and Massinger the revengers are seeking vengeance for the long past seduction of their sisters. Both villains slander the reputations of the women whom they love in order to further their designs.

Revenge in *Sicily and Naples*, while not perfunctorily treated as in *Aglaura*, is definitely—as in *Alphonsus, Emperor of Germany*—made subsidiary to the interest in Ursini's villainous intrigue. Zisco is another in the growing list of tool-revengers so popular in these years. His blood-revenge, the most serious in the play, is presented early (I.iv) but it is totally lacking in intrigue, and except for a few casual appearances he drops out of the action until it is time for him to precipitate the bloody catastrophe. Thus in his second entrance (II.iii) he merely recalls his injuries, thinks he sees the ghosts of his father and mother reproaching him for his delay, and promises to hasten his vengeance. Yet he does not appear again until the fifth scene of the fourth act when he once again reproaches himself for his delay. For the first time the audience is given the hint that he has been held back by Ursini's orders, for when Ursini enters and prepares him for action, he eagerly seizes the villainous plan for the rape of Calantha.

To Ursini's ambitious plots and Zisco's revenge against Ferrando is added a second revenge when Calantha, discovering Ferrando's intrigue with Felicia after she herself has been betrothed to him, unites with Felicia to revenge Felicia's injury and the insult to herself. This revenge is softened when Felicia hopes to convert Ferrando by substituting herself for Calantha in the marriage bed, a plan which proves disastrous when the two revenges meet and Zisco unwittingly ravishes and kills his own sister. The third revenge is the counter-revenge of Valenzo against Ursini, who has tried to remove him from Charintha's love. This revenge enters late and serves merely to kill off the remaining villains.

Like that of *The Fatal Contract* the plot is complicated by disguise, information withheld, and several fatal misunderstandings which are unravelled only at the close. The catastrophe surpasses anything in Elizabethan tragedy for the piling of blood on horror. Ursini and Ferrando draw the curtain and find Felicia, who they think is Calantha, ravished and slain. Zisco stabs Ferrando in the names of his father and Felicia, and, doffing his disguise, he and Ursini triumph over the dying Ferrando. In his rage Zisco stabs the helpless king again. As in *The Fatal Contract* Valenzo and his soldiers break in on the tragic scene; the revenger Valenzo stabs Ursini, and his friend stabs Ursini's accomplice. Zisco triumphantly announces his crime to them, but the appearance of the living Calantha throws him into confusion. Calantha rejoices over the still living Ferrando, who passionately affirms his innocence of Felicia's rape. The identity of Felicia is discovered, and Zisco realizes that he has raped and murdered his own sister. Ursini, who had previously expressed atheistical sentiments, perceives the workings of God and confesses Ferrando is guiltless and that it was he who in his guise seduced Felicia. At this point Ferrando expires. Zisco runs mad and stabs himself, Calantha's senses leave her and she kills Ursini; finally Zisco in his madness murders Calantha and falls himself.

Such an indiscriminate wading in blood by a young dilettante allies the play to *Aglaura* and *The Fatal Contract*. In all three the treatment of revenge is practically the same. All use the motive of blood-revenge for the death of a father, but in each the revenger is a tool-accomplice and the central interest is not in his revenge although the theme has been announced early in the play in *Aglaura* and *Sicily and Naples*. Each dramatist recognized the convenience of revenge not as a truly tragic motivation but merely as a means to blood and horror. The analytical seriousness of Kydian revenge is entirely missing, to be replaced by the superficial theatricality of external melodrama. Conventionality has quite stifled inspiration. The older ethical spirit is nonexistent.

Revenge for Honour was apparently written by Henry Glapthorne about 1640, although an earlier version of the play may go back to 1624 or even as early as 1619.[7] The plot is based on the familiar structure of the rise of an ambitious villain to power. As in *Claudius Tiberius Nero,* the villain Abrahen tricks his father into killing the brother who stands between him and the crown. In this play, however, the villain succeeds in disposing of his father as well, even though a Fletcherian coup finally reveals that the brother Abilqualit has really saved himself from death by bribing the executioners.

The first strand of the revenge plot is the revenge of Mura on Abilqualit for the asserted rape of his wife Caropia. This vengeance is, as usual, fostered and employed for his own ends by the villain Abrahen. Mura, in spite of temporary qualms about revenging himself on the blood-royal, finally adopts a legal revenge by petition to the king, but the apparent success of his revenge is nullified by the eventual preservation of Abilqualit. Mura's revenge provokes the counter-vengeance of his wife Caropia for the supposed death of her lover Abilqualit. The third is the abortive revenge of Caropia on Abrahen, and the fourth that of Abilqualit on Abrahen. This last is linked to the fifth and titular revenge of Caropia on Abilqualit for the slaying of Abrahen to whom she had transferred her affections.

Of these revenges, the only ones which are not conceived on the moment or in which there is any dramatic intrigue are the revenge of Mura and the relinquished revenge of Caropia on Abrahen. But since the first is so closely linked to the villainous plans of Abrahen to dispose of Abilqualit, and the second begins only with the end of the fourth act, the sole interest of the play for four acts is centered in the various villainies of Abrahen which are not connected with any revenge intrigue. Indeed, the titular

[7] J. H. Walter, "Revenge for Honour: Date, Authorship and Sources," *Review of English Studies,* Vol. XIII (1937), pp. 425-37; F. T. Bowers, "The Date of Revenge for Honour," *Modern Language Notes,* Vol. LII (1937), pp. 192-6, and "Correspondence," *Review of English Studies,* Vol. XIV (1938), pp. 329-30.

revenge, so ridiculous in its foundation, comes as a complete surprise without any preliminaries.[8]

The plot is made up of borrowings from Fletcher's *Cupid's Revenge, Maid's Tragedy,* and *Bloody Brother,* from Carlell's *Osmund the Great Turk* (which must have been known in manuscript), *Claudius Tiberius Nero,* and Drue's *Bloody Banquet.* The main influence is undoubtedly that of Fletcher, but the play is little better than other exercises in dramatic ingenuity which have been considered. The utter confusion of morality is exemplified by the close. Caropia, who had been a revenger for Abilqualit on Abrahen, quickly gives up her vengeance when she becomes the mistress of the villain, and transfers her animus to her former lover on whom she conceives a mortal revenge for first corrupting her honor. Abilqualit's acceptance of the justice of her deed,

> O I am slain, Caropia,
> And by thy hand. Heavens, you are just; this is
> Revenge for thy dear honour, which I murder'd,
> Though thou wert consenting to it,

is a problem for a metaphysician.

Andromana, by one J.S., was written about 1642. The author evidently has tried to write a villain play,[9] but the prominence of the hero Plangus in his source [*The Arcadia,* Book II, Chap. XV] and the author's own interest in Plangus's character and revengeful motives, have led him to a fatal compromise between the villain play and revenge tragedy. The exigencies of space and the dramatist's own inexpertness have resulted in a portrait of Andromana which is incomplete and too hurried; correspondingly, the

---

[8] It is of interest to note that the play was registered for publication as "The Parracide," with "Revenge for Honour" its original subtitle.

[9] See the subtitle, "The Fatal and Deserved End of Disloyalty and Ambition," and the closing lines of the play,

> "When this is told, let after-ages say,
> But Andromana none could have begun it,
> And none but Andromana could have done it."

action of Plangus is never fully worked out. The play abounds in conventional dramatic situations and motives which are planned but never finished. When the dramatist is guided by his source the play progresses, but in the elaboration of Plangus's revenge, the portrait of Andromana's accomplice Libacer, and the ordering of the catastrophe, missing from *The Arcadia,* the writer is forced back on his own resources. As may be expected, he turns to traditional material and achieves only incoherence.

The story in *The Arcadia* is entirely lacking in conflict and dramatic conclusion. To provide the first, the author opposes Plangus in the rôle of revenger to the villainess Andromana. For the second, Andromana is given motives of revenge which she had not possessed in Sidney. The clash of these two revenges produces the catastrophe. Andromana is presented from the start as a desperately revengeful woman. Her first thought is of revenge, even at the expense of her life, when Ephorbas the king discovers her intrigue with Plangus, but this vengeance is halted by the king's proposal of marriage. When she has married the father and the son spurns with horror her incestuous invitation, she determines on Plangus's death and also on that of Ephorbas, as she says, "Because he is his father." The first plan, nevertheless, does not include Ephorbas and it is only in desperation after its failure that the villains contrive a plot to kill him and to accuse Plangus of the murder. Eventually it is decided to trick the king into slaying his own son by arousing his jealousy and fear. Plangus is rescued by his friends, whereupon Libacer plans to expose Andromana to the king after the murder of Plangus, for which new schemes are on foot, and thus to reap a rich reward. Andromana, herself, plans to dispose of Libacer, but neither of these plots materializes.

Plangus as a revenger for the injuries heaped on him by the villains and the tricked king is a pitiable spectacle. On his return home to find his mistress Andromana married to his father, he breathes fire and vengeance, hesitates, and then endeavors to commit suicide, since it is because of his lies that his father is living in incest with her. His friend Inophilus punctures his revengeful mood with common sense satire, but Plangus retires still harboring revenge although torn between his emotions and filial duty. An absurd speech occurs in this scene when, about to kill himself, he tells Inophilus,

> Be sure, when I am dead, to meet my ghost,
> And do as that instructs thee. 'Twill tell all the particulars
> Of my revenge, who must die first, who last, and
> What way too.

In the next scene he is still undecided. His father's sentence of death leaves him resigned, but on his next appearance he has once again resolved on a revenge which will include Ephorbas and Andromana. Ephorbas is scarcely less wavering. One moment he believes Plangus guilty; the next, innocent.

The catastrophe is almost farcical in its crowded deaths. The respective revenges of Plangus and Andromana clash when Plangus overhears Libacer and Andromana plotting his destruction and rushes in to kill Libacer. Andromana shouts a rape and Ephorbas enters and stabs Plangus. Plangus is at last happy since he has found by his own death the revenge which he had originally planned. He reveals Andromana's incest and perfidy. Andromana goes berserk, throws Plangus's dagger at the king, stabs Inophilus who has just entered, and then, when the lords rush in, kills herself in a wild frenzy of destructiveness, shouting,

> I wouldn't live a minute longer
> Unless to act my ills again, for all Iberia.

Andromana makes a feeble effort to reproduce in the perplexities and hesitations of Plangus the strain on the emotions of the Kydian hero-revenger placed in an impossible situation. The puerility of the conception and of the basic situation, however, robs the characterization of all its natural force. In the portrait of Andromana the dramatist wavers feebly between showing a purely ambitious and revengeful woman and a furiously destructive Machiavellian villainess. The indecision of method inevitably produces a fatal incoherence. The motivation of revenge was forced upon the author when he decided to turn the story of his source into a bloody tragedy, but the weight of conventional incident proved too heavy. Faced with a superfluity of traditional situation and motivation which had ceased to be living and inspirational material, he did not know what to do with it. The characters have the usual sentiments but do not know how to put them into action. In the complete failure of this attempt to fill in a story with material drawn from the older revenge tragedy, is revealed the dramatist's lack of understanding and total conventionality—indeed his complete loss of inspiration—in the treatment of revenge as subject matter for tragedy.

The Marriage Night by George Cary Viscount Falkland, written at some indeterminate date after 1642, could be dismissed in a sentence were it not for its value as a final object lesson typifying the complete disintegration of the revenge play. This reason must serve as excuse for the following pages.

Like *The Fatal Contract, Aglaura,* and *Sicily and Naples, The Marriage Night* is dilettante work, and like them it is excessively complicated and artificial. All four have a character seeking blood-revenge for the death of his father, but subordinate this plot to the interest in a love story and in a villainous intrigue. *The Marriage Night* resembles most closely *Sicily and Naples,* since in each play vital information is withheld in a similar fashion. In both plays it is only with the death of the villain that we learn that he has motivated the blood-revenger by murdering his father and seducing a woman dear to him. The trend towards extreme complication is carried in Cary's tragedy to the point of utmost confusion. The characters become mere automatons who make and unmake love, determine revenge, and kill each other as the whim of the author conceives a new turn in the plot. Motivation is almost wholly missing; sudden surprises, resurrections from the dead, calculated withholding of important information all abound.

The main revenge, presumably, is that of the brothers Dessandro and De Castro for the execution of their father for treason. Dessandro is the moving spirit, a malcontent whose melancholy has been increased by the recent loss of command of the citadel, a deprivation which he feels as an insult to himself and to his father's memory. He vows revenge on those persons who betrayed his father to death, but he is forced to hesitate since he does not know their identity. A soliloquy promises his future course of action:

But I'll observe
And creep into men's souls: hug my dear anger
To myself, until it gnaw my entrails through,
That men may court my patience and discourse,
As now they shun it.
And when black night has stretch'd her gloomy limbs,
And laid her head upon some mountain-top,
Bound up in foggy mists, then keep my haunts
By some dull-groaning stream, with screeching owls
And bats; there pay my broken thoughts
Unto thy ghost, Velasco!—
Echo shall wake, and midnight, to help me curse their souls,
That thrust thee to thy grave.

Thus deep Kydian gloom overcomes him; he soon after drinks poison and is saved only by the ministrations of the servants of his master, the duke.[10]

Dessandro's next appearance shows him attempting to seduce Claudilla. He is betrothed to Cleara (the sister of De Flame, who is betrothed to Claudilla) and this lust for his future sister-in-law is apparently a sudden impulse. Certainly it is unmotivated, since he has never previously paid any attention to her. When Claudilla refuses him, he somewhat illogically swears a bloody revenge on De Flame,

[10] As an example of the slipshod plotting of the play this incident may be elaborated. Immediately after the soliloquy quoted, the duke enters and invites Dessandro to accompany him on a visit to the Duchess Claudilla. The two depart on their errand, and in the next act arrive at her house. While there Dessandro announces that he has poisoned himself, and faints. No indication is given of his change of heart from the plans proposed in his soliloquy, nor is any motivation given for the act. Indeed, no account is given of how he managed to drink poison while accompanying the duke to the house.

> I must prepare for thunder and
> Thy revenge, De Flame, as horrid as thought can
> Shape it.

In spite of this threat, his revenge on De Flame never materializes.

Dessandro appears to suspect the king of causing his father's death and his own disgrace. He talks darkly of public revenges on tyrants and of regicide. Apparently the author is shaping him into a villain.[11] He wins the more phlegmatic De Castro to join him and they swear a solemn and bloodthirsty oath on the hilt of Dessandro's sword to revenge their father. Dessandro mentions a plan which he will unfold later. The audience allies this promised scheme to his apparent designs for vengeance on his sovereign, yet no further mention is ever made that Dessandro suspects anyone or that he has laid out a single course of action. Indeed, from this point the theme of the revenge for a father is entirely dismissed. It never at any time has an influence on the plotting of the play, and is brought in at the catastrophe only in the duke's exultant summing up of his villainies. Dessandro from now on is entangled in his love for Claudilla and the resulting complications ending in his marriage to her, and her assassination.

De Castro, the second revenger, is a wholly colorless individual. A hanger-on of the duke, his only action is the swearing of the oath with Dessandro and finally the betrayal of the duke's villainous plots against the life of the king.

De Flame is the third revenger. His sister Cleara has been betrothed to Dessandro and he and Dessandro have been firm friends. Dessandro's unaccountable and suddenly conceived passion for De Flame's betrothed Claudilla has led to a break with Cleara. Upon this news De Flame sends a challenge to Dessandro,

---

11 Comments of chorus characters on Dessandro's marriage further this conception, as does his cavalier treatment of De Flame. Yet in the latter stages of the play no indication is given that he is to be considered as anything but a faulty hero with too strong passions. Certainly if he had been criminally guilty it would have been he and not De Flame who would have suffered death in the catastrophe. Cary's whole conception of Dessandro's character and actions, however, is so incoherent and unfinished that speculation is useless.

who, giving him a negligent reply, insults the messenger and wounds him against all laws of arms. De Flame later breaks in on Dessandro and Claudilla (who has now accepted her new lover and cast off De Flame) and, being jeered at for his pains, withdraws without satisfaction for his challenge. The nuptials of the two furnish his opportunity to avenge the injuries done himself and his sister. In disguise he and Cleara await the newly married pair. His intentions are bloody but, in his opinion, just.

> Sure, heaven will not
> Lose the glory of such a justice, and by a hand so
> Justly engaged.

The married pair are surprised in their sleep. De Flame plans to wake them and give them time to repent, but Cleara thrusts forward and stabs Claudilla. Dessandro awakes in time to receive a stab from the dagger which is thereupon turned against her own breast. De Flame scorns to flee:

> I am
> Too proud of my revenge to start from it:
> Let the law frown, and fall in tempests on me.
> Cowards repent
> When valiant blood ne'er pales at the event.

Before the court of justices he outfaces the judges. Learning from the trapped duke that Claudilla had been his whore, he is enraged that he should have been originally chosen to marry her. Shouting that "Castile shall . . . name me With her patriots for taking this foul monster From her bosom," he stabs the duke just as the duke stabs him. The king exclaims in horror, "Desperate atheists!"

The duke is the fourth and last revenger. Following Massinger's device of withholding as a surprise the fact that a character is a revenger (a trick copied in *The Fatal Contract* and to some extent in *Sicily and Naples*), Cary does not reveal the full scope or motives of the duke's machinations until the very end. The first hint of his true nature comes in the second act at the conclusion of the scene in which Dessandro has poisoned himself. He endeavors to kiss Claudilla's hand, and vows to be revenged on her when she refuses him. In a very confused manner this retaliation is bound up with his revelation that he is ambitious for the throne. Subsequent references indicate that no new complicating strand of the plot has been started against Claudilla, however, but simply that she has previously been his mistress. He asserts that he is advancing, and perhaps has instigated, Dessandro's love for her, and that he wants them married because Dessandro, as a soldier, will be absent more than De Flame and their intrigue may thus be continued more safely. No subsequent reference is made to his promised revenge on Claudilla for spurning him.

The duke comes into the open when he commissions De Castro to poison the king. Betrayed by his accomplice, he defends himself spiritedly and with success until the sudden appearance of Dessandro, rescued from supposed death by Cleara's stab, confirms De Castro's accusations. The trap is closed, the duke exults in his villainy, and in revenge on De Castro reveals that it was he who because of jealousy plotted his father's downfall. Moreover, he allied Dessandro with Claudilla in the hope that De Flame would kill him and thus give the duke his revenge on Dessandro, although the reason for this revenge is veiled in mystery. Dessandro, in spite of his earlier bloody vows, takes the news quite calmly. It is De Flame who is infuriated by the revelation that Claudilla has been the duke's mistress and who stabs the duke. Dessandro, asking leave to retire to live in meditation on Cleara's virtue, is ordered to a monastery by the king, and De Castro is advanced in royal favor.

The chief confusion results from the crowding of three major themes, each sufficient for a single play, into one drama: the blood-revenge of Dessandro and De Castro; the rise of the ambitious villain, the duke, with his varied intrigues; and the revenge of a brother for the insult to his sister. An extreme ethical confusion arises from the anomalous action. Dessandro wavers between the conception of a hero and that of a villain. De Flame's status is never clear. With the king's excited characterization of his desperate murder of the duke, may be compared the more balanced judgment of two courtiers on his revenge for his sister:

> *De Loome*. The count's resolution had too much blood and cruelty in't.
>
> *Pirez*. Dessandro urged as much as mortal sense could groan with.

Cleara, who with jealous resolution had killed Claudilla sleeping without opportunity to save her soul by repentance, is regarded as a saint. De Flame, who had assisted in the murder of Claudilla, kills the duke because he had made her his mistress. Dessandro, cured in an instant of his love for Claudilla by the duke's revelation, spends the rest of his life mourning the suicide of the woman he had jilted without compunction and who had almost killed him for it.

The final imbecility of plotting is apparent when the various intrigues are closely examined. The duke's hidden intrigue against Dessandro causes every complication in the play, yet it is conducted entirely off-stage and without the knowledge of the audience. Furthermore, the motive for his serious revenge is never explained. One must imagine it was caused by general hatred of the whole family because of his jealousy of the father, since no hint is given that the duke feared Dessandro's discovery of his secret. In this case the whole Kydian formula of murdered father, melancholy son oppressed to the point of suicide by the weight of his duty and solemn oaths of vengeance, has been utilized merely as a spectacular background for the villain's hatred of the father which has secretly descended to the son, although no action by the duke against Dessandro can be detected during the course of the play. Certainly the space devoted to Dessandro's plans for blood-revenge early in the work and the emphasis on Kydian emotional spectacle was entirely too great as simple motivation for the surprise appearance of the revived Dessandro which proved the ruin of the duke, particularly since the duke is slain by another revenger for a different matter. We must not overlook also the loose ends of motivation for actions which never appear, such as Dessandro's plans to dissemble until he can detect the murderer, and his dark threats apparently directed at the king.

The theme of revenge for a father had in *Aglaura* and *The Fatal Contract* fallen into a convention which was useful only to provide the blood of the catastrophe, but never before had it sunk to the depths of *The Marriage Night* where it is a useless excrescence on the plot. *The Marriage Night,* to all intents the last of the Elizabethan revenge tragedies, exemplifies the final triumph of amateur ingenuity working in the Fletcherian vein of complicated intrigue, villainy, sexual entanglements, and surprise, over the dramatic motivation of revenge as a source for the action of high tragedy of the embattled soul.

CHAPTER VIII

CONCLUSION

IN spite of the prominence and well marked character of the tragedy of revenge as a literary type, the Elizabethans gave it no critical recognition. True, Anthony Copley in 1596 styles his personified Revenge "the pith of Tragedies,"[1] but it is not clear whether Tragedy is here just a literary word for murder or whether he means stage plays or that literary form exploited by the authors of *A Mirror for Magistrates*. Even if Copley is definitely referring to plays, there is no proof that he is speaking of the English drama rather than of Seneca or the bloody and revengeful neo-Senecan tragedies of Italy where he had spent most of his life. Thomas Nashe makes his Cutwolfe exclaim, "Reuenge in our tragedies is continually raised from hell: of hell doe I esteeme better than heauen if it afford me reuenge" (1594).[2] Yet there remains the doubt whether Nashe, in the person of the Italian Cutwolfe, is speaking of Italian or of English tragedies. If of the latter, Nashe must be referring—in spite of the exaggerative "continually"—to the prologue and *entr'acte* scenes of *The Spanish Tragedy*.

The Elizabethans recognized that the basis of Seneca's tragedies was deeds of violence. "The *Tragedie* [of the Romans]," writes J. Greene in 1615, "discourseth of lamentable fortunes, extream affects [i.e. passions], horrible villanies, rapines, murthers, spoils, tyrannies, and the like."[3] Thomas Adams (1614) uses the horror of classical tragic stories to point his moral on another subject: "no spectator at those horrid Tragedies, where *Oedipus* is beheld the Incestuous Husband of his owne Mother, or Thyestes, drunke with the blood of his owne Children, or at any of the bleeding Bankets of *Medea's,* can receiue those horrours at the Windores

[1] *A Fig for Fortune* (Spenser Society, 1883), p. 17.
[2] "The Unfortunate Traveller," *Works,* Vol. II, p. 324.
[3] I. G[reene], *A Refutation of the Apology for Actors* (1615), p. 22.

of his senses, without terrour to his bowels, and trembling to his bones."[4]

Elizabethan observers, following the Senecan conception, agreed in describing scenes of violence and blood as the essentials of English tragic plot, with correspondingly bloodthirsty and vicious persons for the characters.

> Thalia, come and bring
> Thy Buskin'd sister, that of Blood doth sting,

writes Thomas Randolph in 1630, and, again,

> *Trag.* The subject of my Scene is in the persons
> Greater, as in the vices; Atheists, Tyrants,
> O'er-daring Favorites, Traytours, Parasites,
> The Wolves and Cats of State, which in a language
> High as the men, and loud as are their crimes
> I thunder forth with terror and amazement
> Unto the ghostly wond'ring audience.[5]

An anonymous author of 1625 thus summarizes: "Whereas Stage-playes ordinarily goe under the name either of Tragedies or els of comedies; we are to understand that the argument or matter acted in tragedies is murther, treason, rebellion, and such like"; and, later, the "argument . . . is . . . murther and mischief in tragedies."[6]

The Puritan opponents of the stage naturally painted the picture as black as they could. Stubbes, in 1583, argues against plays specifically on the ground of the tragic plots: "But if there were no euill in them saue this, namely, that the arguments of tragedies is anger, wrath, immunitie, crueltie, iniurie, incest, murther, & such like, the Persons or Actors are Goddes, Goddesses, Furies, Fyends, Hagges, Kings, Queens, or Potentates."[7] That Stubbes was chiefly arguing on classical precedents rather than native

---

[4] *The Diuells Banket* (1614), p. 42.
[5] *The Muses Looking Glass*, Act I, sc. iii, iv.
[6] *A Short Treatise against Stage-Playes* (1625), pp. 11, 16.
[7] *Anatomie of Abuses*, p. 143.

tradition is clear, since this list, like that of Gosson before him,[8] is based chiefly on Lactantius. It remained for Greene in 1615 to issue the longest list: "The matter of *Tragedies* is haughtinesse, arrogancy, ambition, pride, iniury, anger, wrath, enuy, hatred, contention, warre, murther, cruelty, rapine, incest, rouings, depredations, piracyes, spoyles, roberies, rebellions, treasons, killing, hewing, stabbing, dagger-drawing, fighting, butchery, trechery, villany &c. and all kinds of heroyck euils whatsoeuer."[9] The purpose of such lists was to enforce the argument that the representation of revenge and murder and villainy on the stage encouraged the spectators to violence in real life.

Defenders of tragedies and their plots adopted two methods of reply. The first consisted of denying the evil effects of the violent scenes. The second defended tragedy on the highest moral grounds as inculcating virtue by showing the inevitable downfall of vice. Perhaps the best known pronouncement of this kind is Thomas Heywood's in 1612, backed by various authentic cases: "If we present a tragedy, we include the fatall and abortive ends of such as commit notorious murderes, which is aggravated and acted with all the art that may be to terrifie men from the like abhorred practises."[10] Heywood laid no claim to originality. From the days of Aristotle, tragedy was supposed to reward virtue and to punish vice. But while Aristotle's dictum was based more on aesthetic than on moral grounds and served chiefly to introduce his conception of the highest type of tragic character as "a man who is not eminently good and just, yet whose misfortune is brought about not by vice or depravity, but by some error or frailty"[11] (a conception which few Elizabethans except Shakespeare thoroughly understood), the Elizabethans discarded the aesthetic grounds for the ethical. To them tragedy in the main was supposed to show God's vengeance on sin and crime.

[8] "Plays Confuted in Five Actions," *The English Drama and Stage under the Tudor and Stuart Princes,* ed. W. C. Hazlitt (Roxburghe Library, 1869), pp. 180-1.

[9] *A Refutation of the Apology for Actors* (1615), pp. 55-6.

[10] *An Apology for Actors,* p. 53.

[11] *Poetics,* XIII, 2-3.

Puttenham (?) wrote in 1589 of "their [Kings who had lived evil lives] miserable ends [which are] painted out in playes and pageants to shew the mutabilitie of fortune, and iust punishment of God in reuenge of a vicious and euill life."[12] Nashe (1592) remarked, "In Playes, all coosonages, all cunning drifts ouerguylded with outward holinesse, all stratagems of warre, all the cankerworms that breede on the rust of peace, are most liuely anatomiz'd: they shew the ill success of treason, the fall of hastie climbers, the wretched end of vsurpers, the miserie of ciuill dissention, and how iust God is euermore in punishing of murther."[13] The religious and moral reasons adduced by John Reynolds for writing *The Triumph of Gods Revenge Against Murther* (1621-1624) form a precise parallel:

"Considering I say the foulness of their facts in procuring the deaths of their Christian Brethren, some through blood, others through poyson: as also Gods miraculous detection and severe punishment thereof, in revenging blood for blood, and death for death: yea many times repaying it home with interest, and rewarding one death with many; that the consideration of these bloody and mournfull Tragedies, may by their examples, strike astonishment to our thoughts, and amazement to our senses, that the horror and terrour thereof may hereafter retain and keep us within the lists of charity towards men, and the bounds of filial and religious obedience towards God, who tells us by his Royal Prophet, that *whosoever maketh a pit for others shall fall into it himself: for his mischief will return upon his own head, and his cruelty fall upon his own pate.*"[14]

---

[12] *Puttenham's Art of Poesie*, ed. Arber (London, 1869), Vol. I, pp. xv, 49.

[13] "Pierce Penilesse," *Works*, Vol. I, p. 213. See also Randolph's *Muses Looking Glass*, Act I, sc. iv. Even this defense, that men were made better by viewing on the stage the actions of God's justice was attacked by the Puritans: "It is not lawfull for Christians to sporte themselues eyther with the dreadfull iudgements of God, or with the abhominable sinnes of men. But in Stage-playes there are acted sometimes the vile and hatefull sinnes of men, as in comedies. And therefore it is full of horrour seriously to thinke vpon them, and much more to be eyther actor to shew them, or beholder and hearer to laugh at them, or delite in them." *A Short Treatise against Stage-Playes* (1625), pp. 16-17.

[14] "Preface to the Reader" (ed. 1670), sig. A₂.

One may sum up the Elizabethan critical view by saying that tragedy portrayed violent action—deeds of lust, villainy, and murder—but these deeds were always punished at the close. The firm object of Elizabethan tragedy, therefore, was the enacting not only of poetic but, more important, of divine justice.

That the Elizabethans in conceiving of tragedy as replete with violent action were indebted to Seneca is obvious, and the Elizabethan tragedy of revenge undoubtedly drew upon him for its initial inspiration. In the three major tragedies of *Medea, Thyestes,* and *Agamemnon* the Elizabethans found personal revenge as the cause of murder, and thus the keystone of the tragic motivation. Furthermore, the revenge in *Thyestes* and *Agamemnon* is of a peculiar quality since it is, in a sense, supervised by a ghost and is conceived for extremely serious reasons which lie far back in the past. Atreus and Aegisthus are the two great Senecan revengers. Atreus is motivated by the seduction of his wife and the attempted usurpation of his throne by his brother Thyestes. Unknowingly, as well, he is carrying out the curse of Pelops, hastened on by the fury-driven shade of Tantalus, that one brother shall perish by the other's hands. In the dramatization of Aegisthus as a revenger is found the great theme of blood-revenge for murder. Thyestes, to procure revenge on the seed of Atreus, had on the advice of an oracle committed incest with his own daughter, who bore him a son. That son, Aegisthus, seeks revenge on Agamemnon, the son of Atreus. Thus in *Agamemnon* revenge takes on a sacred quality and becomes a bounden duty which must override all other considerations. Filial duty joins with supernatural command, and, since the urge is so compelling, methods are employed which in normal circumstances would be regarded as villainous in the extreme. The most famous of all classical revenge stories, the vengeance of Orestes on Aegisthus and Clytemnestra for the murder of his father, was not treated by Seneca. His *Agamemnon* portrays only the slaying of Agamemnon by the revenger of blood Aegisthus.

A survey of the whole Senecan canon shows that a serious revenge leading to a murder may be conceived for great injuries, rape or adultery, as a result of frantic jealousy or the necessity for self-preservation, or else for murder itself. The revenge may be demanded or urged on by a ghost who in *Agamemnon* appears and speaks directly to the revenger, and in *Thyestes* merely spreads his malign presence over the scene of the forthcoming tragedy. The revengers, with the exception of Atreus and in the main Aegisthus, have moments of ecstasy close to madness. This frenzy is caused by the strong revengeful emotions which have removed them from the category of normal people. Atreus, the most thoroughgoing of Seneca's villains is abnormal only in his towering villainy. Perhaps because of the exigencies of the Orestes story, Aegisthus is of lesser stature; it is inevitable that the unnatural revenge of Clytemnestra should overshadow that of her paramour. Atreus, Aegisthus, and Medea—Seneca's three great revengers—are all villains, and Deïanira of *Hercules Oetaeus,* who is a revenger in error, is cleared of her crime by an expiatory suicide.

Those Elizabethan dramatists who went to Seneca direct found tragedies dealing with great crimes, treated with strong emphasis on blood and horror and tricked out with all the glamorous accessories of dramatic irony, philosophical rhetoric, and scenes of the supernatural. But in *Gorboduc,* written twenty odd years before the *Ur-Hamlet* and *The Spanish Tragedy,* and in *The Misfortunes of Arthur* produced very shortly after Kyd's plays, we find two tragedies manifestly under the influence of Seneca; yet in these plays the blood and violence of Seneca give place to an all-pervading scholastic decorum. Furthermore, the larger movements of history are chosen for the plots rather than one individualized and personal crime as in such plays as *Thyestes, Medea,* and *Agamemnon.* Revenge, therefore, loses its importance as tragic motivation. The *raison d'être* for *Gorboduc* and *The Misfortunes of Arthur* is to be found less in direct imitation of such plays of Seneca as *Phoenissae* or *Troades* (to which they conform most closely in classical decorum and generalized interest) than in the paramount influence of French Senecan plays and the English medieval forms. The French dramatists, influenced by the Renaissance Italian commentators on Aristotle and Horace, built their plays on academic critical formulas. The unyielding demand for a more than classical decorum banished all action, blood, and violence from the stage. The subject-matter was correspondingly affected.

The small clique in England which persisted throughout the whole Elizabethan period in writing these bloodless neo-Senecan tragedies under the influence of French canons of taste is an indication, perhaps, of what might have proved the major trend if Seneca alone had furnished the Elizabethans with tragic material. The early Elizabethan tragic dramatists were graduates of the universities and, in spite of the obvious demands which came from writing for the popular stage, it is possible that academic precedents would have proved too strong had not the dramatists' imaginations been fertilized by the flood of Italian *novelle* introduced into England by Painter and his followers. It is no doubt true that eventually English tragedy would have separated itself from the academicians and have realized itself, for classical stories were too familiar and the incidents of ancient British history too narrow in scope to provide writers very long with dramatic materials. But if we may judge from such attempts to popularize Seneca as *Locrine,* the emancipation would have been delayed and the finest flower of tragedy in the last years of Elizabeth's reign (except for the Marlovian chronicle-history based on *Tamburlaine*) would have been lost had neo-classical authority usurped the place of the *novelle*.

In marked contrast to the stock of lifeless classical subjects or themes from legendary British history, the Elizabethans found in Painter's work a superabundance of stories which were novel and highly interesting to the men of the day. Indeed, the foreign yet contemporary nature of the Italian stories proved their greatest attraction to Elizabethan audiences. It was only from the Italian that the dramatists could procure a stock of tales which would allow the interweaving of many actions into one plot in the characteristic manner of their drama. When to these stories from the *novelle* were added the multitude of shocking accounts from Italian life in the tumultuous Renaissance found in travellers' narratives and histories of Italy, the Elizabethan's equipment needed only the addition of the vivid characterization of Italian villains drawn from Machiavelli and the prejudiced English view of Italian character.

From the *novelle* and the non-fictional accounts of Italian life the Elizabethans took almost every dramatic element that was to be found in Seneca, and more besides. First and foremost they recognized in the Italian character an extreme vindictiveness which manifested itself in a distinct preference for private revenge. This revenge was capable of long concealment, was fostered by an overweening pride, and vented itself, on occasion collectively, by means which were secret, treacherous, and horrible. Not only in the *novelle* but also in the more sober historical accounts they found portraits of passionate jealousy, terrible stories of lust, a shocking lack of religion, a delight in ingenious horror, and countless examples of secret poisonings. Revenge was brutal beyond English experience, particularly in the terrible retaliation exacted for adultery and in the vendetta for murder. Expiatory suicide was also to be found in the *novelle*. In addition to these matters which paralleled Seneca, the Elizabethan in search of dramatic material discovered in the Italian *novelle* and their French imitations the important use of accomplices in the intrigues of revenge, occasional madness arising from an overwrought mind, dramatic errors in poisoning, and the valuable tragic theme of romantic love. Finally, the Elizabethan found in the Italian and French stories a revenger who was weaker than his enemies and so was dependent upon devious and long-drawn-out intrigues for his eventual success.

It is safe to say that owing to their closer contemporaneousness the crimes and the great criminals of Italy caught the Elizabethan imagination with a far surer and more realistic horror than any of the well known classical characters. The fiendishness, in their view, of a Machiavelli and a Caesar Borgia was much nearer to actual experience and thus more fascinating than the villainy of an Atreus. The dramatists could not altogether remove themselves, even if they had wished, from the influence of Seneca, but they were forced by their Italianate subject-matter to go to Seneca direct instead of to the fashionable French tragedies which had emasculated Seneca. And with Seneca himself as their general literary guide, they constructed plays which, in the essentials of plot, characterization, and dramatic incident, were very largely Italianate. No Senecan drama had worked out for them a complete story of revenge or had provided the important lesson of a strong opposing force moving against the revenger. All Senecan revengers were villains, whereas the early Elizabethan stage revengers began as heroes. Finally, the hereditary expiation of evil to provide a reason for a tragic fate—so prominent in Seneca— was discarded under the influence of the Italian, and this change altered in a most fundamental manner the whole English conception of tragedy as compared to the Roman. Naturally, Seneca's rhetoric was copied, since there was no Italian example to follow, but the early tragedies of revenge such as the *Ur-Hamlet, The Spanish Tragedy, Alphonsus, Emperor of Germany, Antonio's Revenge, Hoffman,* and even *Titus Andronicus,* in general owe little to Seneca except their language and flavor.

To warn against an over-emphasis on Senecan influence, however, is not to exalt unduly the effects of the Italian *novelle* on the formation of the characteristic Elizabethan revenge tragedy. Few *novelle* treated blood-revenge, especially that of a hero, and the supernatural compulsion is entirely lacking. On the evidence of *Gismond of Salerne,* the first tragedy drawn from an Italian plot, the *novelle* alone would never have given us *The Spanish Tragedy.* Instead, revenge tragedy was created by a perfect fusing of Seneca and the Italianate. The theme of blood-revenge was not in England a specific borrowing from either Seneca or the Italian, but came from a primitive Germanic story which was found added to a series of Italian *novelle* translated into French by Belleforest. To believe that Kyd was not conscious of the extraordinary parallelism of the Hamlet story with the classical tale of Orestes is impossible. This parallelism, however, cannot change the fact that the *Ur-Hamlet* was indebted for its plot to a Teutonic history. Emphasis on this point is necessary, since the *Ur-Hamlet* was in all likelihood the first English tragedy of revenge, and marked the start, with Marlowe's *Tamburlaine,* of the swift development of Elizabethan tragedy.

Of especial significance for the future of English tragedy was this theme of blood-revenge forced as a dedicated duty upon a revenger who was, at the start, comparatively helpless. Although this theme was parallel to the revenge of Orestes, Seneca had treated only the first part of the story, and could give the English no dramatic model on which to build plays that treated the problems confronting a revenger of the Orestes type. From the available evidence, Elizabethan tragedy might never have employed this central theme of blood-revenge in the manner it was dramatized in such plays as the *Ur-Hamlet* and *The Spanish Tragedy,* as distinct from *The Misfortunes of Arthur* or *Locrine,* if Senecan influences had been chiefly responsible. The importance of this distinction may be realized when we consider that this theme of blood-revenge by a hero who is helpless at the start proved to be the motive which unified the form of Elizabethan tragedy and gave it a suitable tragic situation. The important formula was produced by fusing the Italianate and Senecan in the treatment of the Hamlet story. From the *novelle* and Machiavelli came the villains Claudius and Lorenzo, important as an opposing force; the Italianate revenger Laertes; the romantic woman revenger Bel-Imperia; the general type of intrigue as well as specific incidents; and the pervading atmosphere of vendetta. From Seneca was taken the supernatural enforcement which gave an added tragic dignity, the emotional treatment of characterization, the trappings of rhetoric, and the philosophical approach. The final step came when Kyd, in the middle of *The Spanish Tragedy,* abandoned the reminiscent Senecan theme of revenge for a person who had been murdered before the start of the play and who took part in the drama only in the form of a ghost. The moment he substituted, no matter how confusedly, the revenge for a murder which had been portrayed before the audience's eyes, he gave them characters with whom they could more directly sympathize and a situation which they could appreciate as an incident from real life. At that moment the Elizabethan tragedy became entirely a native drama.

One final point indicating the cleavage may be mentioned. Judging by the example of the Senecan dramas of the Italians and their Latin imitations (such as *Roxana*) in England, if Seneca had not been drained of violence in the French manner the earlier English dramatists would have followed the Italian in accentuating the villainous deeds of the protagonists. These evil actions would have usurped the plot and so would have taken the place of the working-out of a hero's revenge. When revenge was used as a dramatic motive it would have been a malicious revenge, not a sympathetic revenge for murder, and as a result the revenge motives would have been definitely subsidiary to the exhibition of tyrannous villainy and sexual corruption. Owing to its derivation from the Hamlet story, however, the Kydian school of English dramatists adopted a hero as protagonist, in sharp contrast to the three most important of Seneca's plays and the normal Italian development from them. That these Elizabethan tragic revenger heroes gradually gave place to villains was not, in general, the result of any specifically Senecan influence.

When Kyd came to dramatize the loose story of Hamlet found in Belleforest, he broke wide not only with the classical story of Orestes but also with the Senecan development of situation. In brief, a murder is committed secretly before the play opens; the name of the murderer is given to the revenger by a medium which he distrusts, thus causing some delay; additional facts corroborate the identification, but then the revenger is hampered by the counter-intrigue of his enemies and all perish in the catastrophe. The sheer brilliance of Kyd's dramatic ingenuity accounts for two of the most vital changes from the Orestes story: first, the secrecy of the murder and the revenger's consequent ignorance of his enemy, which gives a functional use as the revealer of the crime to the Senecan prologue ghost; second, the invention of a powerful opposing force to hamper and eventually to destroy the protagonist. The victims of Seneca's revengers are like lambs led to the slaughter, but Kyd develops a true contest between his hero and villain.

The previous discussion of the growth of the plots of *Hamlet* and *The Spanish Tragedy* has indicated the course Kyd followed which led him away from Senecan to Italianate incidents for the series of situations which composed his plots. The most important influence was that of Machiavelli. While Atreus is as crafty and treacherous as any Machiavellian villain, neither the king in *Hamlet* nor Lorenzo in *The Spanish Tragedy* is the protagonist, neither is such an inherently evil person, and neither has the tyrannous power which Atreus wields nor the strong motive which leads to his villainous course of action. Atreus, of course, does not follow the formal system of Machiavellian ethics, a mark distinguishing Kyd's villains. There was frequently a distinct tinge of pettiness in the Elizabethan Machiavellian villain which led him to take offense at trivial injuries and to favor roundabout methods of intrigues, sometimes through necessity and sometimes through choice. He was frequently an atheist and always a thoroughgoing villain, but since his wrongs were slight the ghoulish evil inherent in Atreus's terrible retaliation is missing.

Kyd's villains have no trace of Seneca. This fact is the more apparent since they are Machiavellians; indeed, Lorenzo may possibly have been modelled on the Italianate portrait of Leicester in Father Parson's (?) *Copie of a Letter* (1584). Even Marston's Piero, who is the villain of a play which is more directly under Senecan influence than any of Kyd's, is entirely Italianate. The feigned madness which Kyd found in the story of Hamlet played an important part in his break with Seneca, as did in *The Spanish Tragedy* the Italian theme of romantic love and the elaborate Italianate devices by which the villain disposed of his accomplices. This last is of the keenest interest because of its effect on Marlowe's *Jew of Malta*.

Some writers on Elizabethan drama have tried to distinguish two types of revenge tragedy with separate bases and separate development. These are the Kydian tragedy in which the protagonist is a hero who is a revenger of blood, and the tragedy in which the protagonist is a villain who may or may not be a revenger in a play in which revenge takes an active part in resolving the catastrophe. The first type comes from Kyd and the second from Marlowe, with *The Spanish Tragedy* and *The Jew of Malta* as the basic plays for each class. These two types are said to have kept surprisingly far apart throughout their development.

We may be very chary of accepting any such definite division. Between its production in 1589 and its publication in 1633, many changes were made to keep *The Jew of Malta* up to date; but in spite of reasonable doubt about the original details of the plot in the last three acts, the central fact remains that *The Jew of Malta* is a villain play, with a villainous protagonist the center of chief interest. In spite of this essential contrast to Kyd's tragedy, it may well be a matter of serious doubt whether *The Jew of Malta* as we have it would have been written if it had not been preceded by *The Spanish Tragedy*. The earlier discussion of Marlowe's play has indicated that the main framework of the plot is actually the form of chronicle-history and that Marlowe merely took over the counter-action of *The Spanish Tragedy* as the main action of *The Jew of Malta*. Marlowe's intention of writing a play revolving about one central character who is a Machiavellian villain left him at a loss for appropriate action once the villain's major piece of retaliation had been accomplished in the early part of the play. Since his conception of dramatic technique had not yet recognized the need for a strong counter-action, he pieced out his work by adopting and multiplying a device—the disposal of accomplices—which Kyd had previously invented. Whether Marlowe's study of Machiavellism would have led him to the same result if he had not had *The Spanish Tragedy* as example is open to question. In essential character, and certainly in his actions, Barabas is simply a Marlovian inflation and extension of Lorenzo. The confusion in plotting experienced in the play resulted from the change of such a character from opposing force to protagonist.

That *The Jew of Malta* was in many ways influenced by *The Spanish Tragedy* and cannot be called an entirely original creation does not, however, alter the question of its influence in starting a school of tragedy which, by its adoption of a villain as protagonist, may seem to differentiate itself from the Kydian type. Yet a swift glance at representative tragedies for some twenty years after the production of *The Spanish Tragedy* and *The Jew of Malta* does not tend to establish any very strong and specific Marlovian influence on the villain-play. *The Battle of Alcazar* (1589) and *Locrine* (1591) owe nothing to *The Jew. Selimus* (1591-1594), a variation on the type of *Tamburlaine,* adopts a villain as protagonist; but this villain's character and intrigues are not in the least reminiscent of Barabas, while the scene of his exploits suggests rather the influence of *Soliman and Perseda. Titus Andronicus* (1594) is strictly in the tradition of Kyd. Only Aaron, in the inflation of his villainy, has felt the impress of Barabas. This influence, however, does not affect the type of the play but merely the conception of a few details in a villainous character who is not the protagonist.

An interesting test case comes with *Alphonsus, Emperor of Germany* (1597-1599), where Marlowe's influence is clear in the portrait of the Machiavellian tyrant Alphonsus, the protagonist. Yet Marlowe's influence on the plot is distinctly subsidiary to that of the *Ur-Hamlet* and of *Titus Andronicus,* for the main action is manifestly an expansion of the counter-action of a Hamlet play. Moreover, since the young revenger Alexander seems to have been drawn from both Hamlet and Laertes, there is more than a slight probability that the character of Alphonsus was based on the early Claudius, with simple overtones of Barabas and Aaron. The play departs far from the type of Kyd in its portrayal of a villain king and a villainous revenger of blood as protagonists, but their debt to an early *Hamlet* indicates merely that the Kydian play was their foundation and not *The Jew of Malta. Antonio's Revenge* (1599-1601) is purely Kydian, and *Julius Caesar* owes nothing to Marlowe.

Lust's Dominion (1600) is the first play in which the thoroughgoing influence of *The Jew of Malta* is clearly discernible. Here the major interest lies in the intrigues of an ambitious villain set in the outline of what may be regarded as a chronicle-history.

Yet Kydian reminiscences, such as the villain's subsidiary motive of blood-revenge and his lustful relations with the mother of his victim, can be found in the play. In addition, since Eleazar is a Moor, *Titus Andronicus* probably had a part in the larger inspiration for the action; furthermore, the conqueror play cannot be omitted when one considers the sources of the character of the protagonist Eleazar. In the last analysis, however, the close parallels to Barabas cannot be overlooked. Like Barabas, Eleazar is a deep-dyed Machiavellian villain who has a certain power and greatness in his conception which is lacking in Lorenzo and the king of the *Ur-Hamlet*. By devious intrigues he endeavors not only to retaliate on his enemies for certain injuries, but also to raise his position to one of complete power and authority. Like Barabas he succeeds for a time but is finally tricked and overthrown at the moment of success, chiefly by means of an unfaithful accomplice. In *Lust's Dominion* there can be no doubt that Marlowe's influence is paramount.

Shakespeare's *Hamlet* (1601-1603) is in the Kydian manner, as is Chettle's *Hoffman* (c. 1602), even though Chettle's protagonist is a villain. Heywood's *A Woman Killed with Kindness* (1603) is not affected by either school. *The First Part of Jeronimo* (1604) attempts to capitalize the popularity of *The Spanish Tragedy*. *Othello* (1604) has no relation to Marlowe, nor have *The Malcontent* (1604), *Bussy D'Ambois* (1604), or *Macbeth* (1605-1606). *The Revenger's Tragedy* (1606-1607) follows the internal modifications of the Kydian form that were developing naturally. *Claudius Tiberius Nero* (c. 1607), although a villain-play, is more influenced by *The Malcontent* and perhaps Jonson's *Sejanus* than by Marlowe, and totally lacks the greatness of conception or the major situation of *The Jew*. Barnes's *Devil's Charter* (1607) did not need Marlowe to point the way to Caesar Borgia. *The Turk* (1607-1608) by Mason has a perceptible Kydian flavor and the intrigues of its villain protagonists do not point to Marlowe. *The Triumph of Death* (1608) and *The Insatiate Countess* (1610) have their obvious inspiration in Italian *novelle,* while *The Revenge of Bussy D'Ambois* (1610) and *The Atheist's Tragedy*

(1607-1611) are both Kydian. So far the influence of Kyd is much the stronger on plot and structure, and Marlowe has had little direct influence. Nor can Marlowe's hand be traced in subsequent villain-plays like *The White Devil, Women Beware Women, Valentinian, The Bloody Brother,* and *Thierry and Theodoret.*

The account of the development of Kydian tragedy has emphasized the narrowness of the form both in plotting and characterization. Dramatists very quickly found that there were only two possible variations. Even in the pure Kydian form the villain's intrigue against the protagonist revenger was of extreme importance in the construction of the plot, and might, as in *The Spanish Tragedy,* demand almost as much space as the intrigue of the hero. The first variation, to scrap the hero and concentrate exclusively on the Kydian villain, was devised almost immediately by Marlowe in pursuance of his dramatic theory for gaining unity. Marlowe was content to drape a number of loosely related incidents about a protagonist who was guided by one overwhelming emotion. Barabas the Jew is such a Marlovian protagonist treated as a villain, since he follows the tenets of Machiavelli.

The other alternative for varying the Kydian formula was to extend the part of the villain, and consequently to decrease the emphasis on the intrigue of the revenging hero. *Titus Andronicus,* the first extant revenge tragedy after *The Spanish Tragedy,* follows this course. No one can doubt that the influence of Kyd is predominant, but equally perceptible is the fact that greater space is devoted to the action of the villains than to Titus's tardy revenge. Correspondingly clear is the fact that Barabas has influenced the characterization of such an inhuman villain as Aaron. The structure of the Kydian plot has thereby been modified, but not essentially. Lorenzo and Claudius had each committed only one murder which was to be revenged, but Aaron, Tamora, and Chiron and Demetrius progress from murder to murder and villainy to villainy. The action which dramatizes these holds the central interest until the revenge of Titus for this multitude of crimes is started. Marston's *Antonio's Revenge* rejects the multiple villain and returns to the single character of Kyd, but Piero's ambitious designs are so increased in scope that he more than shares the interest with the hero Antonio. Chettle's *Hoffman* completes the obvious trend. Realizing the increasing preference of the audience for magnificent villainy, Chettle was yet loath to give up the popular feature of blood-revenge. The two combined, with a villain as a revenger of blood, produced a revolutionary play. A villain as a blood-revenger was an integral part of the counter-action in the early *Hamlet,* whence it had been taken as a feature of the main plot of *Alphonsus, Emperor of Germany.* Chettle carried this hint to its logical conclusion, and wrote a unique tragedy.

This progression of Kydian hero to villain-revenger was inevitable, owing to the standards of English morality, although several later playwrights were to attempt an unsuccessful compromise which shows clearly the public temper. Irrespective of the causes, however, Chettle's protagonist is strictly a combination of the characteristics of the Kydian hero and villain, with no outside influence operating from Marlowe. Chettle's example was followed in *The Revenger's Tragedy* and to some extent in *Valentinian,* and his type of play was extremely popular in the later years of the period as in *The Fatal Contract* and *Orestes.* His innovation of the disguised revenger was even more popular as a distinct contribution to the sum of Kydian devices by which to tell a story of revenge. With Chettle we arrive at an influential play which has a bloodthirsty villain as protagonist in the supposed Marlovian manner, yet this villain has been constructed entirely within the Kydian form.

Another very popular type of villain was the ambitious villain accomplice, who had no prototype either in Seneca or in Marlowe. The accomplices in *The Spanish Tragedy* had been tools who were disposed of as soon as their usefulness had ended. In Laertes of the early *Hamlet* and Alexander of *Alphonsus, Emperor of Germany* the accomplice has an integral part in the plot yet there is no hint of personal ambition. An excellent classical model, familiar to all, was dramatized in 1603 in Jonson's *Sejanus* and by Marston one year later in Mendoza of *The Malcontent. Claudius*

Tiberius Nero developed the Sejanus story in popular form, and this type of villain had a long and honorable career on the Elizabethan stage. Mason's *Turk* has felt its influence, and so have the later *Duke of Milan, The Unnatural Combat, The Changeling, The Bloody Banquet, The Traitor, Sicily and Naples,* and *Revenge for Honour.* Ithamore's comparative independence of his master, in *The Jew of Malta,* is too slight a foundation to be considered a source for the later villainous accomplice who may even be the protagonist of the play. Jonson and Marston are his creators, and once again Marlowe has had no influence on a type of protagonist villain.

The type of villain known as the bloody tyrant probably had its origin in the stories of such classical tyrants as Nero, although the impetus to present them on the stage may have come, as with *Selimus,* from *Tamburlaine.* Yet *Cambyses* had been presented long before, and the influence of Roman history is strong in *Claudius Tiberius Nero,* the anonymous *Nero,* and *The Roman Actor.* The lustful tyrant of such plays as *The Maid's Tragedy, The Second Maiden's Tragedy, Valentinian,* and *All's Lost by Lust* is a Fletcherian development. Finally, such desperately revengeful women as appear in *The Turk, The Noble Spanish Soldier, Women Beware Women, The Bloody Brother,* and *Thierry and Theodoret* were never treated by Marlowe, and are in the line of descent from Bel-Imperia and Tamora. Equally free from specific Marlovian influence are various unclassifiable villains like the cardinal in *The Duchess of Malfi,* and Soranzo in *'Tis Pity She's a Whore.*

The theory of Marlowe's vast influence on Elizabethan villains and the villain-play, together with the distinct and lasting separation of the Kydian and Marlovian types, has been over-emphasized. There can be no doubt, of course, that such a prominent play as *The Jew of Malta* exercised a considerable effect in popularizing villainy on the stage, and may even have hastened, as forecast in the figure of Aaron, the Kydian development of the villain to the position of protagonist. Barabas provided some touches in the characterization of later villains, but such an influence is at best superficial when viewed in the light of the main-line development within the Kydian form. The extremely fluid quality of the Elizabethan drama defies the exact pigeonholing of influences. That Marlowe earlier had written a popular play with a villain as protagonist would not be forgotten, but lines of influence flow together so rapidly that it is dangerous to isolate him as the main influence on later dramatists. Marlowe merges in *Alphonsus, Emperor of Germany, Titus Andronicus, Lust's Dominion*; Jonson's *Sejanus* is popularized in *Claudius Tiberius Nero, Nero,* and *The Malcontent*; while Kyd's influence was everywhere.

The superimposition of villain on hero in *Hoffman* and *The Revenger's Tragedy* produced a moral chaos which could not long be endured. Tourneur in *The Atheist's Tragedy* made a desperate attempt at a compromise which would still contain the central Kydian feature of blood-revenge by making his protagonist the popular villain, here a Marlovian inflation, who is motivated by ambition and malice. But instead of following the formula of Marlowe and the modified Kydian formulas of Chettle in which the villain intrigues successfully and without appreciable opposition, he reverses the strict Kydian structure and counterpoises a Kydian hero as the combative force. In this way the continual dramatic conflict of Kydian tragedy replaces the single interest of Marlowe's form. The account of *The Atheist's Tragedy* has sketched the reasons why the attempt was unsuccessful: the structure was sound except for the characterization of Charlemont and his delay, which was at once the crux and the weakest point of Kydian plot.

The villain-play after *The Atheist's Tragedy* weakened the opposing force to the villain protagonist, as in *The Second Maiden's Tragedy, The Duchess of Malfi,* and *The Bloody Brother,* but still retained the conflict—particularly in the fifth act—which led to the catastrophe when the two forces clashed, as these forces had really failed to do in Marlowe. The other alternative was that adopted by Middleton in *Women Beware Women*, by Fletcher in *Thierry and Theodoret*, and to some extent by Webster in *The White Devil,* to compose a play in which all the major characters are villains and in which they work their mutual destruction.

Marlowe's *Jew of Malta* by its denial of the Kydian principle of conflict did not start a rival school of revenge tragedy. The play where the protagonist is a villain developed, instead, through the main line of Shakespeare, Marston, Chettle, and Tourneur. Marlowe's characterization helped the development, but his specific contributions were always merged by dramatists with the stronger influence of Kyd whence they had originally sprung, and in that Kydian setting were borrowed and altered. The direct line of modification of the Kydian formula led to the villain protagonist in a revenge play, and thence to the complete villain-play.

Not only was the sole possible dramatic development of revenge tragedy towards the portrayal of villainy, but the moral impulses of the plays also made necessary such a change. The tragedy of revenge began as a moral and philosophical drama on the great theme of personal revenge for blood and God's punishment of crime. Shakespeare's *Hamlet* is the supreme achievement of the form since he made the issue turn on the character of the revenger[15] and thus gave ample scope for the philosophical consideration of life, death, and human endeavor inherent in the central situation from the days of Aeschylus. Lesser dramatists could attack the high problem forecast in Kyd and treated with finality by Shakespeare only on the lower plane of secular morality. The hero-revenger's death was at first considered a sufficient expiation for the twisted course he was forced to pursue against his more powerful opponent; moreover, no feeling of injustice was produced by the death of such a hero, since though inherently good, he was warped and twisted to abnormality by the intolerable stress of his almost impossible situation. But characters like Titus could no longer be considered as heroes, and realization was forced on audience and dramatists that a good man would

[15] Percy Simpson, "The Theme of Revenge in Elizabethan Tragedy," *Proceedings of the British Academy,* Vol. XXI (1935), p. 114.

not revenge by such terrible and dishonorable means. The change from hero to villain in *Hoffman* and *The Revenger's Tragedy* was as much dictated by the impossibility of portraying hysterical revengers of blood as heroes as by the necessity for dramatic variation. The public utterances of moralists and preachers insisted that revenge was evil, and the dramatists soon bowed to the doctrine. Such late survivors as *The Atheist's Tragedy, The Revenge of Bussy D'Ambois,* and *Valentinian* were forced to adopt for the first a painful compromise, for the second a metaphysical sophistry, and for the third an artificial and unmotivated reversal of character.

The early period of Kydian revenge-tragedy, with the exception of these three plays, came to an end with *The Revenger's Tragedy* in 1606-1607. From 1607 to 1620 the villain holds the stage. Revenge has no advocates in this period. It is the prerogative of the villains, and when the catastrophe is brought about by the counter-revenge of the good characters the action is hurried over and their characterization bears few traces of the tormented Kydian revenger. The chief interest lies almost wholly in the intrigues of the villains against the sympathetic persons or against each other. Since the villains' intrigues may be only partially motivated by revenge, and since the revenge is for less serious grounds than murder, the interest of the audience is demanded by other matters than the working-out of a revenge, and revenge motives may enter very late in the play. Yet this outwardly different form is a lineal descendant of the Kydian play which had come to emphasize the villain, and in almost every case a revenge plot provides the dénouement. The difference is really one of emphasis, and there is scarcely a villain-play which would not have had a radically different form were the motivation of revenge missing.

These villain plays show a disapproval of revenge by the use to which they put it in the hands of the villains, but in general this disapproval is more implied than expressed. However, dramatists did not long remain silent in their consideration of the moral and philosophical ethics of private revenge. *The Maid's Tragedy* had weighed the problem of a revenge on kings, and *The Athe-*

ist's Tragedy had outspokenly demanded that revenge for earthly injuries be left to God. From 1620 to 1630 a whole series of plays attacks the problem of the morality of revenge. *A Fair Quarrel* treats of duelling; *The Fatal Dowry* in a straightforward manner warns that injured persons should settle their differences by law instead of private revenge. Massinger's *Unnatural Combat* shows God restraining a private revenge and executing vengeance Himself. Ford and Middleton took as their morals the cruelty, uselessness, and evil effects of revenges.

Comparatively speaking the outburst was sudden. The revenge-tragedy of the school of Kyd had been fundamentally moral and philosophical in its treatment. The sacred duty of blood-revenge lent a semi-religious tone to the plays, and the atmosphere was correspondingly serious. The revengers of blood undertook an enormously difficult task hampered by every conceivable obstacle. The insistence of their duty, the imperfectness of their means, their frequent lack of knowledge of whom to seek, and their comparative helplessness in the grip of circumstance, stretched them on the rack of human emotions and made them peer into the causes of their action and the great questions of life and death.[16] The villain-plays have no such serious content, inevitably, and their sole contribution is an occasional moral that God in the catastrophe has punished vice.

The moral insistence of the plays of the third period is more didactic than the philosophical questionings of the first, and there-

[16] The moral purpose of Kydian drama is too frequently obscured by critics. For example, Tucker Brooke writes: "What became of the moral purpose which . . . the earlier writers of Senecan drama [Sackville, Hughes, etc.] considered the reason for their productions? The answer is simple: it disappeared. The 'tragedy of blood' or the 'revenge play,' the logical successors of the early Seneca, is amoral, avowedly so; there is no thought of picturing the avengers as more amiable or more noble minded than their victims. The tone of the play is frankly that of the vendetta and the author accepts the savage conditions as he finds them without essaying any interpretation of life's problems." *The Tudor Drama* (Boston: Houghton Mifflin Co., 1911), p. 210. W. Thorp, since his investigation is actually of the didactic element in the drama, is content to repeat this statement in *The Triumph of Realism in Elizabethan Drama 1558-1612* (Princeton University Press, 1928), p. 33.

fore dramatists attempt to solve the problem on a lower plane, whereas there was no practical solution to the more general philosophizing and the ethical examination of character in the first. A vast gulf stretches between *Hamlet* and *The Fatal Dowry*.

Three causes seem to have contributed to the change. The first was the insistence by James I on the doctrine of Divine Right which highlighted questions of revenge as a practical aspect of the relations between sovereign and subject. Secondly, the propaganda against duelling arising from the determined opposition of church and state to private combat popularized a number of powerful arguments against revenge. The importance of this movement cannot be overestimated in its effect on the thinking of the age. James's first proclamation against duelling was issued in 1610, his famous *Edict* in 1613, and his *Peacemaker* in 1618. Bacon in 1614 prosecuted with great vigor and equal publicity the charges against Priest and Wright. A flood of pamphlets, mostly inimical to duelling, resulted from the concerted efforts of crown and church, and the arguments against duelling, with their detailed investigation of the religious and moral laws opposed to private revenge, were widely disseminated. Strong emphasis was laid on the evils resulting from rash quarrels, and on the fact that most murders were undertaken for absurdly slight causes. Men were vigorously warned to make sure of the justness of their grounds before entering an altercation which might have such serious results.

The government urged its citizens to let the law judge their quarrels and not to resort to private vengeance. Most important was the continual iteration of the powerful religious prohibition of revenge found in the Bible. Over and over again God's dictum, "Vengeance is mine," was thundered forth.

The great tragic theme of the sixteenth—and seventeenth—century teaching is this theme of God's revenge for sin. Writers of tragedies, both dramatic and non-dramatic tragedies, were necessarily preoccupied with this fundamental teaching. And all

Elizabethan tragedy must appear as fundamentally a tragedy of revenge if the extent of the idea of revenge be but grasped. The threefold aspect of revenge must, however, be always held in mind; and revenge must be reckoned as including God's revenge, public revenge committed to the rulers by God, and private revenge forbidden alike by God and by the state as his representative.[17]

The average thinking man was inevitably affected by the never-ceasing propaganda. For the first time backed by every force of aroused public opinion, private revenge was made a moral issue and its ethics became a public problem of interest to everyone.[18] Dramatic generalization, consequently, gave place to concreteness.

Finally, the Puritan attack on the stage had its effect. Sniping at the stage had been prevalent during the latter half of the sixteenth century, but in the seventeenth century the battle became more general as more apologists for the stage appeared. Actors found their best defense to be the sturdy affirmation of the moral purpose and effect of tragedy. It was but natural that tragedies written during these years of intensified controversy should emphasize the moral consideration of what was a burning question of the day—private revenge.

The fourth and final period of Elizabethan revenge tragedy begins with Shirley's *Traitor* in 1631. The ideals of the third period had faded or become sterile; the decade to the closing of the theaters in 1642 was one almost exclusively of imitation.

[17] L. B. Campbell, "Theories of Revenge in Renaissance England," *Modern Philology,* Vol. XXVIII (1931), p. 290. See also p. 282: "It must be noted, however, that the teaching of the Scriptures seemed to the Elizabethans to include both a command and a promise; not only did God forbid man to recompense evil for evil; he also proclaimed vengeance as his own prerogative, and he proclaimed the everlasting truth that he would repay. No consideration of the attitude toward revenge can, then, be complete which does not see the complementary nature of these two principles which must forever govern man's attitude toward revenge."

[18] The statement is strong but true. For centuries religion and law had echoed disapproval, but in these years for the first time all the force of a real propaganda emanating from the king and applied to a specific and widespread case was trained on the public.

Shirley, the best of the dramatists, concerns himself more with clear-cut plots than with ethical considerations of justice. The fourth period, under the leadership of Shirley, turns back for its inspiration to the great revenge tragedies of the first and second periods, and revenge again takes a prominent place in the motivation of the tragic plot. In consonance with its more practical purposes, the tragedy of the third period had usually treated a revenge for serious injuries rather than for murder, but in the fourth period there comes a renaissance of the great theme of blood-revenge. Unfortunately such dramatists as Suckling, Heminge, and Harding chose this theme less for the profundity of its tragic implication and its concern with character than for its theatrical opportunities.

The minor playwrights of the fourth period had no interest in a tragic hero on the rack of circumstances. The Kydian tragedy, with its great representative in Shakespeare's *Hamlet,* had justified its melodrama by a sympathetic emotional and intellectual penetration into the sources of action and character. But such tragic seriousness had no place in an age dazzled by the shooting stars of Fletcher's artifice, Tourneur's sexual horror, or such plays as Massinger's theatrical *Duke of Milan*. The dramatists could convey no haunting sense of doom, no human pity to relieve tragic suffering in their bloody plots, for the impact of their strained and lurid horrors is felt on the stage not by human beings but by theatrical robots. Revenge entirely loses all ethical consideration, motives become blurred in inexpert hands, heroes and villains exchange characteristics in a bewildering procession. The treatment of the excessively complicated plot is lawless and episodic. The lack of moral standards in the characters produces chaos. Revenge has lost all power of true inspiration and remains only as an artificial incentive to create and, in turn, to resolve strained and bewildering situations. Even Shirley's clarity, so marked in *The Traitor,* was befogged in the conclusion of *The Cardinal*. Decadence is too gentle a word for the insane maze of character, plot, and motive in the minor dramatists; tragedy was actually disintegrating. The closing of the theaters was really a blessing in disguise. In the breathing space afforded by the Commonwealth's inhibition, the tragic drama found a relief from its dependence on empty ingenuity and worn-out tragic conventions which had lost all touch with the problems of human life and ethics, and all interest in the human soul.

INDEX

OTHER TITLES IN LITERATURE
AVAILABLE IN PRINCETON AND
PRINCETON/BOLLINGEN PAPERBACKS

THE IDEA OF A THEATER, by Francis Fergusson (#126), $1.95

THE JAPANESE TRADITION IN BRITISH AND AMERICAN LITERATURE, by Earl Miner (#59), $2.95

JOSEPH CONRAD: A *Psychoanalytic Biography*, by Bernard C. Meyer, M.D. (#188), $2.95

THE LIMITS OF ART: Vol. 1, *From Homer to Chaucer*, edited by Huntington Cairns (P/B #179), $3.95

THE LIMITS OF ART: Vol. 2, *From Villon to Gibbon*, edited by Huntington Cairns (P/B #203), $3.95

THE LIMITS OF ART: Vol. 3, *From Goethe to Joyce*, edited by Huntington Cairns (P/B #217), $3.95

LINGUISTICS AND LITERARY HISTORY: *Essays in Stylistics*, by Leo Spitzer (#88), $2.95

THE LYRICAL NOVEL: *Studies in Hermann Hesse, André Gide, and Virginia Woolf* (#62), $2.95

MIMESIS: *The Representation of Reality in Western Literature*, by Erich Auerbach, translated by Willard R. Trask (#124), $2.95

NEWTON DEMANDS THE MUSE, by Marjorie Hope Nicolson (#31), $2.95

NOTES ON PROSODY *and* ABRAM GANNIBAL, by Vladimir Nabokov (P/B #184), $2.95

THE NOVELS OF FLAUBERT, by Victor Brombert (#164), $2.95

THE NOVELS OF HERMANN HESSE, by Theodore Ziolkowski (#68), $2.95

ON WORDSWORTH'S "PRELUDE," by Herbert Lindenberger (#55), $2.95

ON THE ILIAD, by Rachel Bespaloff, translated by Mary McCarthy (P/B #218), $1.45

THE POETIC ART OF W. H. AUDEN, by John G. Blair (#65), $1.95

THE POETICAL WORKS OF EDWARD TAYLOR, edited by Thomas H. Johnson (#32), $2.95

THE POWER OF SATIRE: *Magic, Ritual, Art*, by Robert C. Elliott (#61), $2.95

A PREFACE TO CHAUCER, by D. W. Robertson, Jr. (#178), $4.95

PREFACES TO SHAKESPEARE, by Harley Granville-Barker (#23, 24, 25, 26), $2.95 each

THE PROSE OF OSIP MANDELSTAM, translated by Clarence Brown (#67), $2.95

RADICAL INNOCENCE: *The Contemporary American Novel*, by Ihab Hassan (#237), $2.95

RELIGIOUS HUMANISM AND THE VICTORIAN NOVEL: *George Eliot, Walter Pater, and Samuel Butler*, by U. C. Knoepflmacher (#187), $2.95